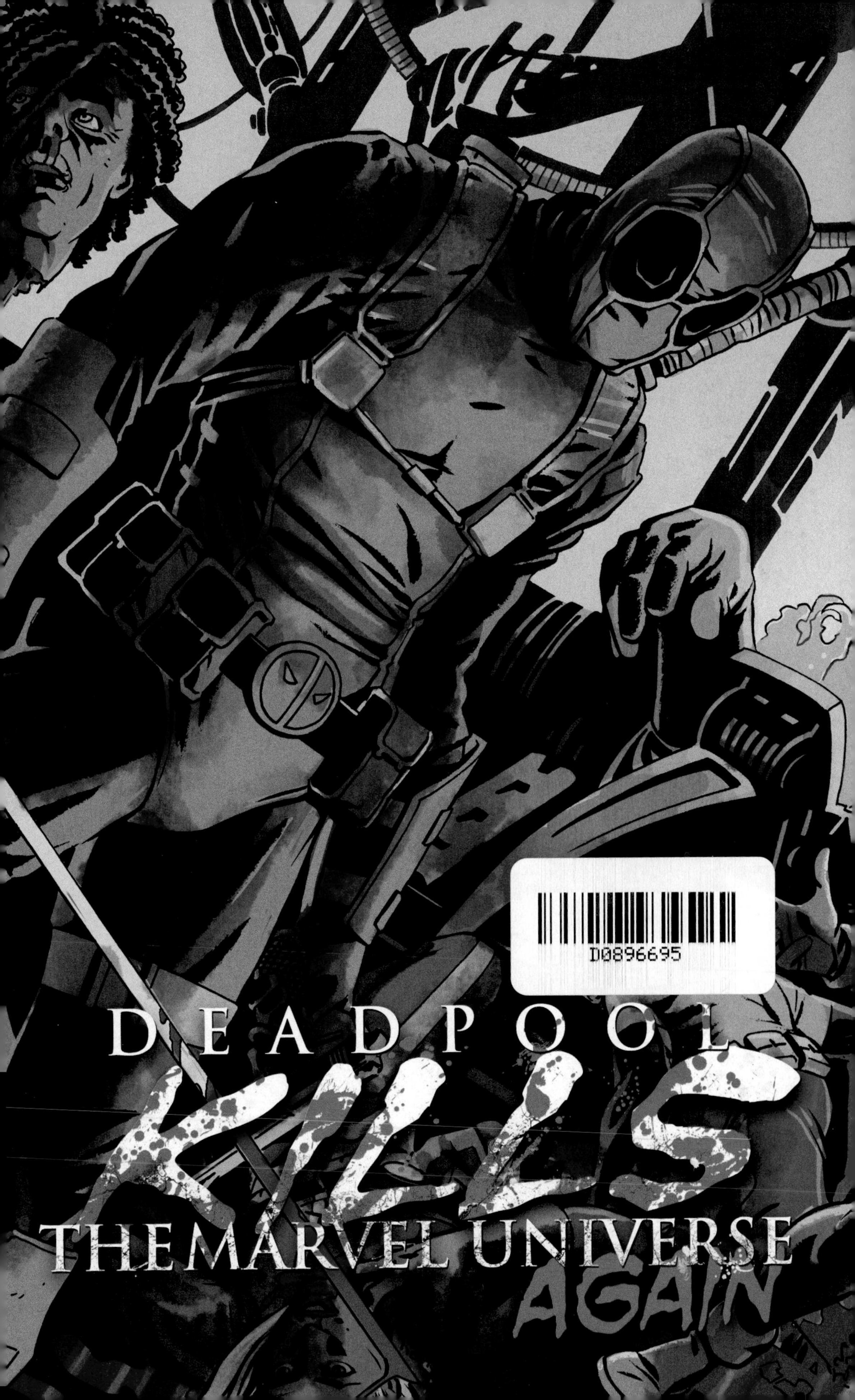
DEADPOOL
KILLS
THE MARVEL UNIVERSE
AGAIN

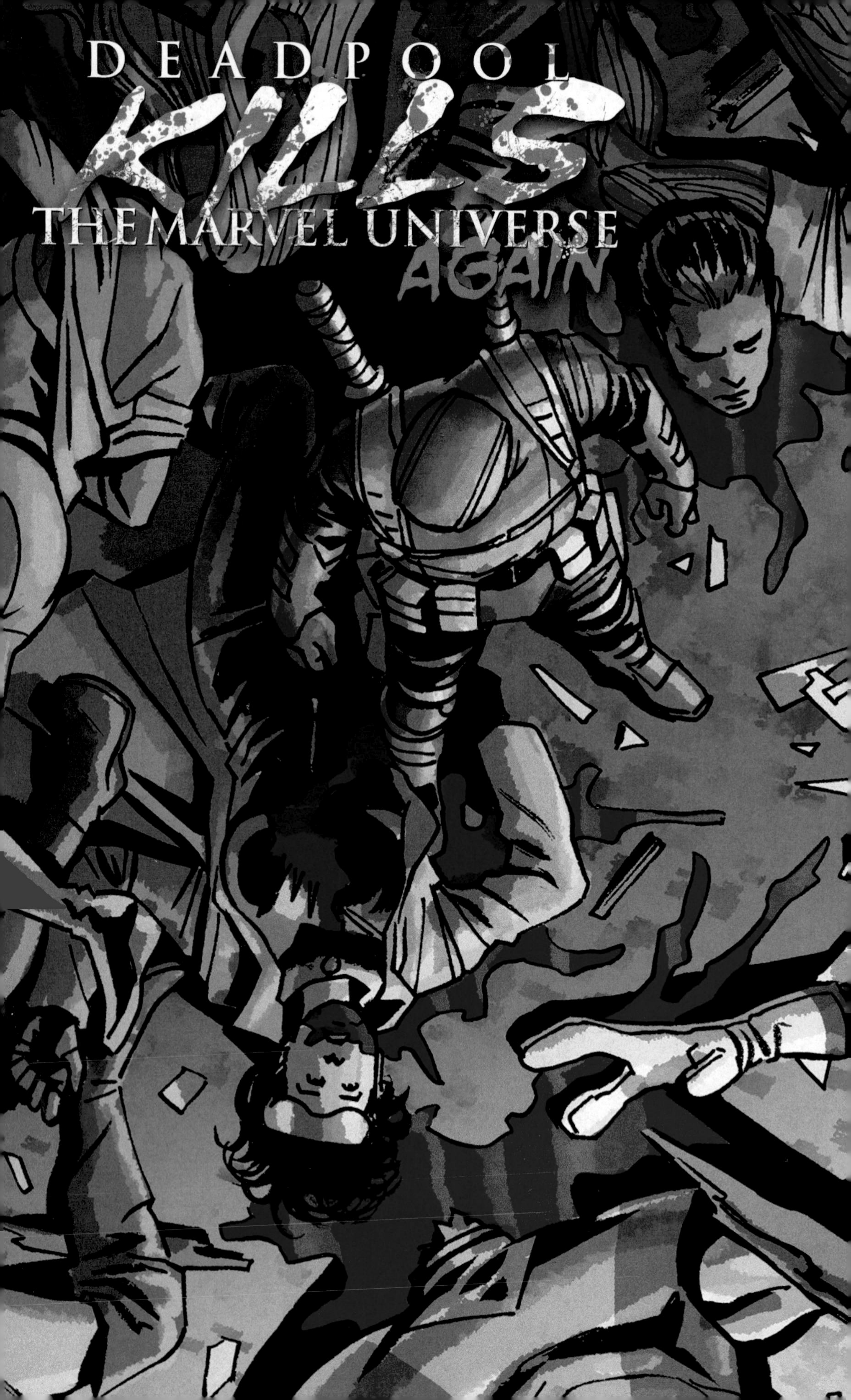
DEADPOOL
KILLS
THE MARVEL UNIVERSE
AGAIN

WRITER
CULLEN BUNN

PENCILER
DALIBOR TALAJIĆ

INKER
GORAN SUDŽUKA

COLORIST
MIROSLAV MRVA

LETTERER
VC's JOE SABINO

COVER ARTIST
DAVE JOHNSON

ASSISTANT EDITOR
HEATHER ANTOS

EDITOR
JORDAN D. WHITE

DEADPOOL CREATED BY ROB LIEFELD & FABIAN NICIEZA

COLLECTION EDITOR MARK D. BEAZLEY
ASSISTANT EDITOR CAITLIN O'CONNELL
ASSOCIATE MANAGING EDITOR KATERI WOODY
SENIOR EDITOR, SPECIAL PROJECTS JENNIFER GRÜNWALD
VP PRODUCTION & SPECIAL PROJECTS JEFF YOUNGQUIST
SVP PRINT, SALES & MARKETING DAVID GABRIEL
BOOK DESIGNER ADAM DEL RE

EDITOR IN CHIEF AXEL ALONSO
CHIEF CREATIVE OFFICER JOE QUESADA
PRESIDENT DAN BUCKLEY
EXECUTIVE PRODUCER ALAN FINE

DEADPOOL KILLS THE MARVEL UNIVERSE AGAIN. Contains material originally published in magazine form as DEADPOOL KILLS THE MARVEL UNIVERSE AGAIN #1-5. First printing 2017. ISBN# 978-1-302-90834-8. Published by MARVEL WORLDWIDE, INC., a subsidiary of MARVEL ENTERTAINMENT, LLC. OFFICE OF PUBLICATION: 135 West 50th Street, New York, NY 10020. Copyright © 2017 MARVEL No similarity between any of the names, characters, persons, and/or institutions in this magazine with those of any living or dead person or institution is intended, and any such similarity which may exist is purely coincidental. Printed in the U.S.A. DAN BUCKLEY, President, Marvel Entertainment; JOE QUESADA, Chief Creative Officer; TOM BREVOORT, SVP of Publishing; DAVID BOGART, SVP of Business Affairs & Operations, Publishing & Partnership; C.B. CEBULSKI, VP of Brand Management & Development, Asia; DAVID GABRIEL, SVP of Sales & Marketing, Publishing; JEFF YOUNGQUIST, VP of Production &

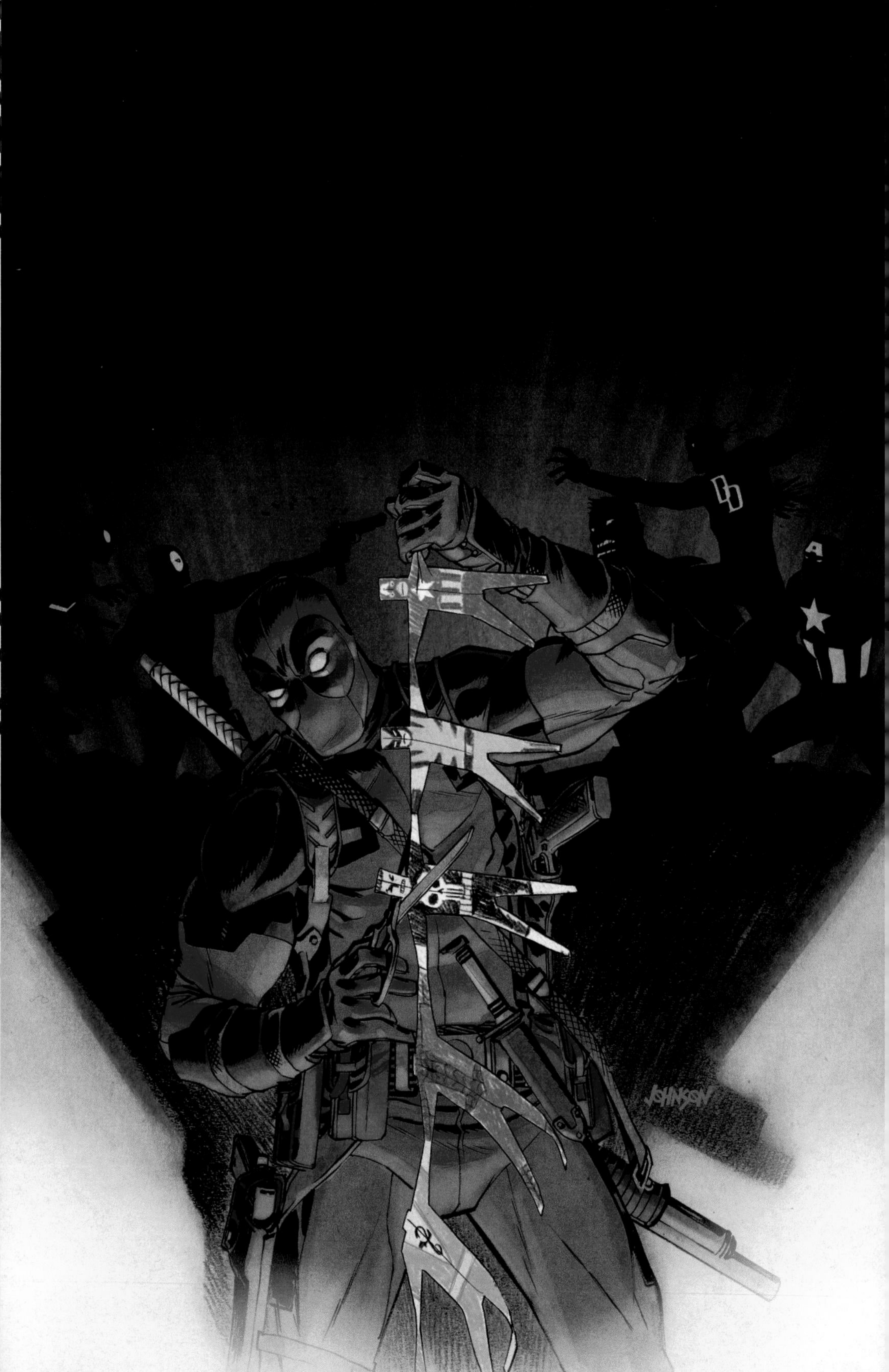
JOHNSON

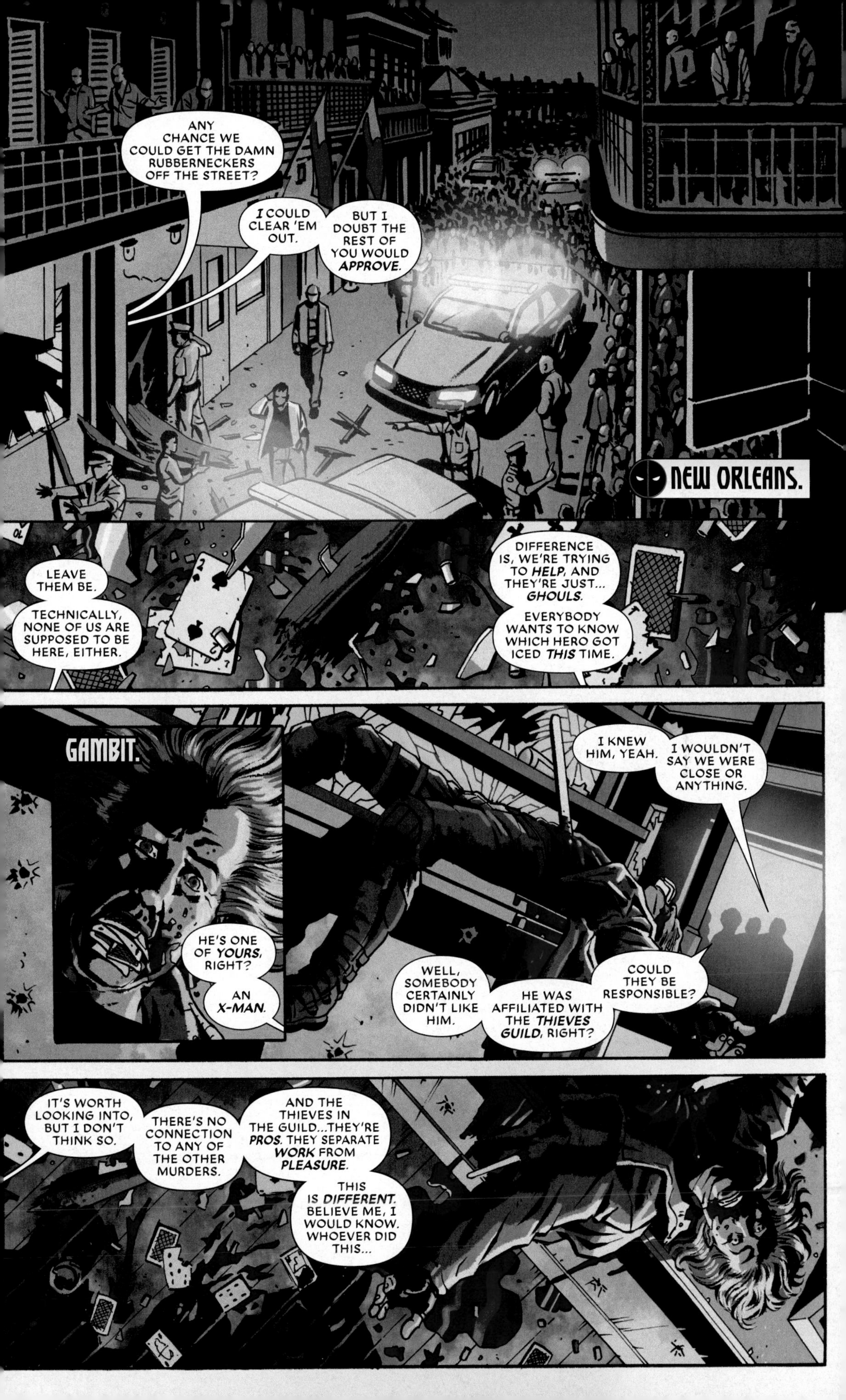

ANY CHANCE WE COULD GET THE DAMN RUBBERNECKERS OFF THE STREET?
I COULD CLEAR 'EM OUT.
BUT I DOUBT THE REST OF YOU WOULD APPROVE.
NEW ORLEANS.
LEAVE THEM BE.
TECHNICALLY, NONE OF US ARE SUPPOSED TO BE HERE, EITHER.
DIFFERENCE IS, WE'RE TRYING TO HELP, AND THEY'RE JUST... GHOULS.
EVERYBODY WANTS TO KNOW WHICH HERO GOT ICED THIS TIME.
GAMBIT.
HE'S ONE OF YOURS, RIGHT?
AN X-MAN.
I KNEW HIM, YEAH.
I WOULDN'T SAY WE WERE CLOSE OR ANYTHING.
WELL, SOMEBODY CERTAINLY DIDN'T LIKE HIM.
HE WAS AFFILIATED WITH THE THIEVES GUILD, RIGHT?
COULD THEY BE RESPONSIBLE?
IT'S WORTH LOOKING INTO, BUT I DON'T THINK SO.
THERE'S NO CONNECTION TO ANY OF THE OTHER MURDERS.
AND THE THIEVES IN THE GUILD...THEY'RE PROS. THEY SEPARATE WORK FROM PLEASURE.
THIS IS DIFFERENT. BELIEVE ME, I WOULD KNOW. WHOEVER DID THIS...

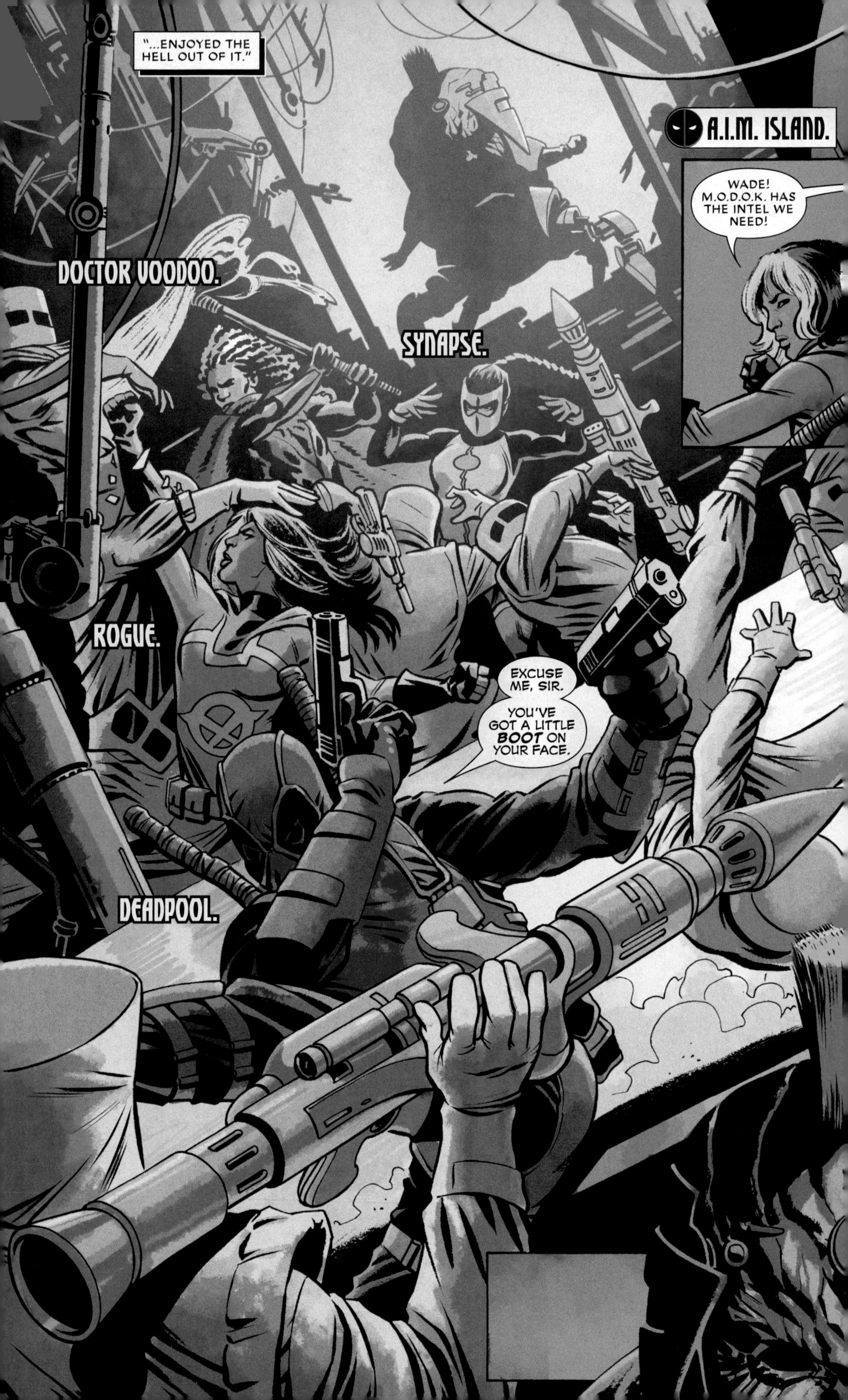
"...ENJOYED THE HELL OUT OF IT."
A.I.M. ISLAND.
WADE! M.O.D.O.K. HAS THE INTEL WE NEED!
DOCTOR VOODOO.
SYNAPSE.
ROGUE.
EXCUSE ME, SIR.
YOU'VE GOT A LITTLE BOOT ON YOUR FACE.
DEADPOOL.

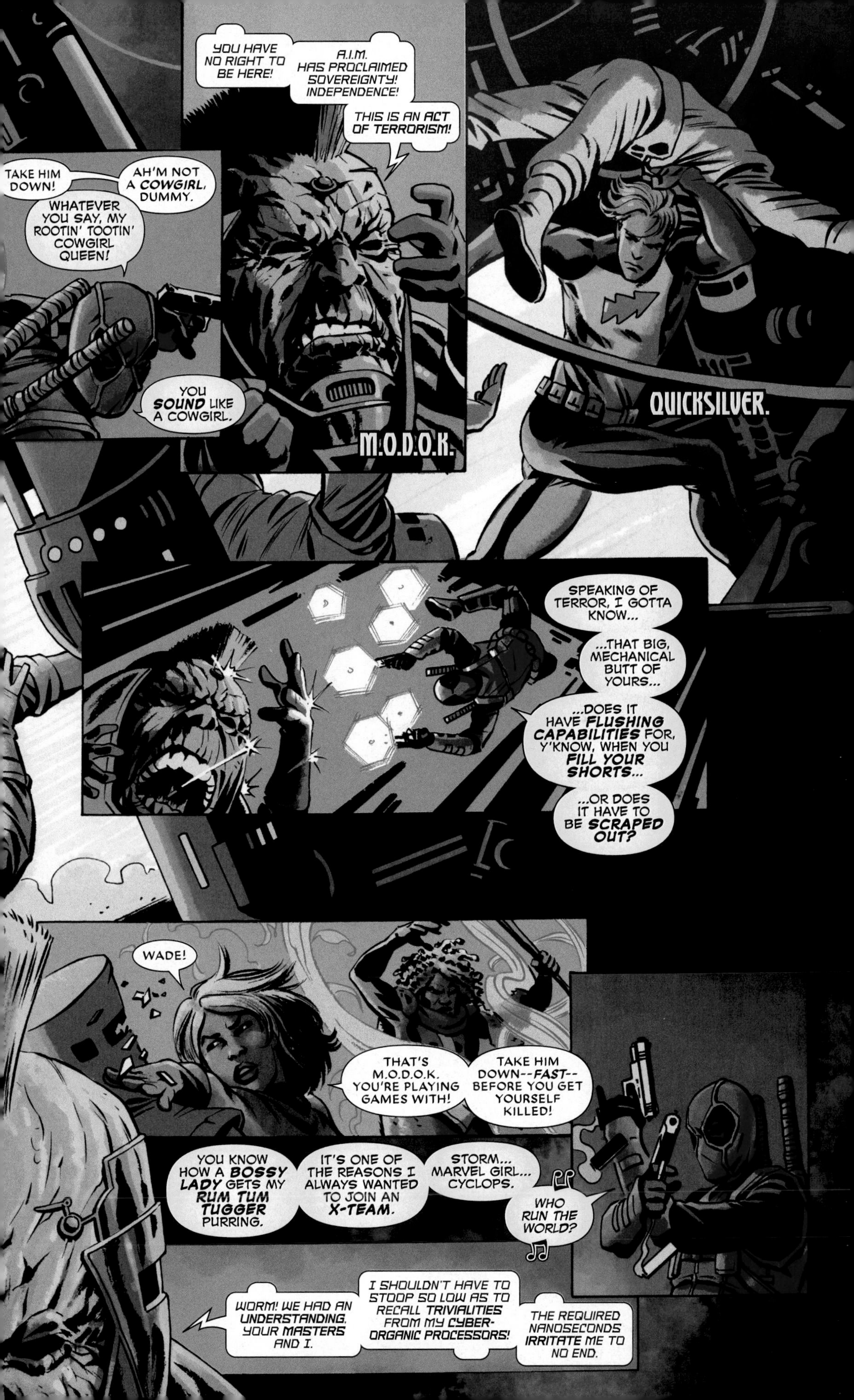

YOU HAVE NO RIGHT TO BE HERE!
A.I.M. HAS PROCLAIMED SOVEREIGNTY! INDEPENDENCE!
THIS IS AN ACT OF TERRORISM!
TAKE HIM DOWN!
AH'M NOT A COWGIRL, DUMMY.
WHATEVER YOU SAY, MY ROOTIN' TOOTIN' COWGIRL QUEEN!
YOU SOUND LIKE A COWGIRL.
M.O.D.O.K.
QUICKSILVER.
SPEAKING OF TERROR, I GOTTA KNOW...
...THAT BIG, MECHANICAL BUTT OF YOURS...
...DOES IT HAVE FLUSHING CAPABILITIES FOR, Y'KNOW, WHEN YOU FILL YOUR SHORTS...
...OR DOES IT HAVE TO BE SCRAPED OUT?
WADE!
THAT'S M.O.D.O.K. YOU'RE PLAYING GAMES WITH!
TAKE HIM DOWN--FAST--BEFORE YOU GET YOURSELF KILLED!
YOU KNOW HOW A BOSSY LADY GETS MY RUM TUM TUGGER PURRING.
IT'S ONE OF THE REASONS I ALWAYS WANTED TO JOIN AN X-TEAM.
STORM... MARVEL GIRL... CYCLOPS.
WHO RUN THE WORLD?
WORM! WE HAD AN UNDERSTANDING, YOUR MASTERS AND I.
I SHOULDN'T HAVE TO STOOP SO LOW AS TO RECALL TRIVIALITIES FROM MY CYBER-ORGANIC PROCESSORS!
THE REQUIRED NANOSECONDS IRRITATE ME TO NO END.

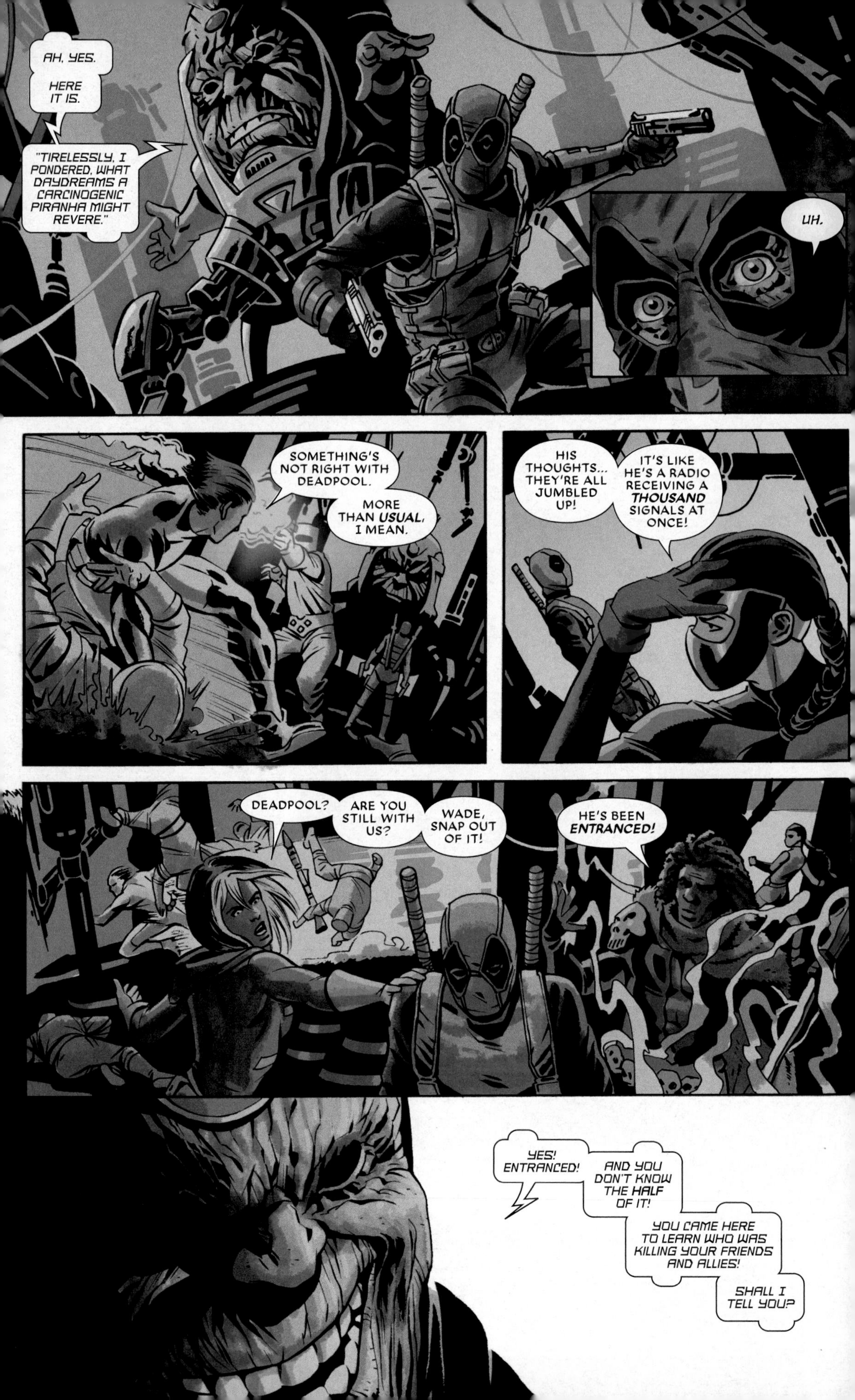
AH, YES.
HERE IT IS.
"TIRELESSLY, I PONDERED, WHAT DAYDREAMS A CARCINOGENIC PIRANHA MIGHT REVERE."
UH.
SOMETHING'S NOT RIGHT WITH DEADPOOL.
MORE THAN USUAL, I MEAN.
HIS THOUGHTS... THEY'RE ALL JUMBLED UP!
IT'S LIKE HE'S A RADIO RECEIVING A THOUSAND SIGNALS AT ONCE!
DEADPOOL?
ARE YOU STILL WITH US?
WADE, SNAP OUT OF IT!
HE'S BEEN ENTRANCED!
YES! ENTRANCED!
AND YOU DON'T KNOW THE HALF OF IT!
YOU CAME HERE TO LEARN WHO WAS KILLING YOUR FRIENDS AND ALLIES!
SHALL I TELL YOU?

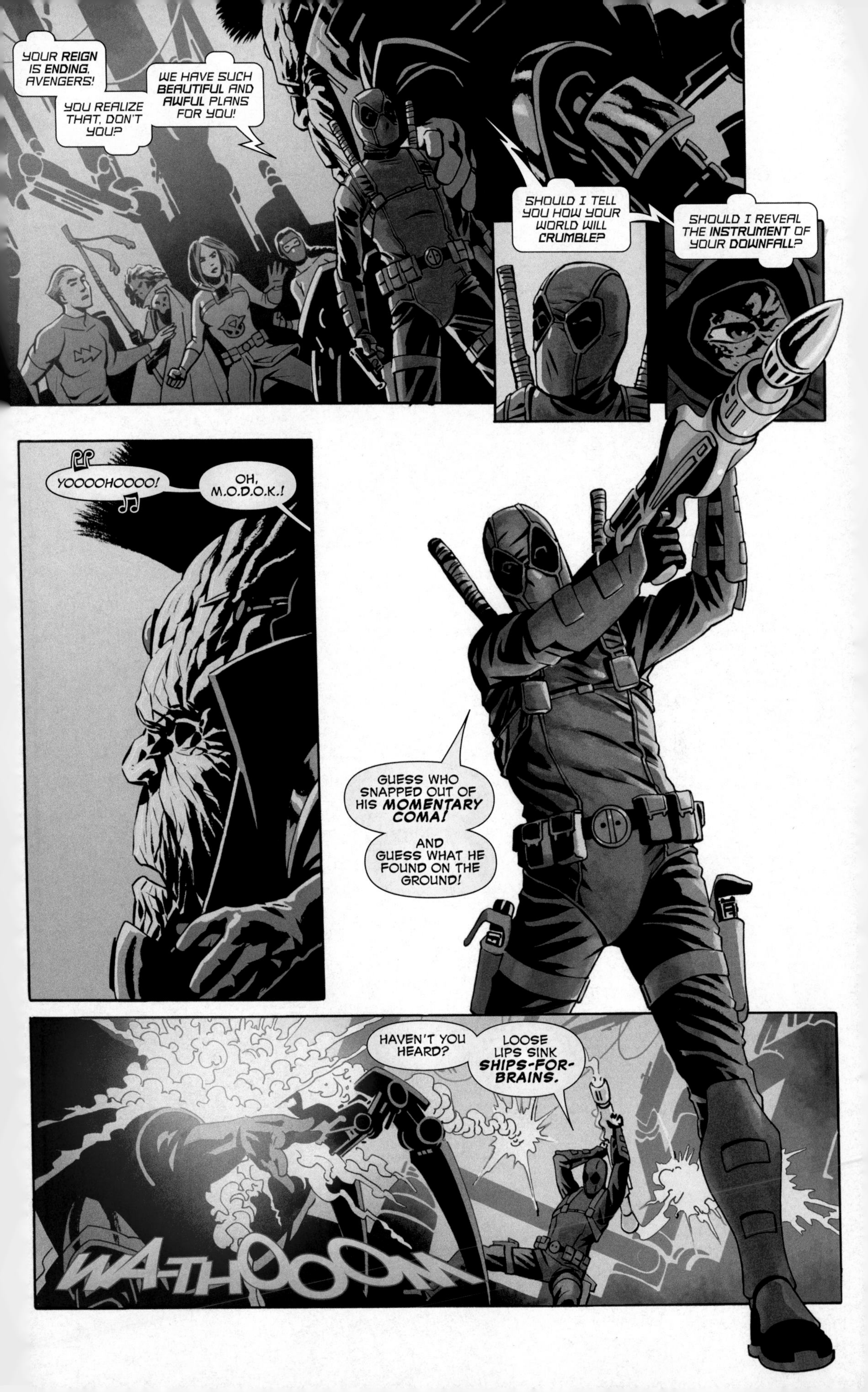
YOUR REIGN IS ENDING, AVENGERS!
YOU REALIZE THAT, DON'T YOU?
WE HAVE SUCH BEAUTIFUL AND AWFUL PLANS FOR YOU!
SHOULD I TELL YOU HOW YOUR WORLD WILL CRUMBLE?
SHOULD I REVEAL THE INSTRUMENT OF YOUR DOWNFALL?
YOOOOHOOOO!
OH, M.O.D.O.K.!
GUESS WHO SNAPPED OUT OF HIS MOMENTARY COMA!
AND GUESS WHAT HE FOUND ON THE GROUND!
HAVEN'T YOU HEARD?
LOOSE LIPS SINK SHIPS-FOR-BRAINS.
WA-THOOOM

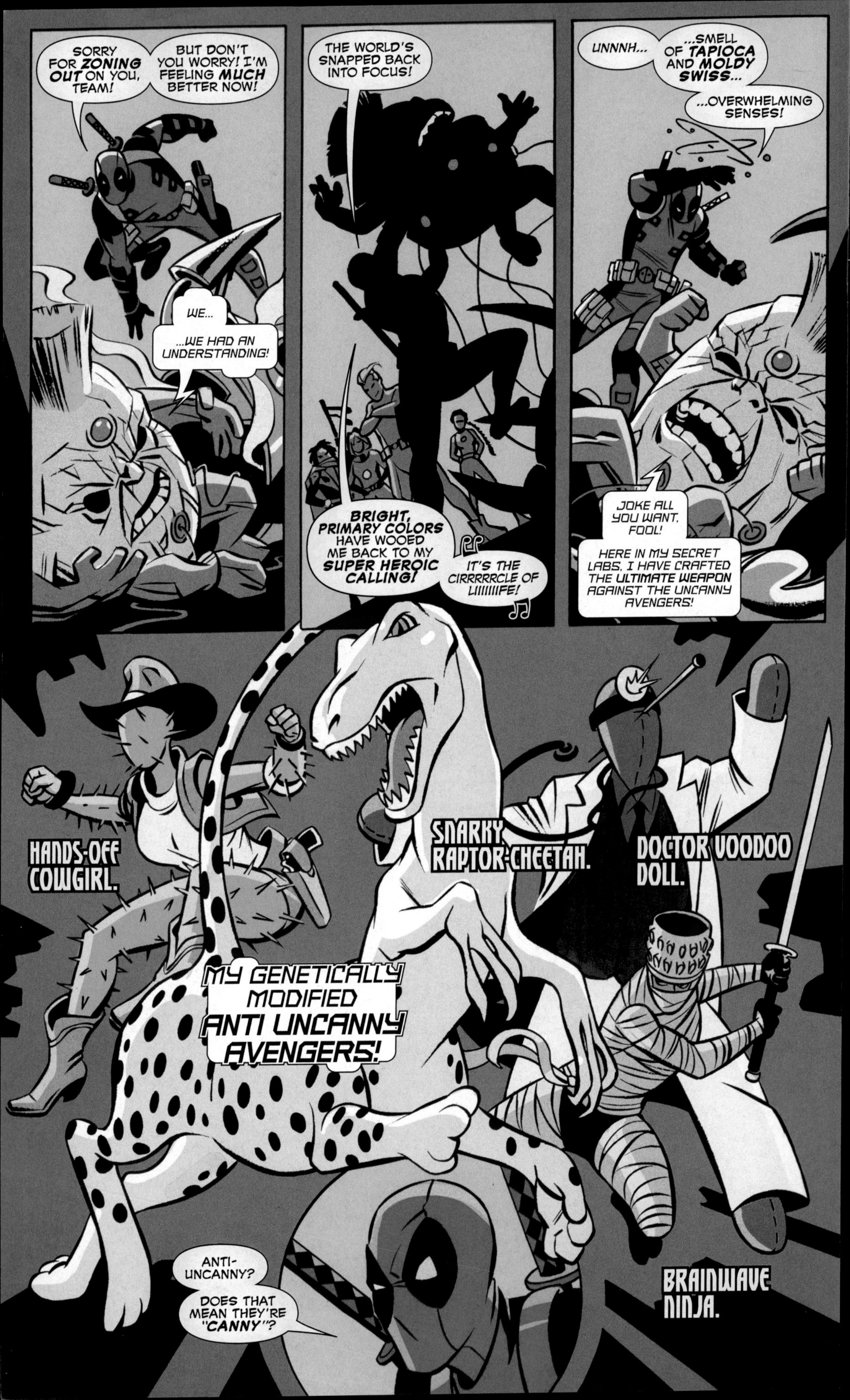
SORRY FOR ZONING OUT ON YOU, TEAM!
BUT DON'T YOU WORRY! I'M FEELING MUCH BETTER NOW!
WE...
...WE HAD AN UNDERSTANDING!
THE WORLD'S SNAPPED BACK INTO FOCUS!
BRIGHT, PRIMARY COLORS HAVE WOOED ME BACK TO MY SUPER HEROIC CALLING!
IT'S THE CIRRRRRCLE OF LIIIIIIFE!
UNNNH...
...SMELL OF TAPIOCA AND MOLDY SWISS...
...OVERWHELMING SENSES!
JOKE ALL YOU WANT, FOOL!
HERE IN MY SECRET LABS, I HAVE CRAFTED THE ULTIMATE WEAPON AGAINST THE UNCANNY AVENGERS!
HANDS-OFF COWGIRL.
SNARKY RAPTOR-CHEETAH.
DOCTOR VOODOO DOLL.
MY GENETICALLY MODIFIED ANTI UNCANNY AVENGERS!
BRAINWAVE NINJA.
ANTI-UNCANNY?
DOES THAT MEAN THEY'RE "CANNY"?

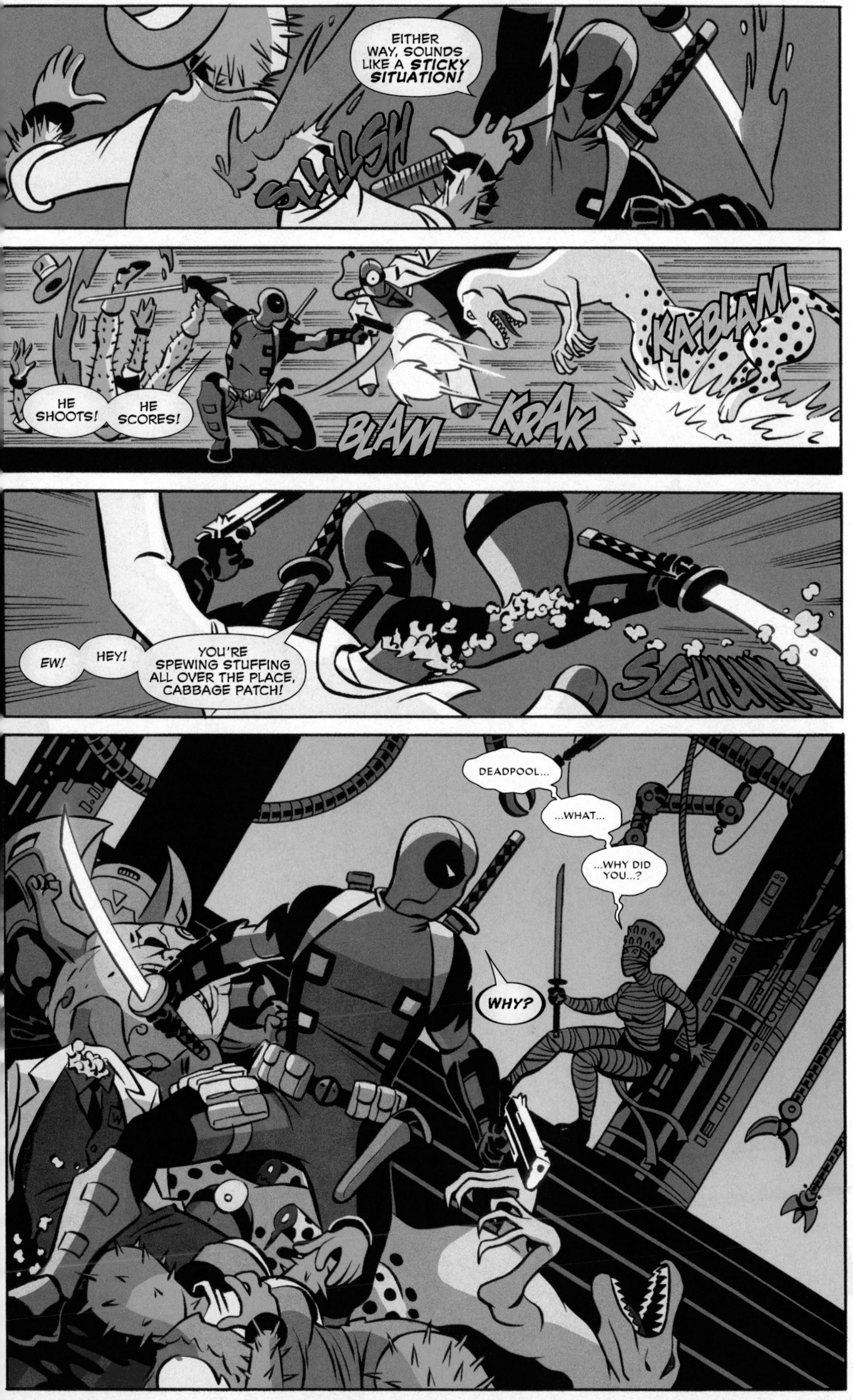

EITHER WAY, SOUNDS LIKE A STICKY SITUATION!
SLLLSH
HE SHOOTS!
HE SCORES!
BLAM
KRAK
KA-BLAM
EW!
HEY!
YOU'RE SPEWING STUFFING ALL OVER THE PLACE, CABBAGE PATCH!
DEADPOOL...
...WHAT...
...WHY DID YOU...?
WHY?

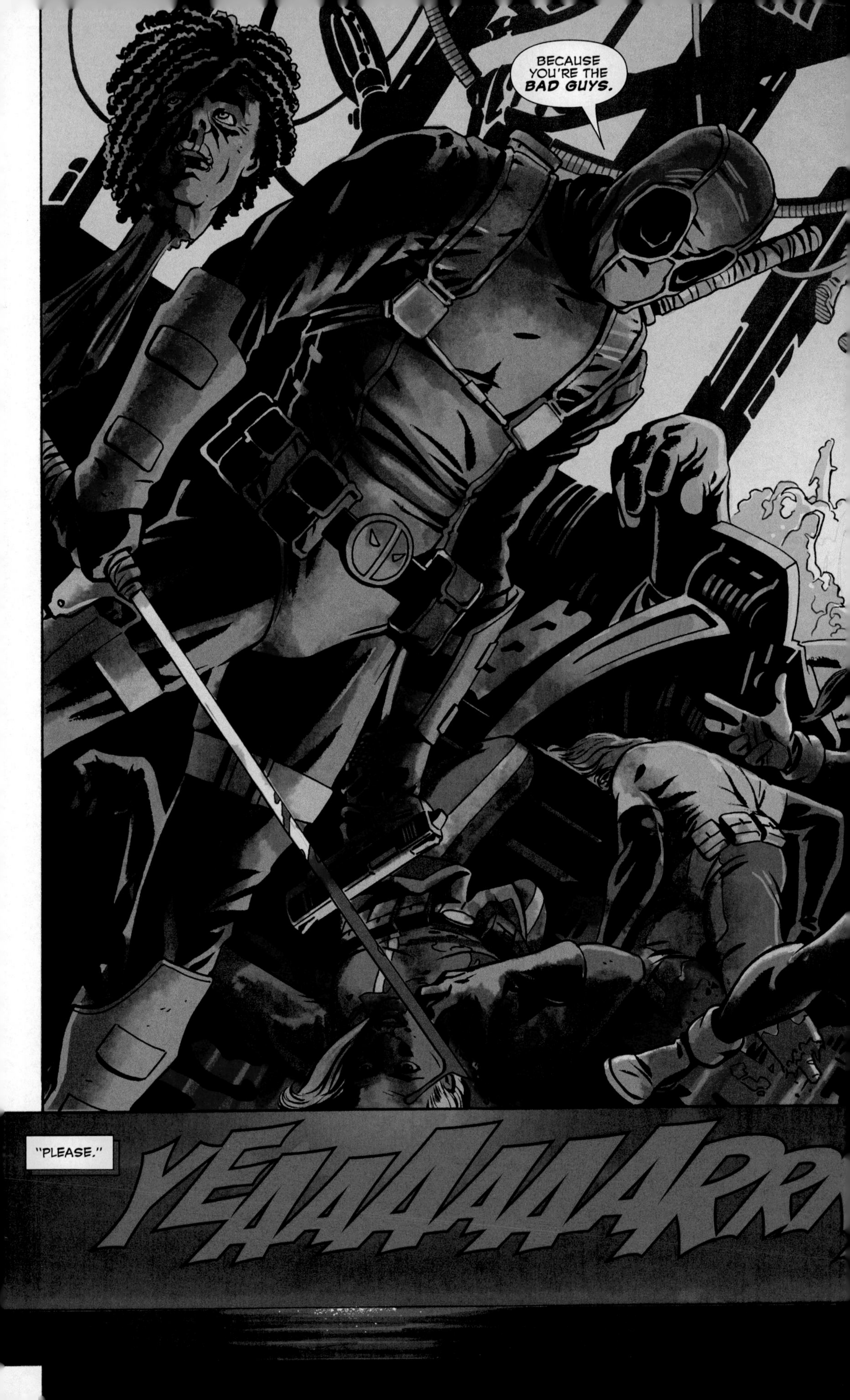

BECAUSE YOU'RE THE BAD GUYS.
"PLEASE."
YEAAAAAARR

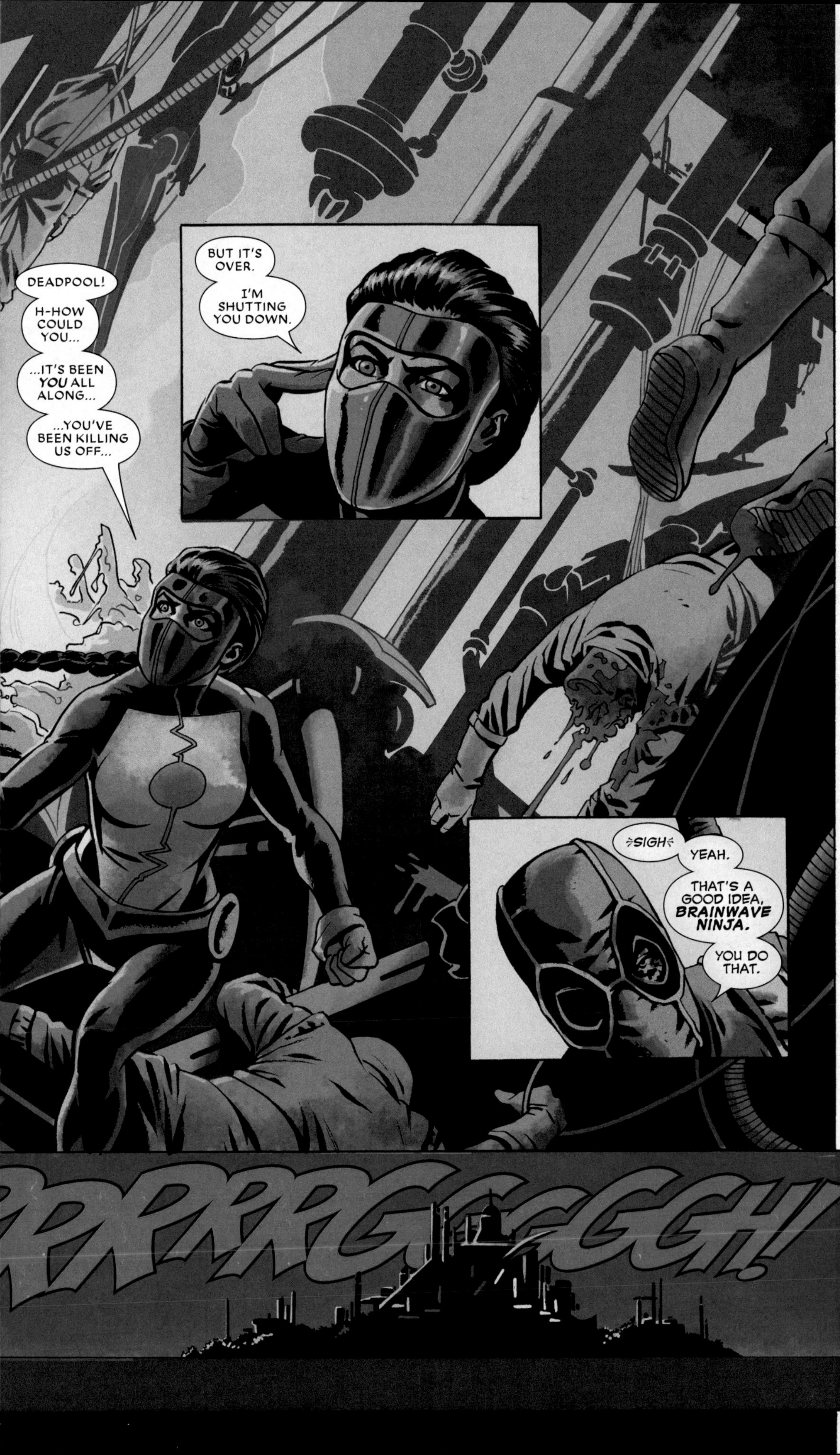

DEADPOOL!
H-HOW COULD YOU...
...IT'S BEEN YOU ALL ALONG...
...YOU'VE BEEN KILLING US OFF...
BUT IT'S OVER.
I'M SHUTTING YOU DOWN.
SIGH
YEAH.
THAT'S A GOOD IDEA, BRAINWAVE NINJA.
YOU DO THAT.
RRRRGGGGH!

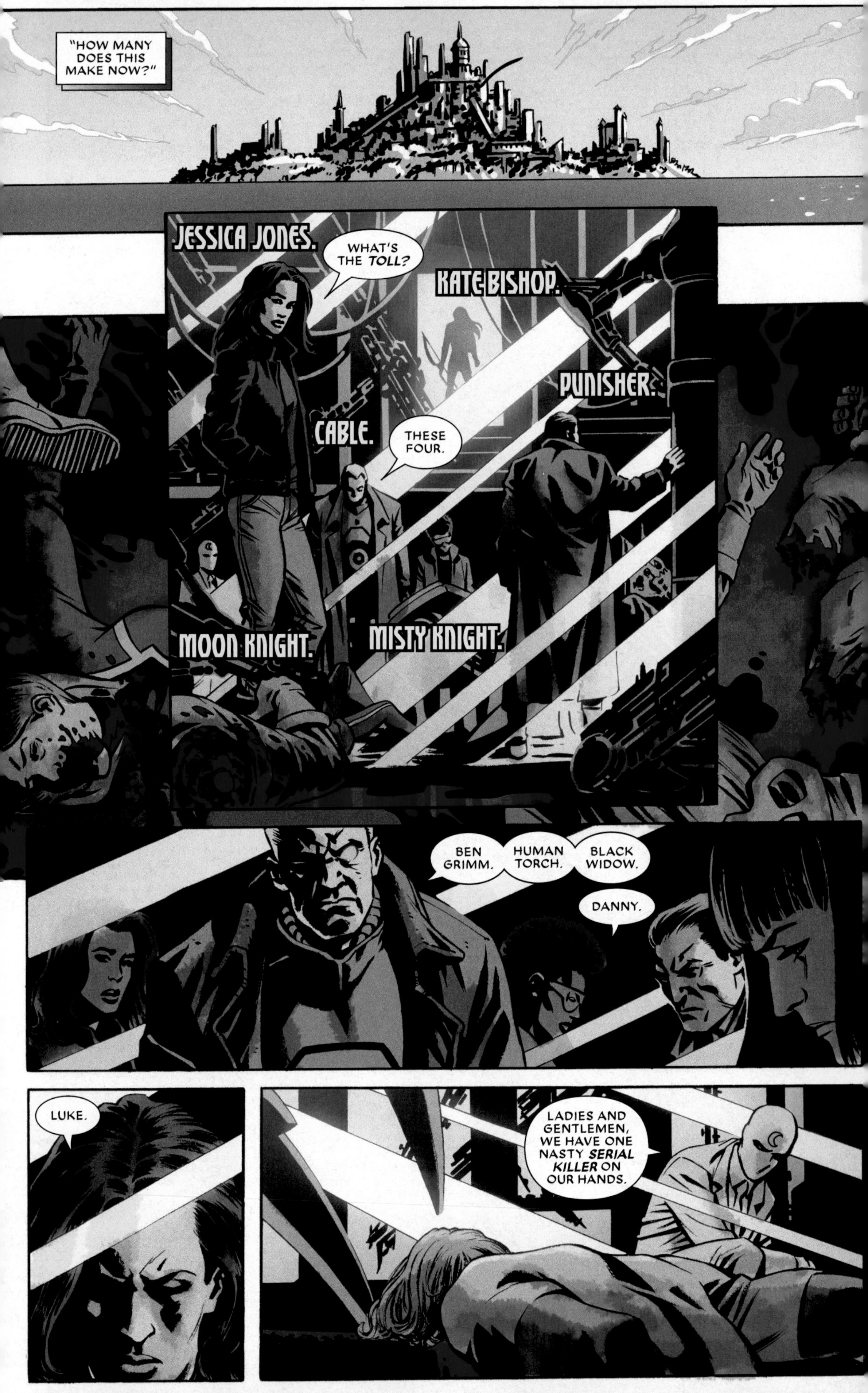
"HOW MANY DOES THIS MAKE NOW?"
JESSICA JONES.
WHAT'S THE *TOLL?*
KATE BISHOP.
PUNISHER.
CABLE.
THESE FOUR.
MOON KNIGHT.
MISTY KNIGHT.
BEN GRIMM.
HUMAN TORCH.
BLACK WIDOW.
DANNY.
LUKE.
LADIES AND GENTLEMEN, WE HAVE ONE NASTY *SERIAL KILLER* ON OUR HANDS.

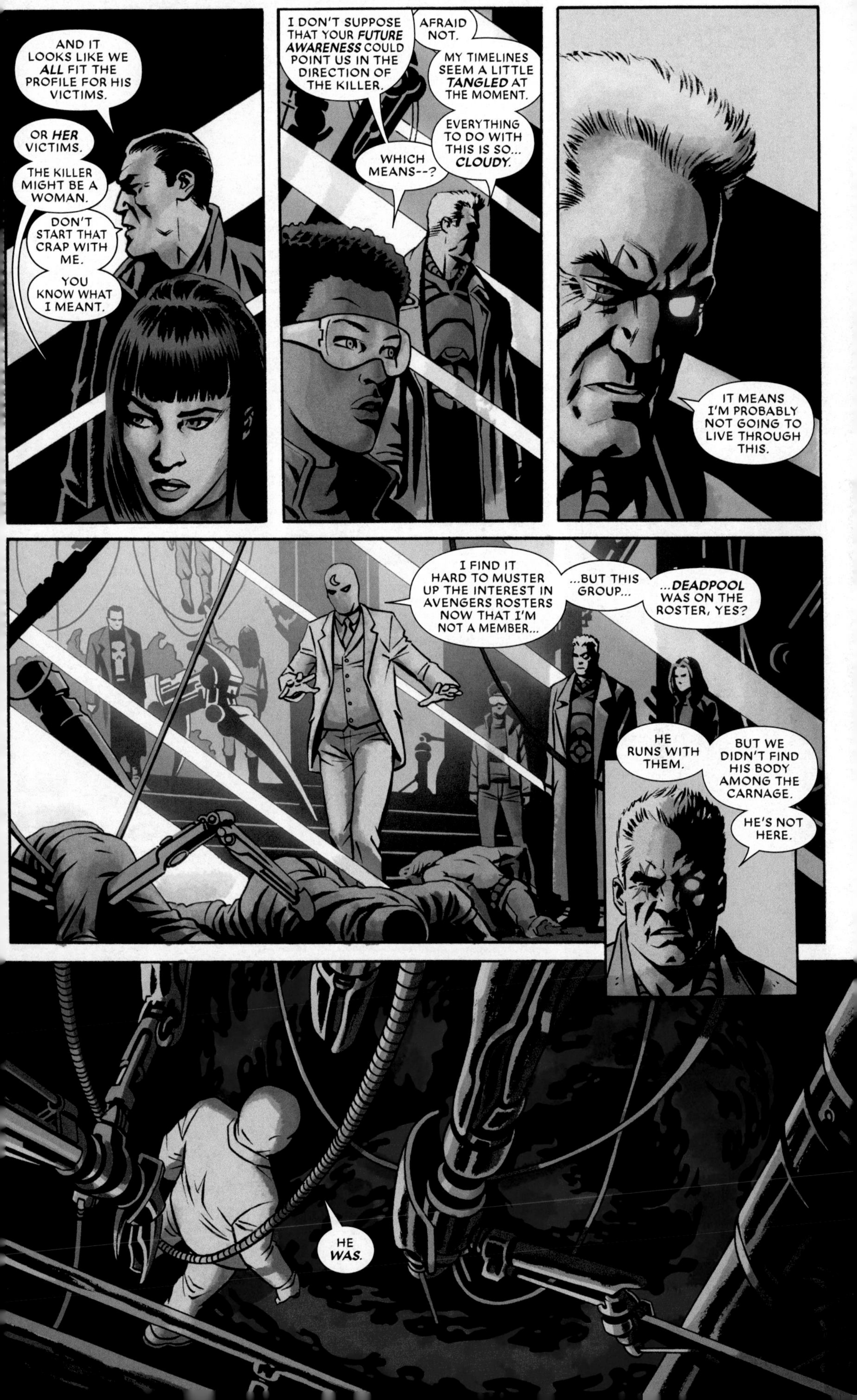
AND IT LOOKS LIKE WE ALL FIT THE PROFILE FOR HIS VICTIMS.
OR HER VICTIMS.
THE KILLER MIGHT BE A WOMAN.
DON'T START THAT CRAP WITH ME.
YOU KNOW WHAT I MEANT.
I DON'T SUPPOSE THAT YOUR FUTURE AWARENESS COULD POINT US IN THE DIRECTION OF THE KILLER.
AFRAID NOT.
MY TIMELINES SEEM A LITTLE TANGLED AT THE MOMENT.
EVERYTHING TO DO WITH THIS IS SO... CLOUDY.
WHICH MEANS--?
IT MEANS I'M PROBABLY NOT GOING TO LIVE THROUGH THIS.
I FIND IT HARD TO MUSTER UP THE INTEREST IN AVENGERS ROSTERS NOW THAT I'M NOT A MEMBER...
...BUT THIS GROUP...
...DEADPOOL WAS ON THE ROSTER, YES?
HE RUNS WITH THEM.
BUT WE DIDN'T FIND HIS BODY AMONG THE CARNAGE.
HE'S NOT HERE.
HE WAS.

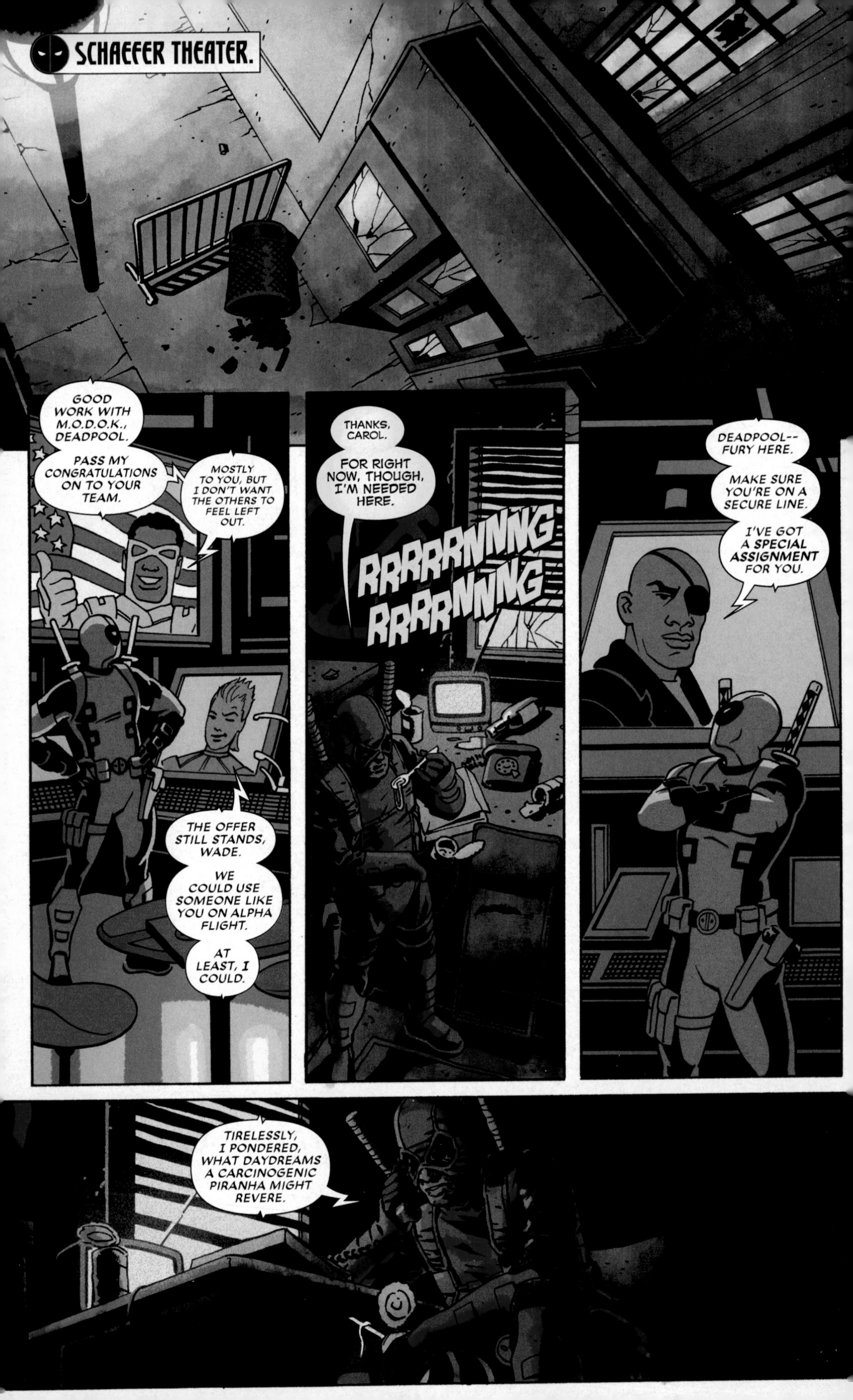
SCHAEFER THEATER.
GOOD WORK WITH M.O.D.O.K., DEADPOOL.
PASS MY CONGRATULATIONS ON TO YOUR TEAM.
MOSTLY TO YOU, BUT I DON'T WANT THE OTHERS TO FEEL LEFT OUT.
THE OFFER STILL STANDS, WADE.
WE COULD USE SOMEONE LIKE YOU ON ALPHA FLIGHT.
AT LEAST, I COULD.
THANKS, CAROL.
FOR RIGHT NOW, THOUGH, I'M NEEDED HERE.
RRRRRNNNG RRRRNNNG
DEADPOOL-- FURY HERE.
MAKE SURE YOU'RE ON A SECURE LINE.
I'VE GOT A **SPECIAL ASSIGNMENT** FOR YOU.
TIRELESSLY, I PONDERED, WHAT DAYDREAMS A CARCINOGENIC PIRANHA MIGHT REVERE.

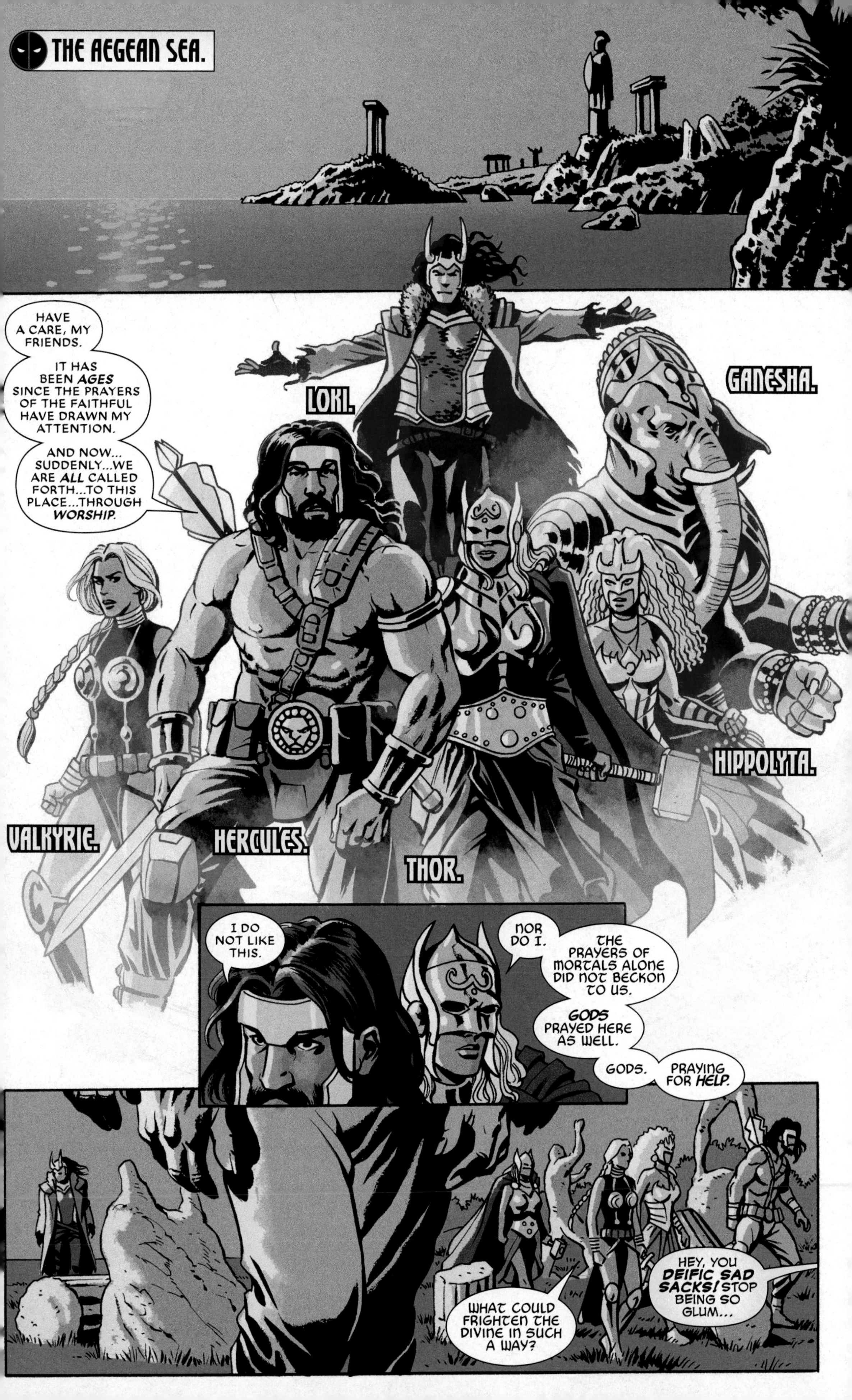
THE AEGEAN SEA.
HAVE A CARE, MY FRIENDS.
IT HAS BEEN AGES SINCE THE PRAYERS OF THE FAITHFUL HAVE DRAWN MY ATTENTION.
AND NOW... SUDDENLY...WE ARE ALL CALLED FORTH...TO THIS PLACE...THROUGH WORSHIP.
LOKI.
GANESHA.
HIPPOLYTA.
VALKYRIE.
HERCULES.
THOR.
I DO NOT LIKE THIS.
NOR DO I.
THE PRAYERS OF MORTALS ALONE DID NOT BECKON TO US.
GODS PRAYED HERE AS WELL.
GODS.
PRAYING FOR HELP.
WHAT COULD FRIGHTEN THE DIVINE IN SUCH A WAY?
HEY, YOU DEIFIC SAD SACKS! STOP BEING SO GLUM...

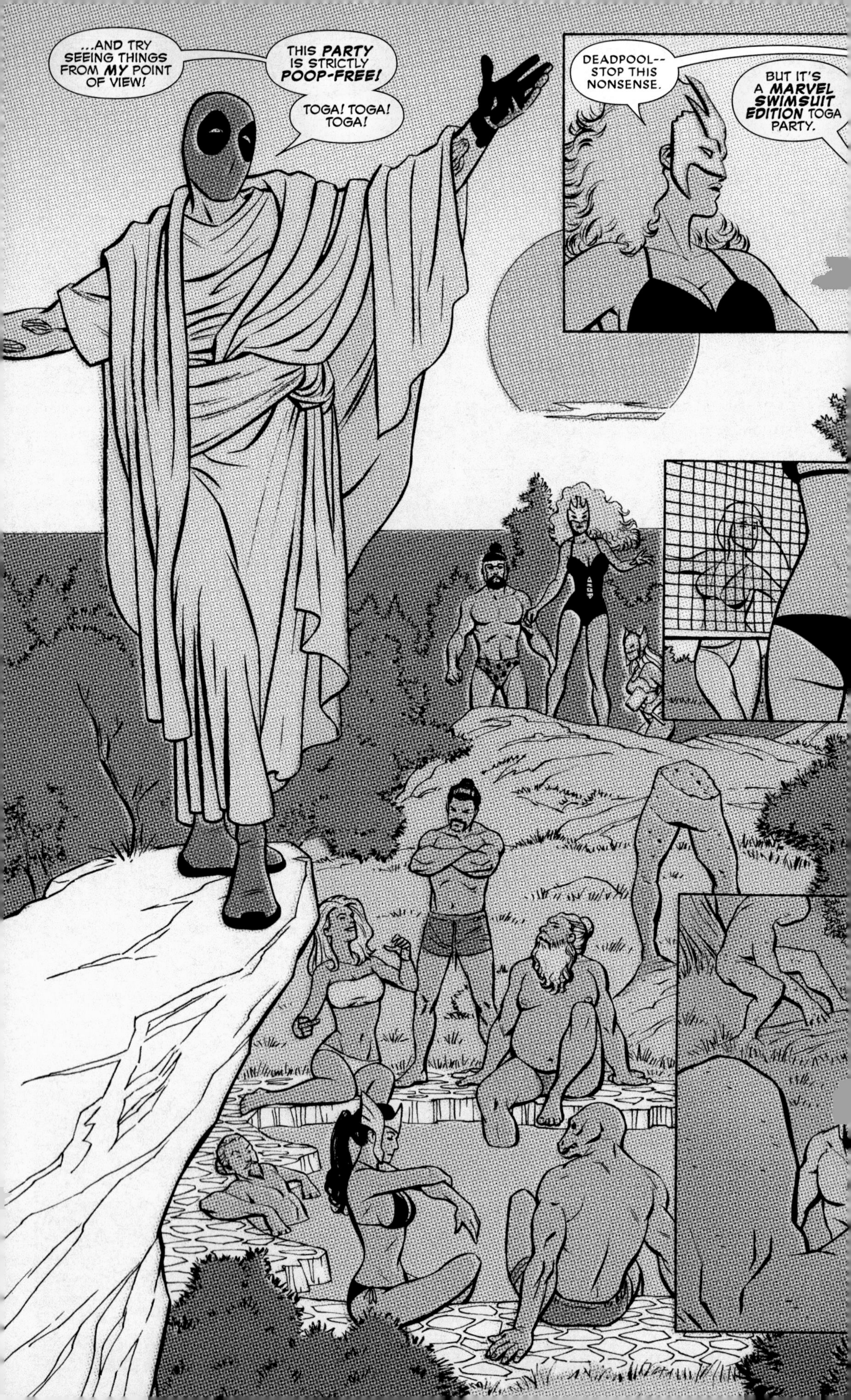

...AND TRY SEEING THINGS FROM MY POINT OF VIEW!
THIS PARTY IS STRICTLY POOP-FREE!
TOGA! TOGA! TOGA!
DEADPOOL-- STOP THIS NONSENSE.
BUT IT'S A MARVEL SWIMSUIT EDITION TOGA PARTY.

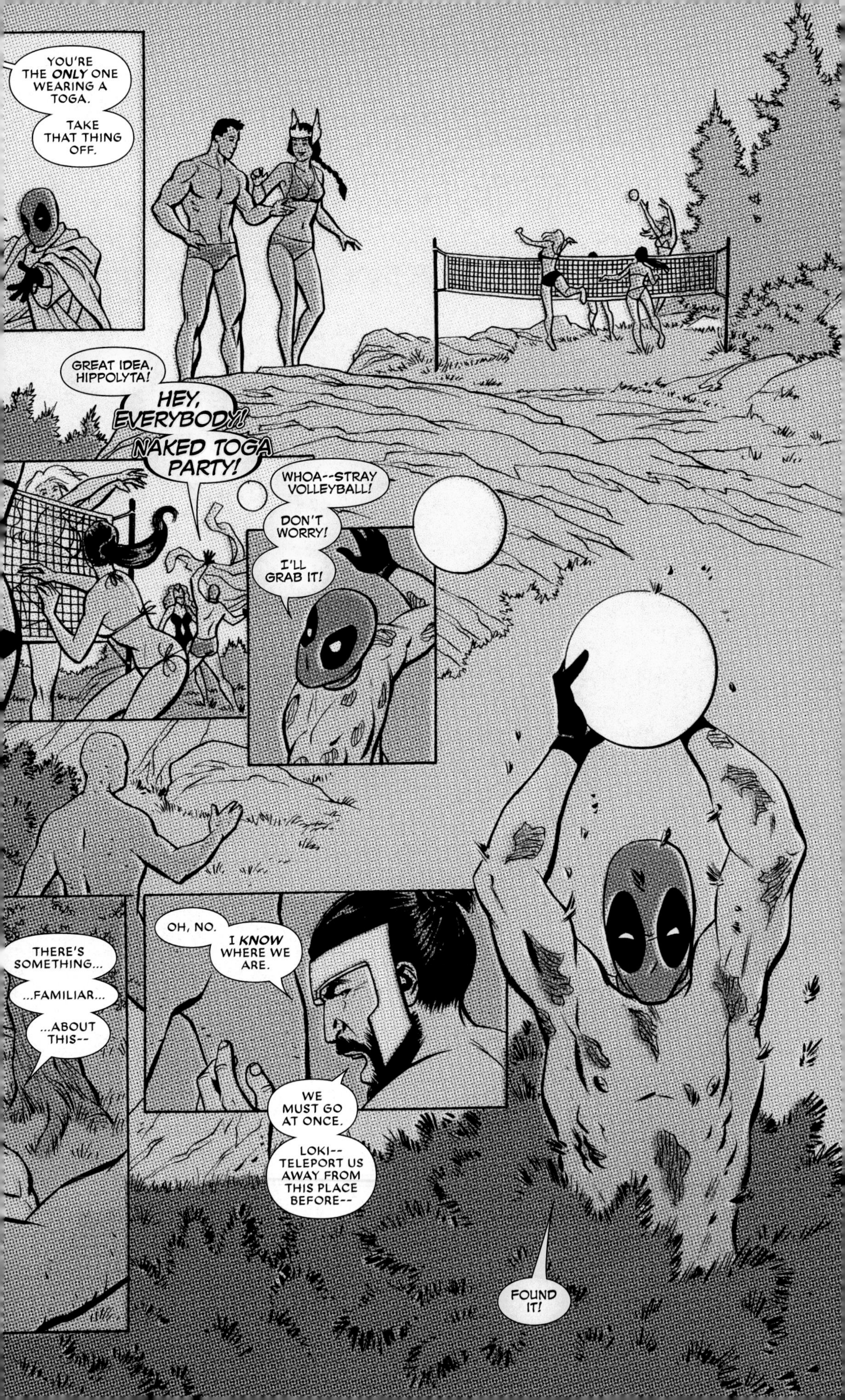
YOU'RE THE ONLY ONE WEARING A TOGA.
TAKE THAT THING OFF.
GREAT IDEA, HIPPOLYTA!
HEY, EVERYBODY!
NAKED TOGA PARTY!
WHOA--STRAY VOLLEYBALL!
DON'T WORRY!
I'LL GRAB IT!
THERE'S SOMETHING...
...FAMILIAR...
...ABOUT THIS--
OH, NO.
I KNOW WHERE WE ARE.
WE MUST GO AT ONCE.
LOKI--TELEPORT US AWAY FROM THIS PLACE BEFORE--
FOUND IT!

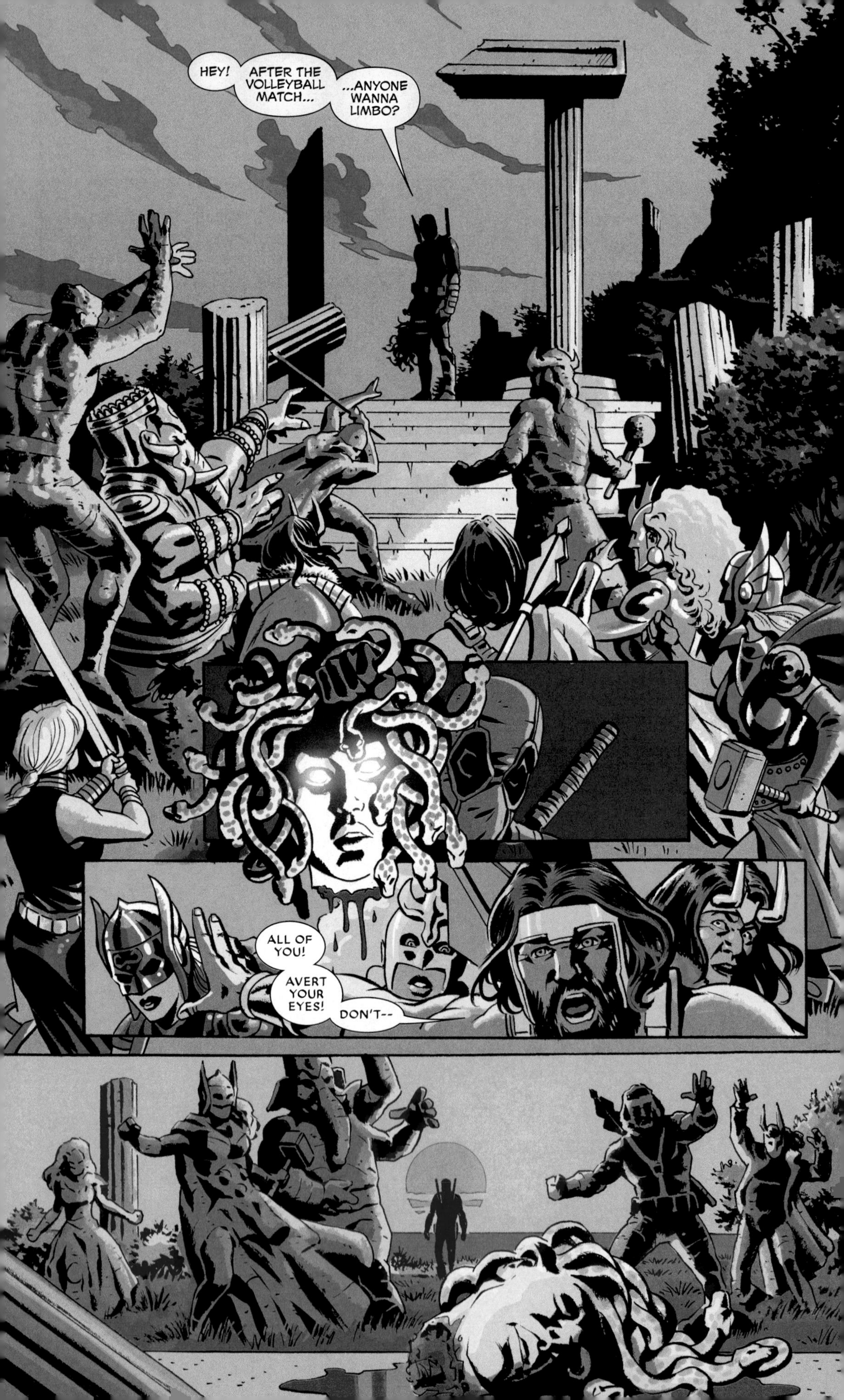
HEY!
AFTER THE VOLLEYBALL MATCH...
...ANYONE WANNA LIMBO?
ALL OF YOU!
AVERT YOUR EYES!
DON'T--

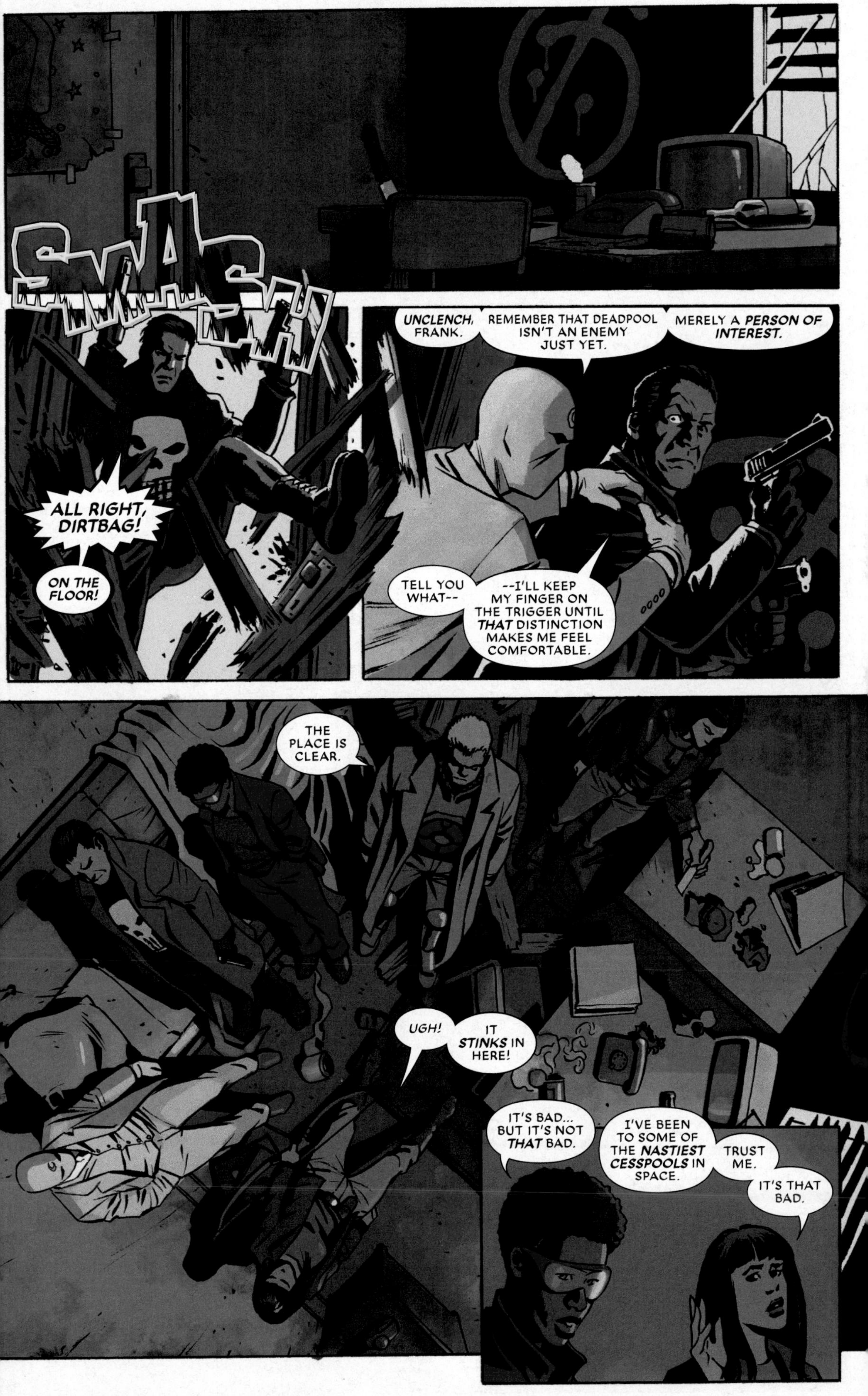
SMASH
ALL RIGHT, DIRTBAG!
ON THE FLOOR!
UNCLENCH, FRANK.
REMEMBER THAT DEADPOOL ISN'T AN ENEMY JUST YET.
MERELY A PERSON OF INTEREST.
TELL YOU WHAT--
--I'LL KEEP MY FINGER ON THE TRIGGER UNTIL THAT DISTINCTION MAKES ME FEEL COMFORTABLE.
THE PLACE IS CLEAR.
UGH!
IT STINKS IN HERE!
IT'S BAD... BUT IT'S NOT THAT BAD.
I'VE BEEN TO SOME OF THE NASTIEST CESSPOOLS IN SPACE.
TRUST ME.
IT'S THAT BAD.

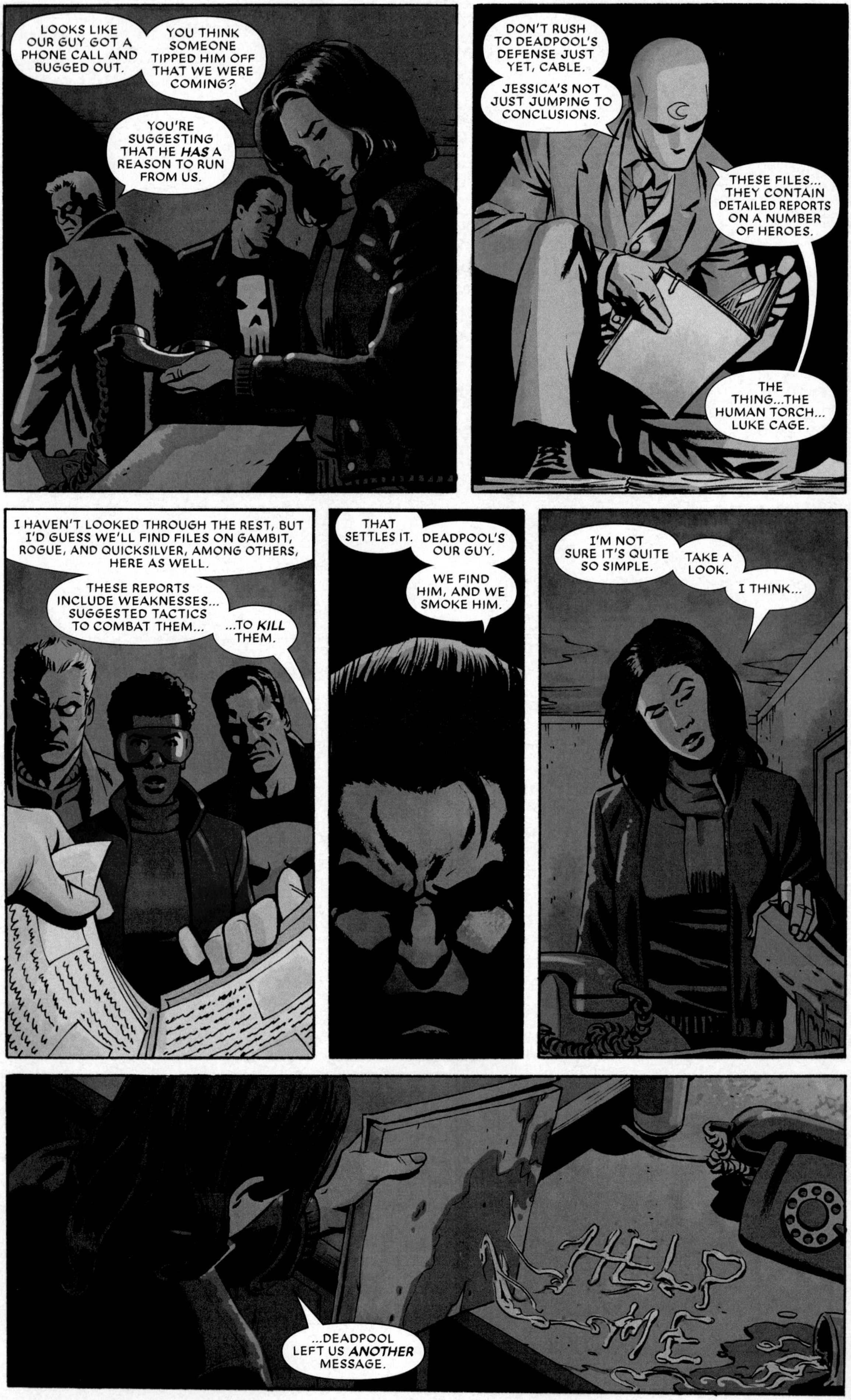
LOOKS LIKE OUR GUY GOT A PHONE CALL AND BUGGED OUT.
YOU THINK SOMEONE TIPPED HIM OFF THAT WE WERE COMING?
YOU'RE SUGGESTING THAT HE *HAS* A REASON TO RUN FROM US.
DON'T RUSH TO DEADPOOL'S DEFENSE JUST YET, CABLE.
JESSICA'S NOT JUST JUMPING TO CONCLUSIONS.
THESE FILES... THEY CONTAIN DETAILED REPORTS ON A NUMBER OF HEROES.
THE THING...THE HUMAN TORCH... LUKE CAGE.
I HAVEN'T LOOKED THROUGH THE REST, BUT I'D GUESS WE'LL FIND FILES ON GAMBIT, ROGUE, AND QUICKSILVER, AMONG OTHERS, HERE AS WELL.
THESE REPORTS INCLUDE WEAKNESSES... SUGGESTED TACTICS TO COMBAT THEM...
...TO *KILL* THEM.
THAT SETTLES IT.
DEADPOOL'S OUR GUY.
WE FIND HIM, AND WE SMOKE HIM.
I'M NOT SURE IT'S QUITE SO SIMPLE.
TAKE A LOOK.
I THINK...
HELP ME
...DEADPOOL LEFT US *ANOTHER* MESSAGE.

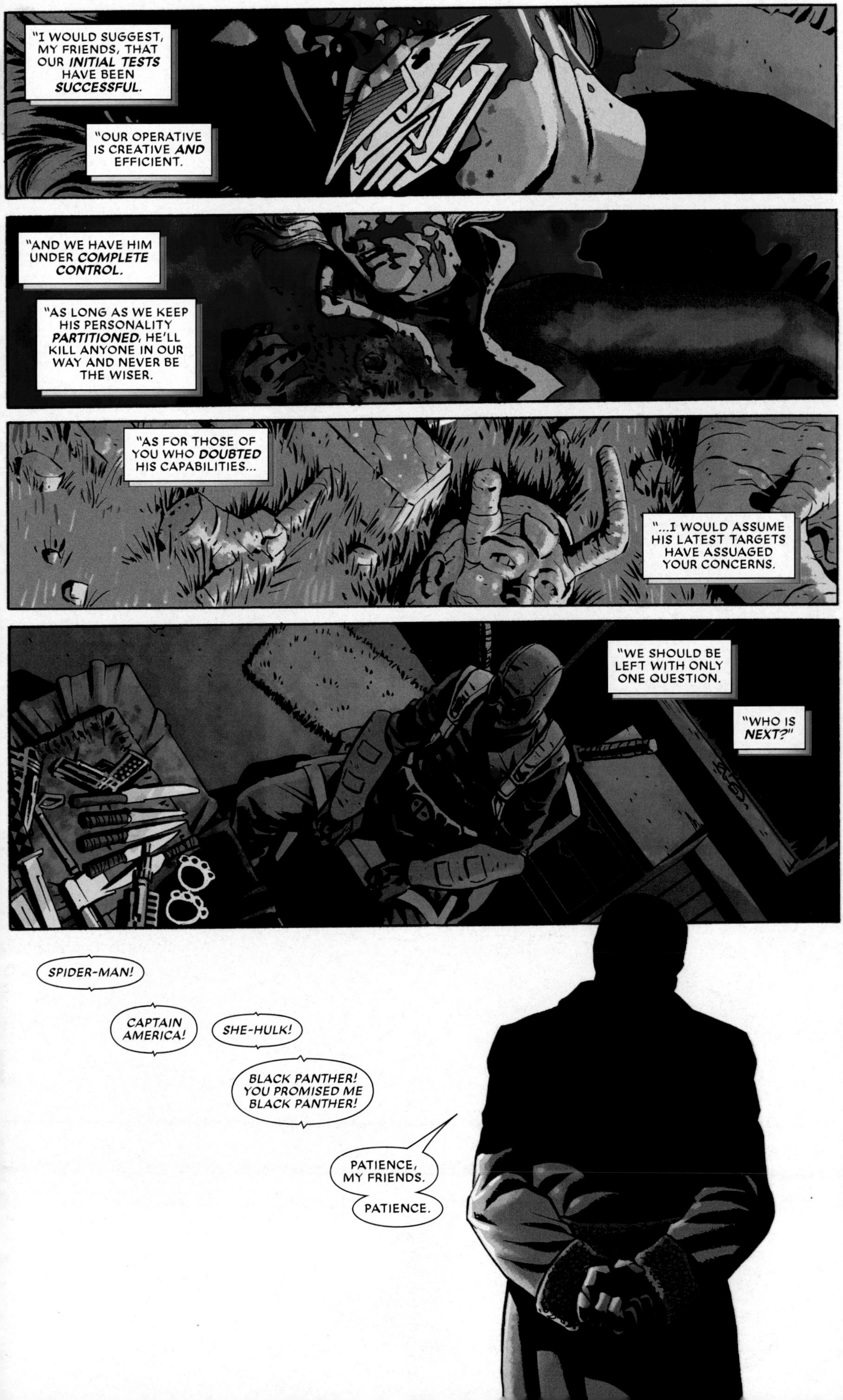

"I WOULD SUGGEST, MY FRIENDS, THAT OUR INITIAL TESTS HAVE BEEN SUCCESSFUL.
"OUR OPERATIVE IS CREATIVE AND EFFICIENT.
"AND WE HAVE HIM UNDER COMPLETE CONTROL.
"AS LONG AS WE KEEP HIS PERSONALITY PARTITIONED, HE'LL KILL ANYONE IN OUR WAY AND NEVER BE THE WISER.
"AS FOR THOSE OF YOU WHO DOUBTED HIS CAPABILITIES...
"...I WOULD ASSUME HIS LATEST TARGETS HAVE ASSUAGED YOUR CONCERNS.
"WE SHOULD BE LEFT WITH ONLY ONE QUESTION.
"WHO IS NEXT?"
SPIDER-MAN!
CAPTAIN AMERICA!
SHE-HULK!
BLACK PANTHER! YOU PROMISED ME BLACK PANTHER!
PATIENCE, MY FRIENDS.
PATIENCE.

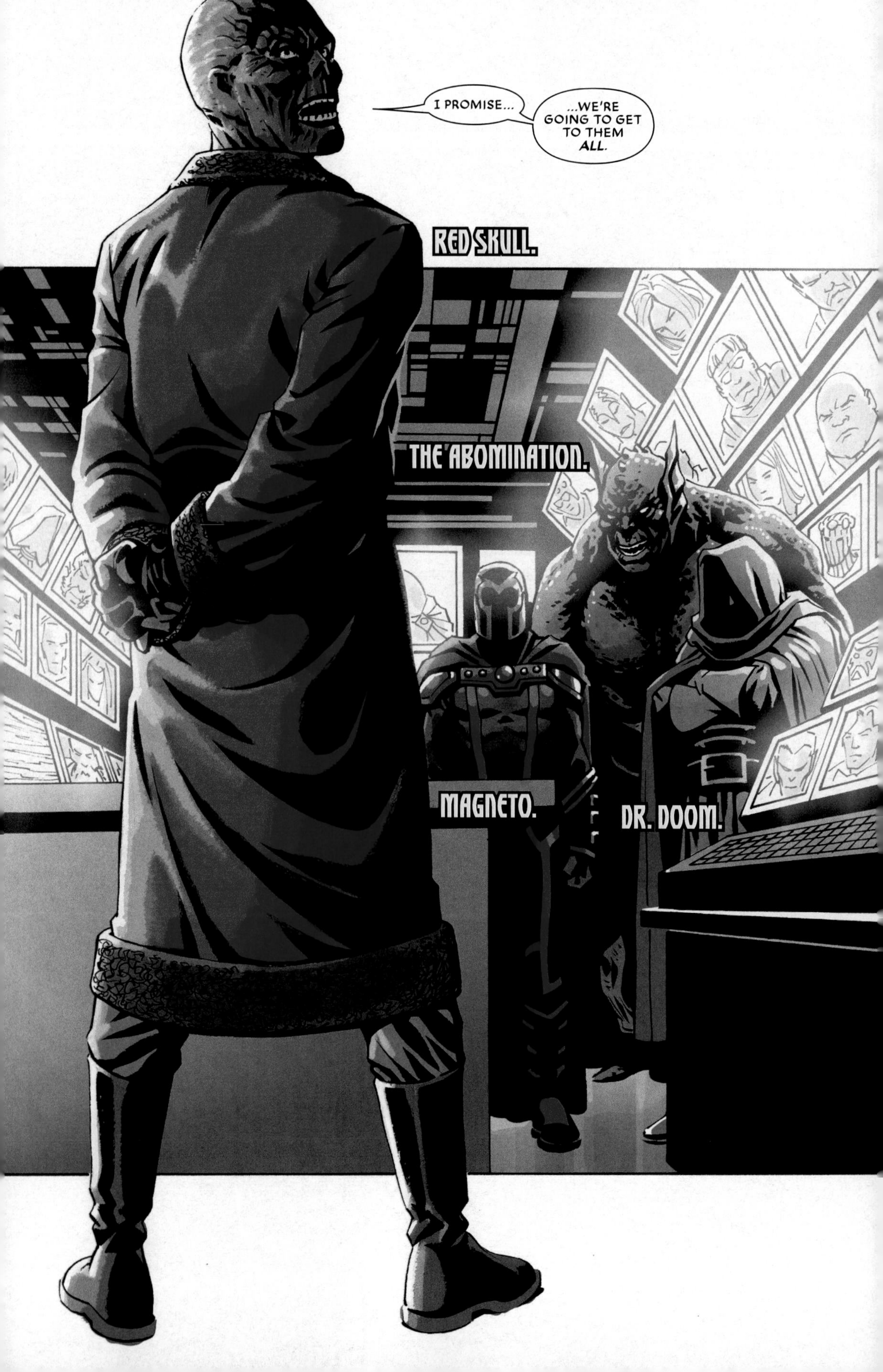
I PROMISE...
...WE'RE GOING TO GET TO THEM ALL.
RED SKULL.
THE ABOMINATION.
MAGNETO.
DR. DOOM.

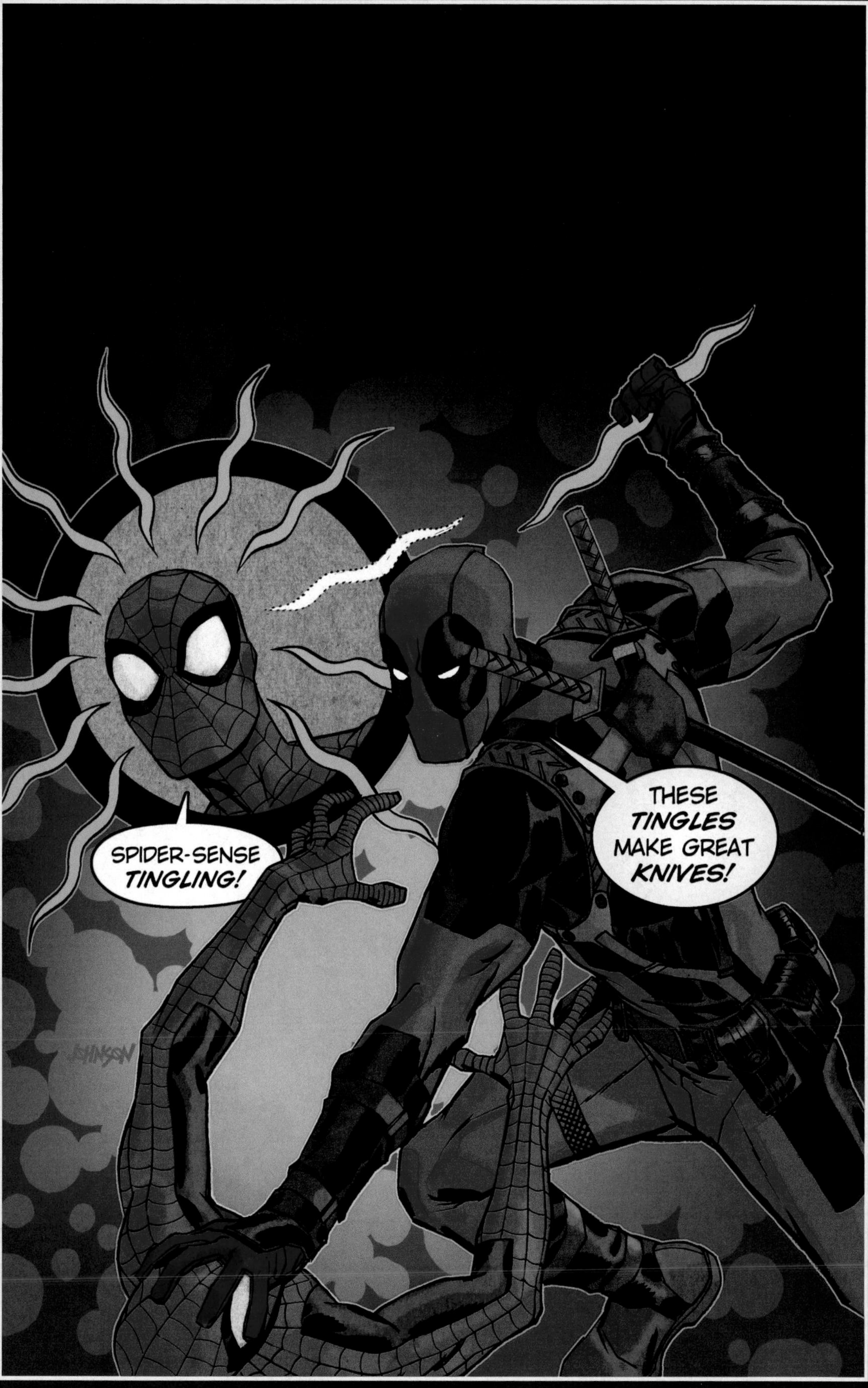
SPIDER-SENSE TINGLING!
THESE TINGLES MAKE GREAT KNIVES!
JOHNSON

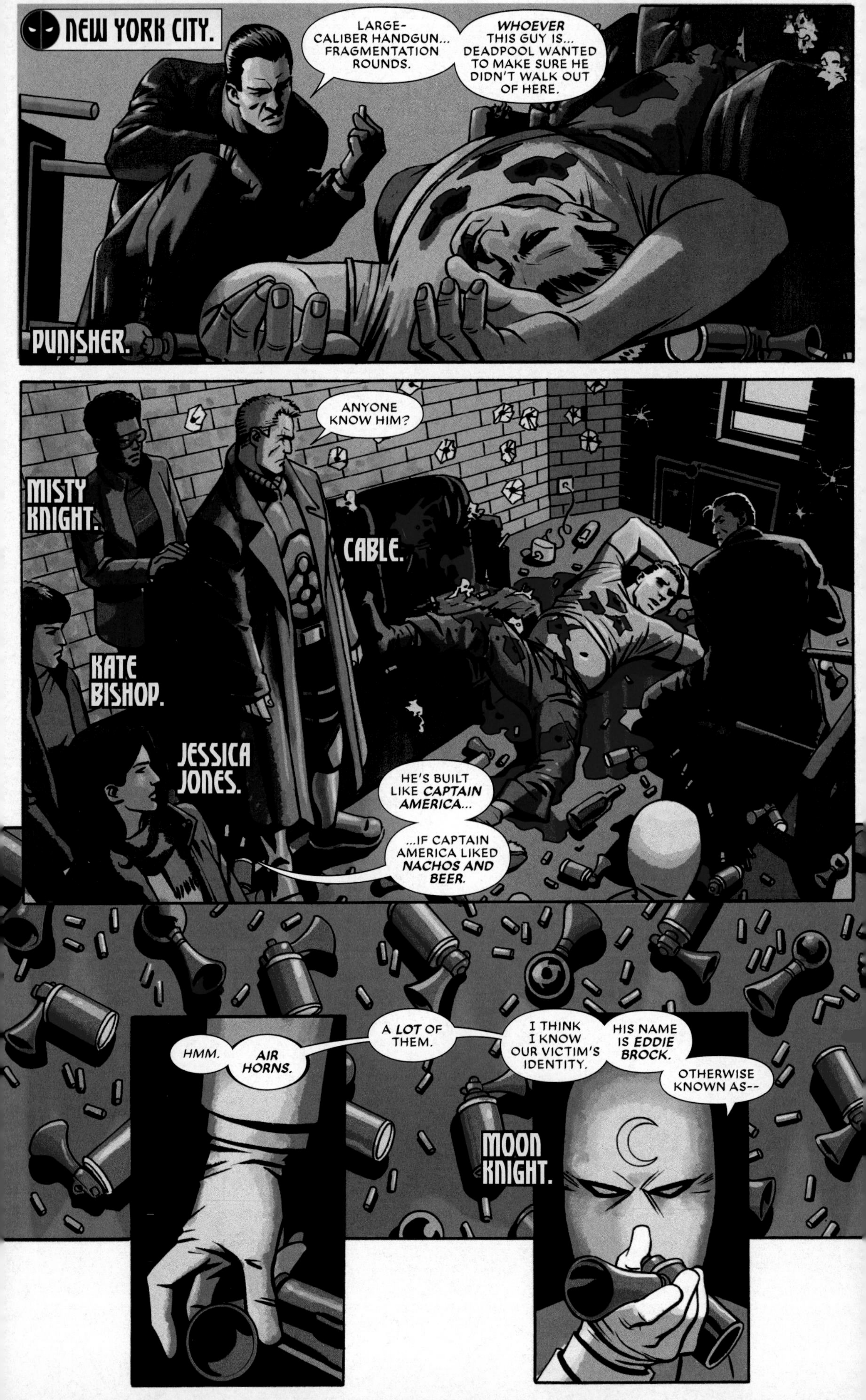

NEW YORK CITY.
LARGE-CALIBER HANDGUN... FRAGMENTATION ROUNDS.
WHOEVER THIS GUY IS... DEADPOOL WANTED TO MAKE SURE HE DIDN'T WALK OUT OF HERE.
PUNISHER.
ANYONE KNOW HIM?
MISTY KNIGHT.
CABLE.
KATE BISHOP.
JESSICA JONES.
HE'S BUILT LIKE CAPTAIN AMERICA...
...IF CAPTAIN AMERICA LIKED NACHOS AND BEER.
HMM.
AIR HORNS.
A LOT OF THEM.
I THINK I KNOW OUR VICTIM'S IDENTITY.
HIS NAME IS EDDIE BROCK.
OTHERWISE KNOWN AS--
MOON KNIGHT.

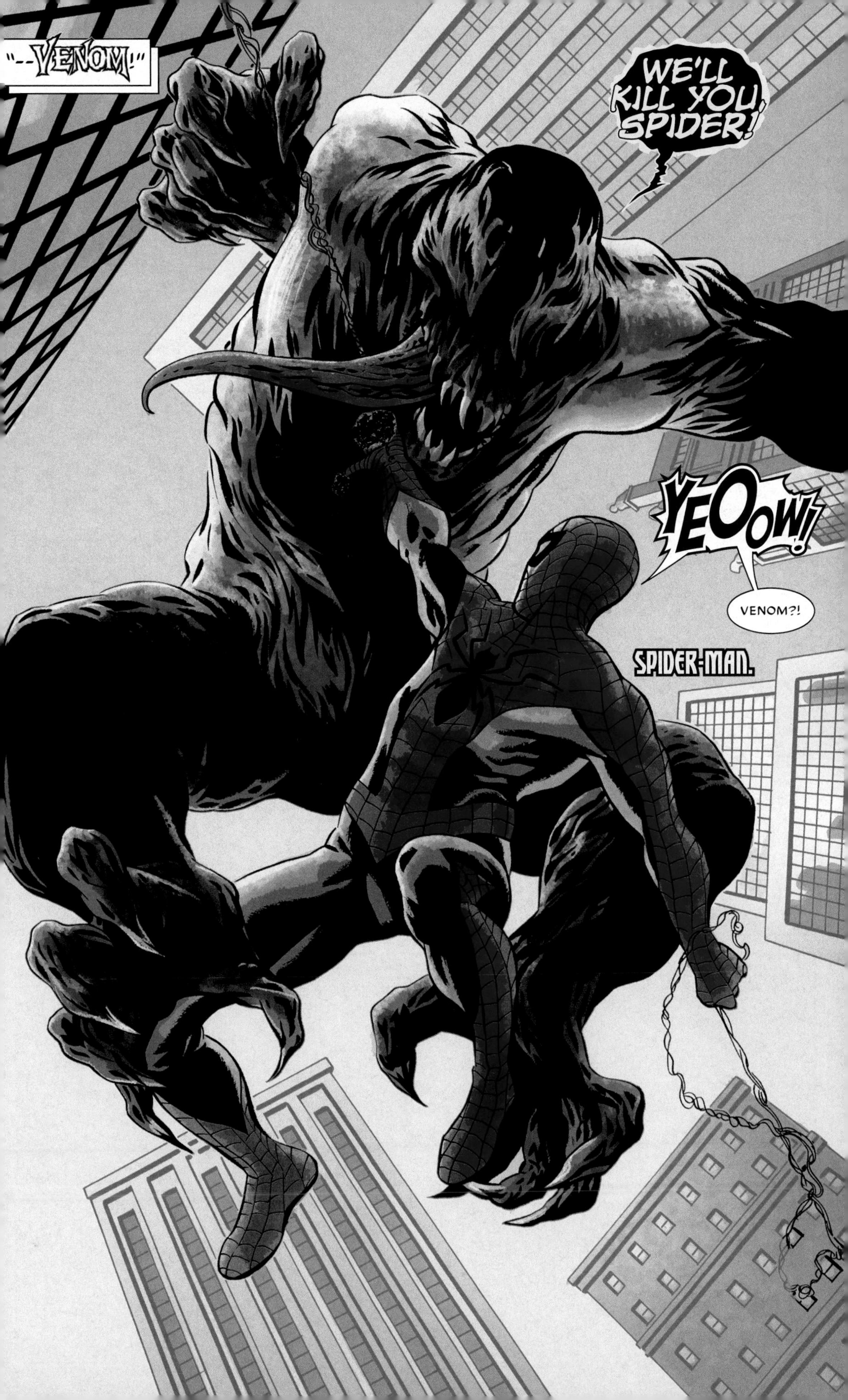
"--VENOM--"
WE'LL KILL YOU, SPIDER!
YEOOW!
VENOM?!
SPIDER-MAN.

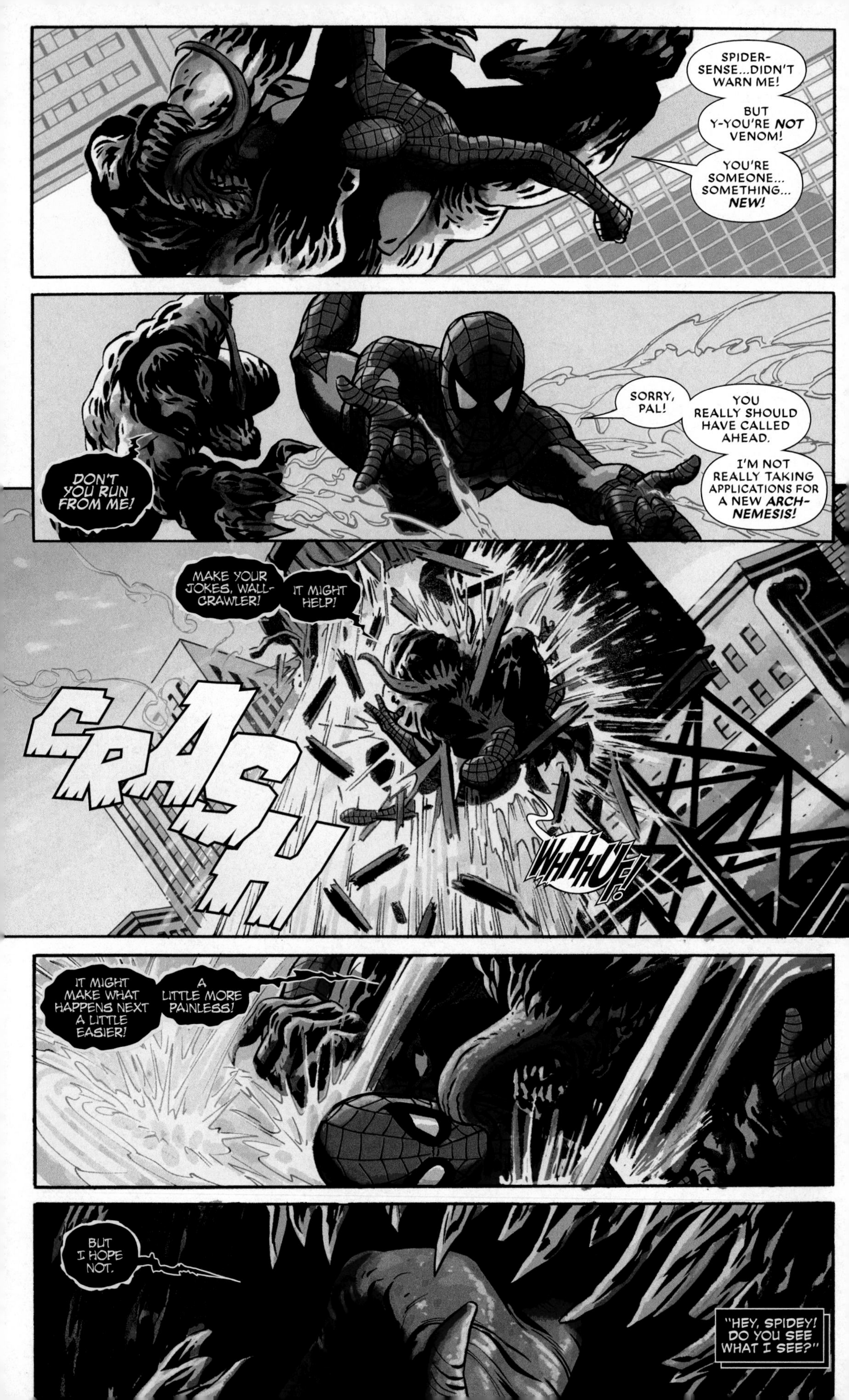
SPIDER-SENSE...DIDN'T WARN ME!
BUT Y-YOU'RE NOT VENOM!
YOU'RE SOMEONE... SOMETHING... NEW!
SORRY, PAL!
YOU REALLY SHOULD HAVE CALLED AHEAD.
I'M NOT REALLY TAKING APPLICATIONS FOR A NEW ARCH-NEMESIS!
DON'T YOU RUN FROM ME!
MAKE YOUR JOKES, WALL-CRAWLER!
IT MIGHT HELP!
CRASH
WHHUF!
IT MIGHT MAKE WHAT HAPPENS NEXT A LITTLE EASIER!
A LITTLE MORE PAINLESS!
BUT I HOPE NOT.
"HEY, SPIDEY! DO YOU SEE WHAT I SEE?"

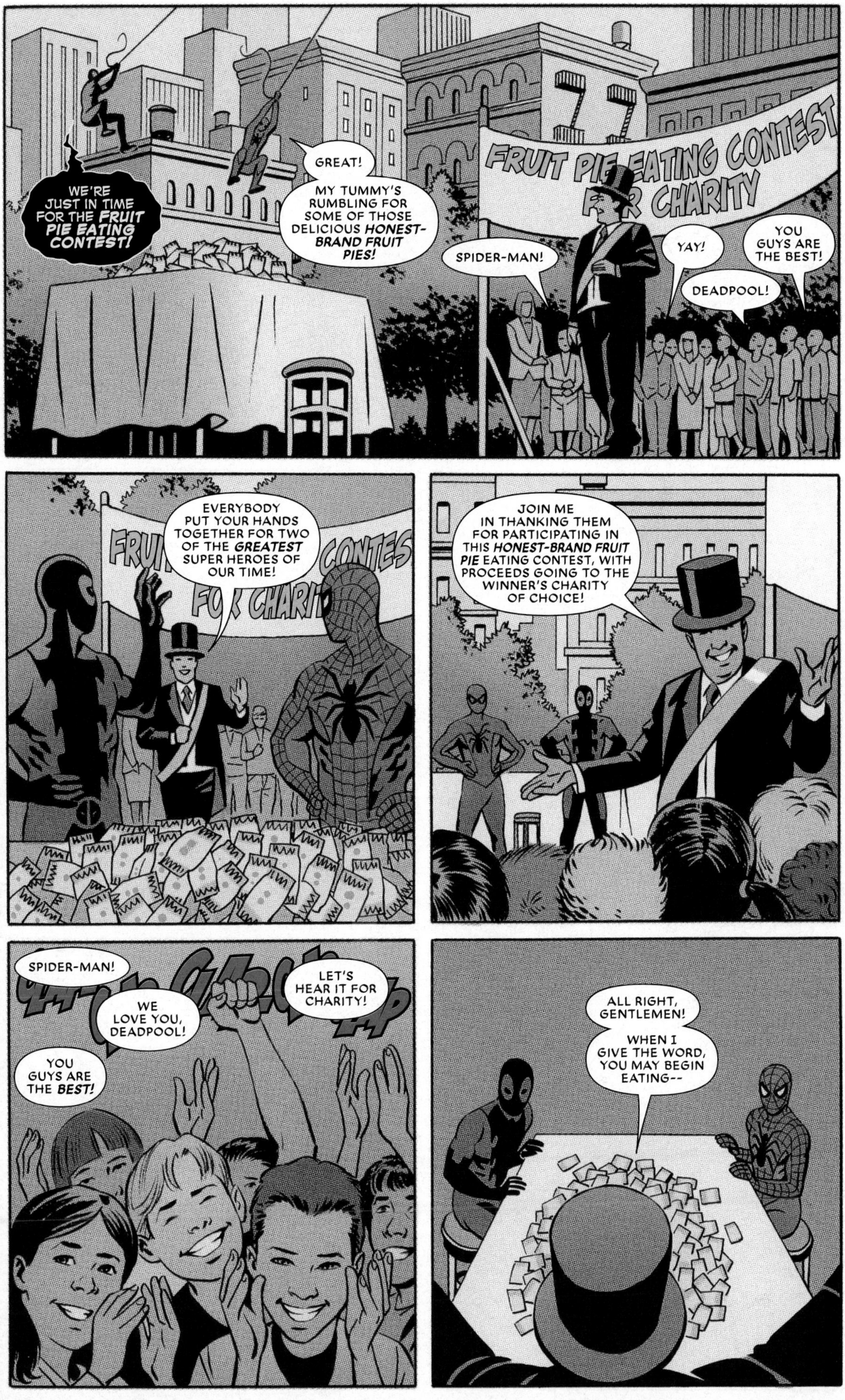
WE'RE JUST IN TIME FOR THE *FRUIT PIE EATING CONTEST!*
GREAT!
MY TUMMY'S RUMBLING FOR SOME OF THOSE DELICIOUS *HONEST-BRAND FRUIT PIES!*
FRUIT PIE EATING CONTEST
SPIDER-MAN!
YAY!
YOU GUYS ARE THE BEST!
DEADPOOL!
EVERYBODY PUT YOUR HANDS TOGETHER FOR TWO OF THE *GREATEST* SUPER HEROES OF OUR TIME!
JOIN ME IN THANKING THEM FOR PARTICIPATING IN THIS *HONEST-BRAND FRUIT PIE* EATING CONTEST, WITH PROCEEDS GOING TO THE WINNER'S CHARITY OF CHOICE!
SPIDER-MAN!
WE LOVE YOU, DEADPOOL!
LET'S HEAR IT FOR CHARITY!
YOU GUYS ARE THE *BEST!*
ALL RIGHT, GENTLEMEN!
WHEN I GIVE THE WORD, YOU MAY BEGIN EATING--

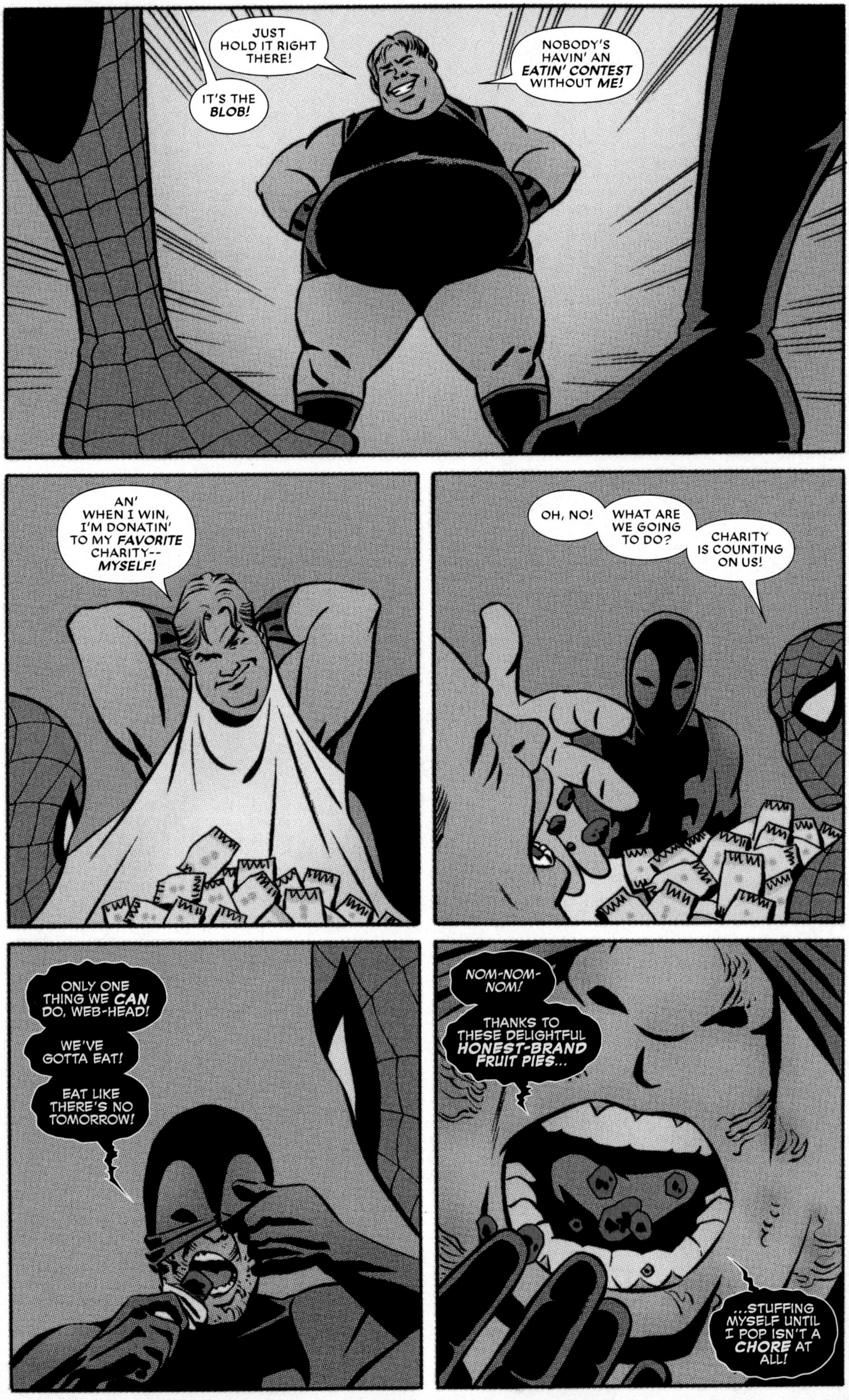
JUST HOLD IT RIGHT THERE!
IT'S THE BLOB!
NOBODY'S HAVIN' AN EATIN' CONTEST WITHOUT ME!
AN' WHEN I WIN, I'M DONATIN' TO MY FAVORITE CHARITY-- MYSELF!
OH, NO!
WHAT ARE WE GOING TO DO?
CHARITY IS COUNTING ON US!
ONLY ONE THING WE CAN DO, WEB-HEAD!
WE'VE GOTTA EAT!
EAT LIKE THERE'S NO TOMORROW!
NOM-NOM-NOM!
THANKS TO THESE DELIGHTFUL HONEST-BRAND FRUIT PIES...
...STUFFING MYSELF UNTIL I POP ISN'T A CHORE AT ALL!

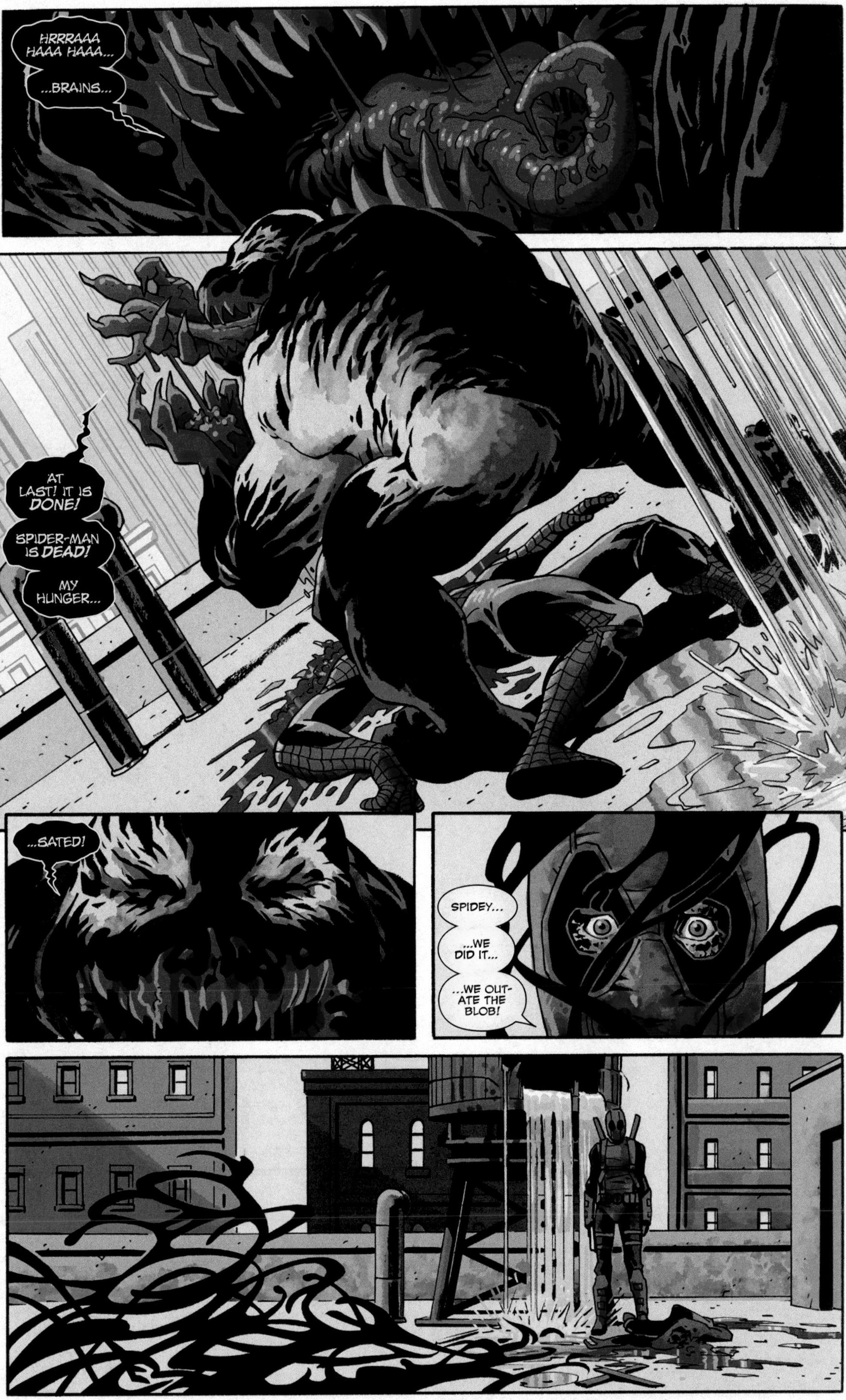
HRRRAAA HAAA HAAA...
...BRAINS...
AT LAST! IT IS DONE!
SPIDER-MAN IS DEAD!
MY HUNGER...
...SATED!
SPIDEY...
...WE DID IT...
...WE OUT-ATE THE BLOB!

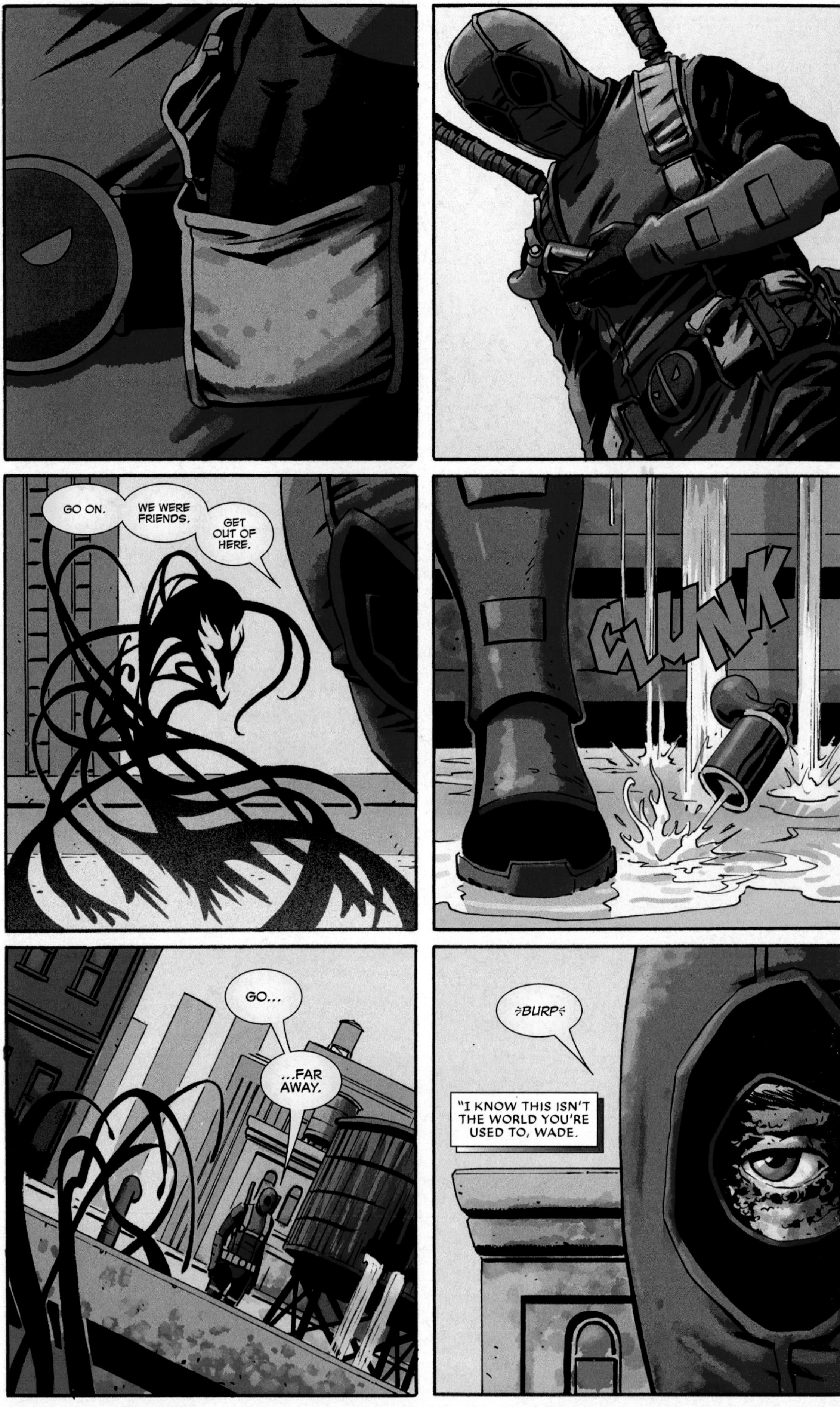
GO ON.
WE WERE FRIENDS.
GET OUT OF HERE.
CLUNK
GO...
...FAR AWAY.
BURP
"I KNOW THIS ISN'T THE WORLD YOU'RE USED TO, WADE.

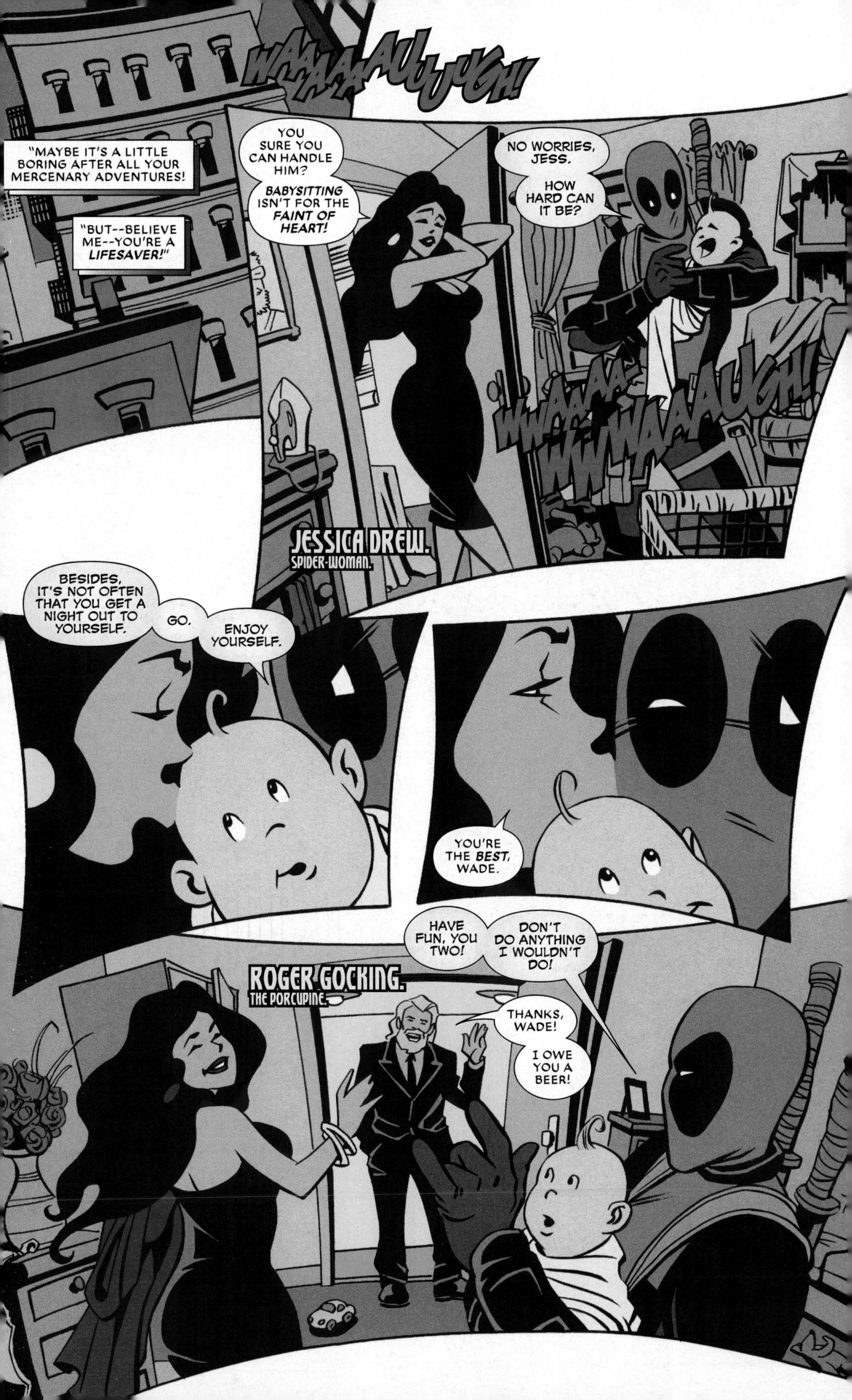
WAAAAAAUUUUGH!
"MAYBE IT'S A LITTLE BORING AFTER ALL YOUR MERCENARY ADVENTURES!
"BUT--BELIEVE ME--YOU'RE A LIFESAVER!"
YOU SURE YOU CAN HANDLE HIM?
BABYSITTING ISN'T FOR THE FAINT OF HEART!
NO WORRIES, JESS.
HOW HARD CAN IT BE?
WWAAAAA-WWWAAAAUGH!
JESSICA DREW.
SPIDER-WOMAN.
BESIDES, IT'S NOT OFTEN THAT YOU GET A NIGHT OUT TO YOURSELF.
GO.
ENJOY YOURSELF.
YOU'RE THE BEST, WADE.
HAVE FUN, YOU TWO!
DON'T DO ANYTHING I WOULDN'T DO!
ROGER GOCKING.
THE PORCUPINE.
THANKS, WADE!
I OWE YOU A BEER!

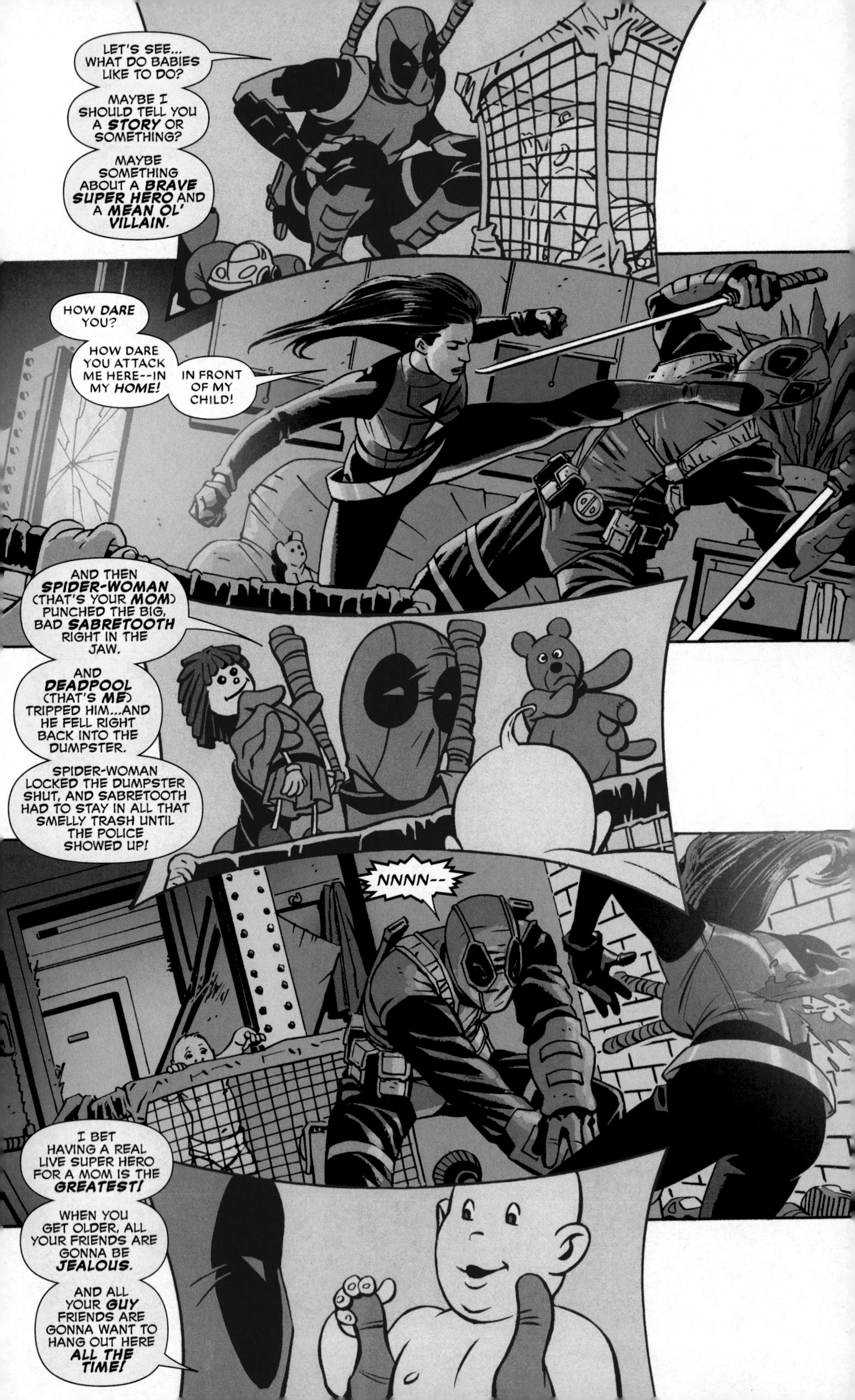

LET'S SEE... WHAT DO BABIES LIKE TO DO?
MAYBE I SHOULD TELL YOU A STORY OR SOMETHING?
MAYBE SOMETHING ABOUT A BRAVE SUPER HERO AND A MEAN OL' VILLAIN.
HOW DARE YOU?
HOW DARE YOU ATTACK ME HERE--IN MY HOME!
IN FRONT OF MY CHILD!
AND THEN SPIDER-WOMAN (THAT'S YOUR MOM) PUNCHED THE BIG, BAD SABRETOOTH RIGHT IN THE JAW.
AND DEADPOOL (THAT'S ME) TRIPPED HIM...AND HE FELL RIGHT BACK INTO THE DUMPSTER.
SPIDER-WOMAN LOCKED THE DUMPSTER SHUT, AND SABRETOOTH HAD TO STAY IN ALL THAT SMELLY TRASH UNTIL THE POLICE SHOWED UP!
NNNN--
I BET HAVING A REAL LIVE SUPER HERO FOR A MOM IS THE GREATEST!
WHEN YOU GET OLDER, ALL YOUR FRIENDS ARE GONNA BE JEALOUS.
AND ALL YOUR GUY FRIENDS ARE GONNA WANT TO HANG OUT HERE ALL THE TIME!

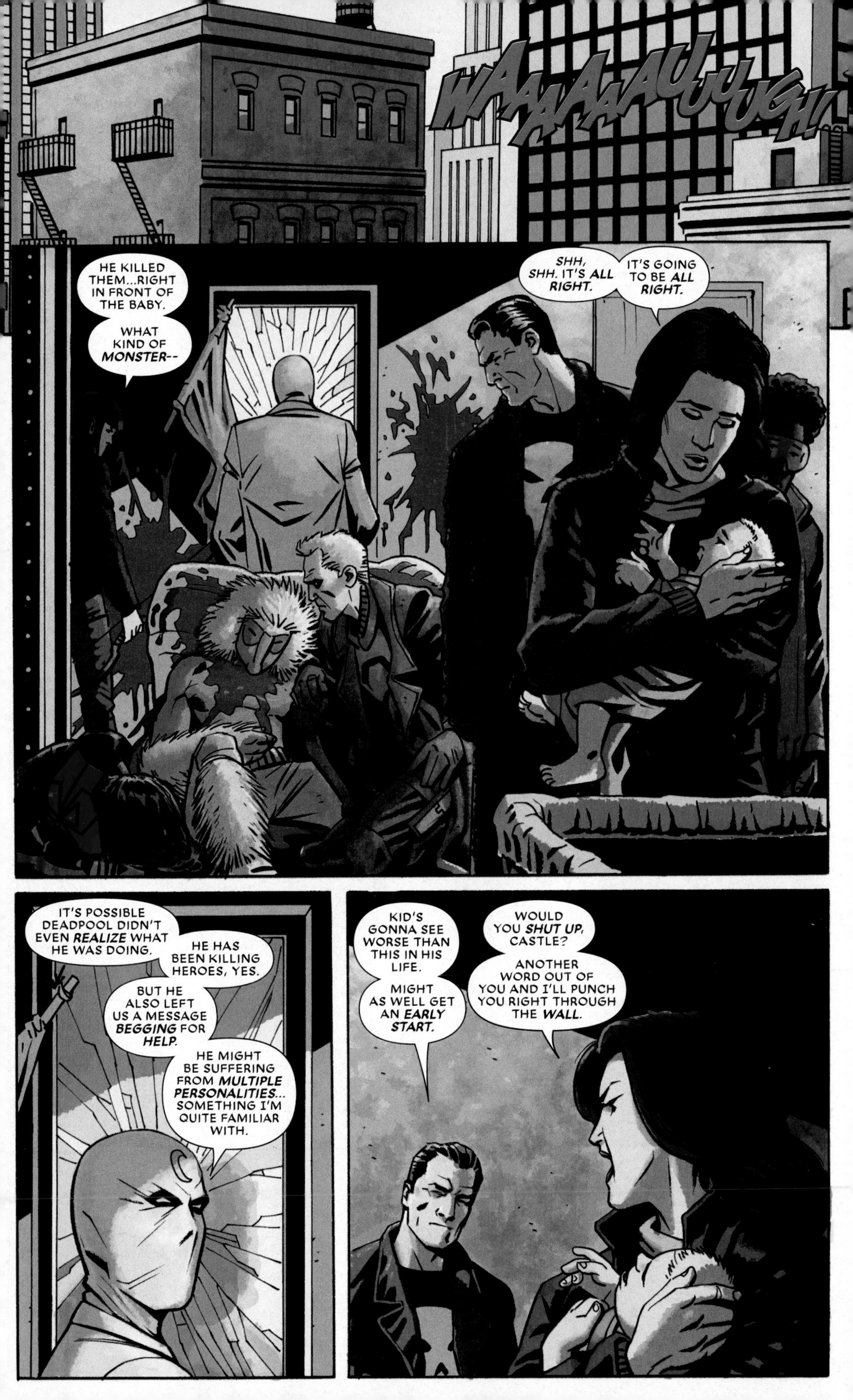
WAAAAAAUUUUGH!
HE KILLED THEM...RIGHT IN FRONT OF THE BABY.
WHAT KIND OF *MONSTER*--
SHH, SHH. IT'S *ALL RIGHT.*
IT'S GOING TO BE *ALL RIGHT.*
IT'S POSSIBLE DEADPOOL DIDN'T EVEN *REALIZE* WHAT HE WAS DOING.
HE HAS BEEN KILLING HEROES, YES.
BUT HE ALSO LEFT US A MESSAGE *BEGGING* FOR *HELP.*
HE MIGHT BE SUFFERING FROM *MULTIPLE PERSONALITIES*... SOMETHING I'M QUITE FAMILIAR WITH.
KID'S GONNA SEE WORSE THAN THIS IN HIS LIFE.
MIGHT AS WELL GET AN *EARLY START.*
WOULD YOU *SHUT UP,* CASTLE?
ANOTHER WORD OUT OF YOU AND I'LL PUNCH YOU RIGHT THROUGH THE *WALL.*

WE'RE ALWAYS A STEP BEHIND HIM.

AND EVERY MINUTE THAT WE DON'T CATCH DEADPOOL, THAT'S *ANOTHER FRIEND* WHO *DIES*.

IT MIGHT BE BEST IF WE *SPLIT UP*...FOLLOW LEADS ON OUR OWN.

I DON'T THINK IT'S A GOOD IDEA FOR US TO GO OFF ON OUR OWN.

MAYBE WE SHOULD USE THE *BUDDY SYSTEM?*

NOT A BAD IDEA.

I CALL ANYONE *BUT* PUNISHER.

WHAT DO YOU SAY, OLD MAN?

A COUPLE OF *BIONIC-ENHANCED BADASSES* WORKING TOGETHER?

WORKS FOR ME.

THAT MEANS MOON KNIGHT AND PUNISHER ARE TOGETHER.

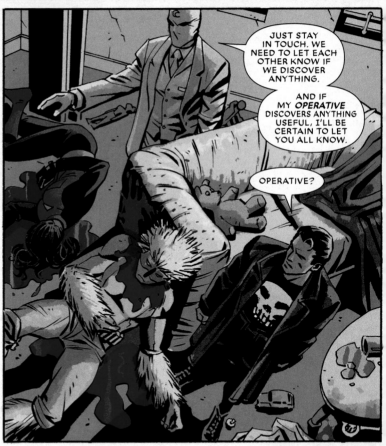

JUST STAY IN TOUCH. WE NEED TO LET EACH OTHER KNOW IF WE DISCOVER ANYTHING.

AND IF MY *OPERATIVE* DISCOVERS ANYTHING USEFUL, I'LL BE CERTAIN TO LET YOU ALL KNOW.

OPERATIVE?

THAT'S RIGHT.

I HAVE *PEOPLE*.

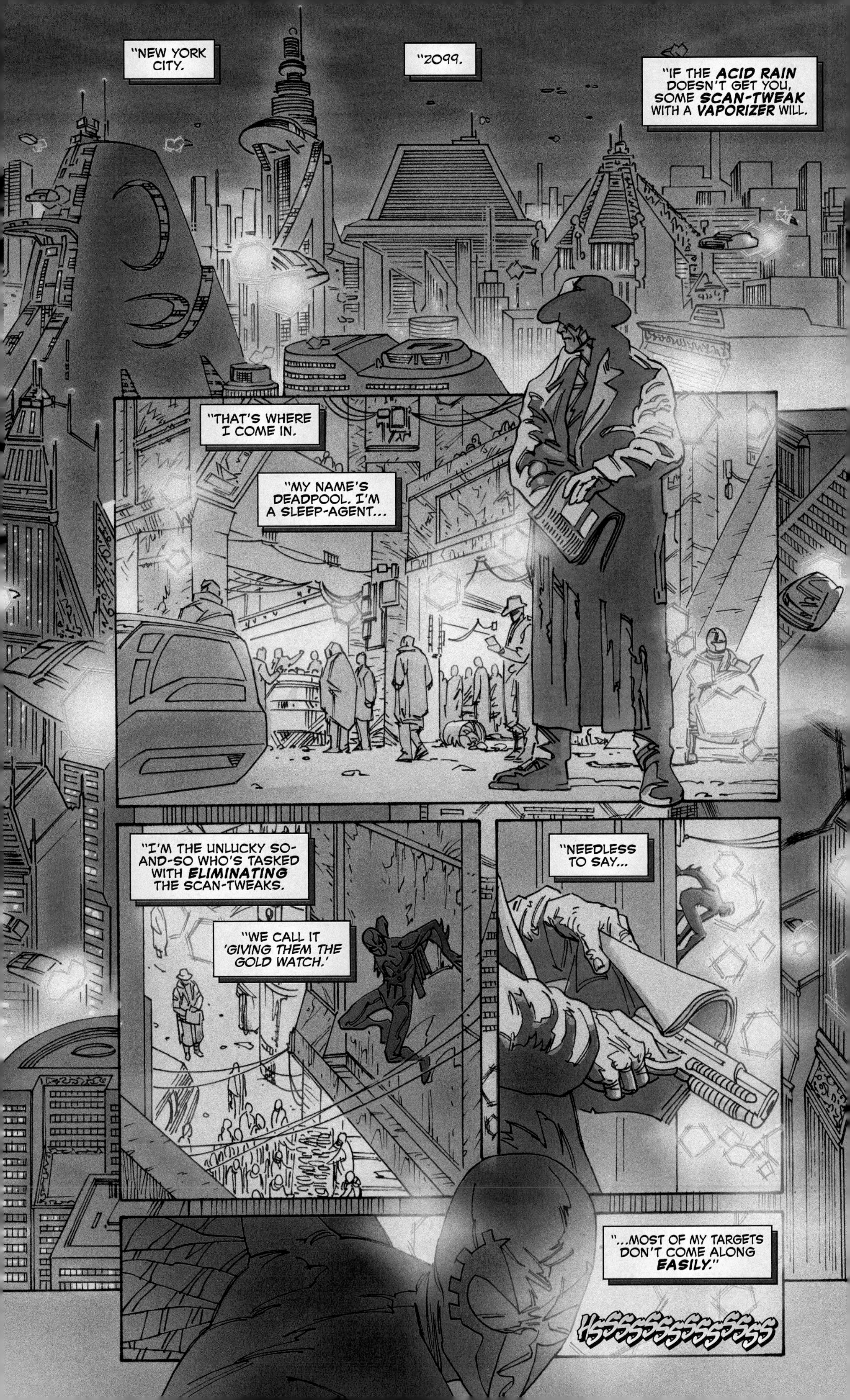
"NEW YORK CITY.
"2099.
"IF THE ACID RAIN DOESN'T GET YOU, SOME SCAN-TWEAK WITH A VAPORIZER WILL.
"THAT'S WHERE I COME IN.
"MY NAME'S DEADPOOL. I'M A SLEEP-AGENT...
"I'M THE UNLUCKY SO-AND-SO WHO'S TASKED WITH ELIMINATING THE SCAN-TWEAKS.
"WE CALL IT 'GIVING THEM THE GOLD WATCH.'
"NEEDLESS TO SAY...
"...MOST OF MY TARGETS DON'T COME ALONG EASILY."
HSSSSSSSSSSSSSS

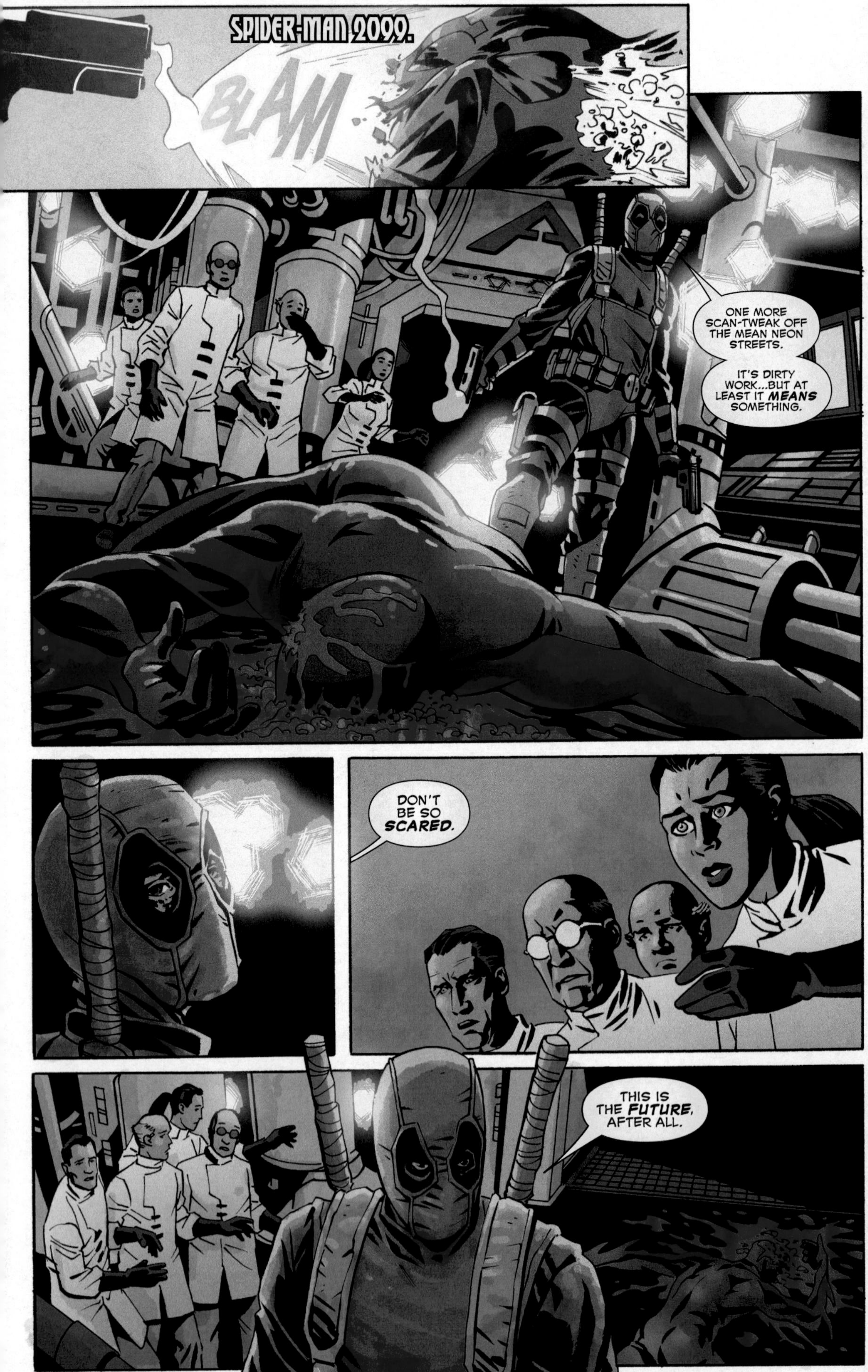
SPIDER-MAN 2099.
BLAM
ONE MORE SCAN-TWEAK OFF THE MEAN NEON STREETS.
IT'S DIRTY WORK...BUT AT LEAST IT MEANS SOMETHING.
DON'T BE SO SCARED.
THIS IS THE FUTURE, AFTER ALL.

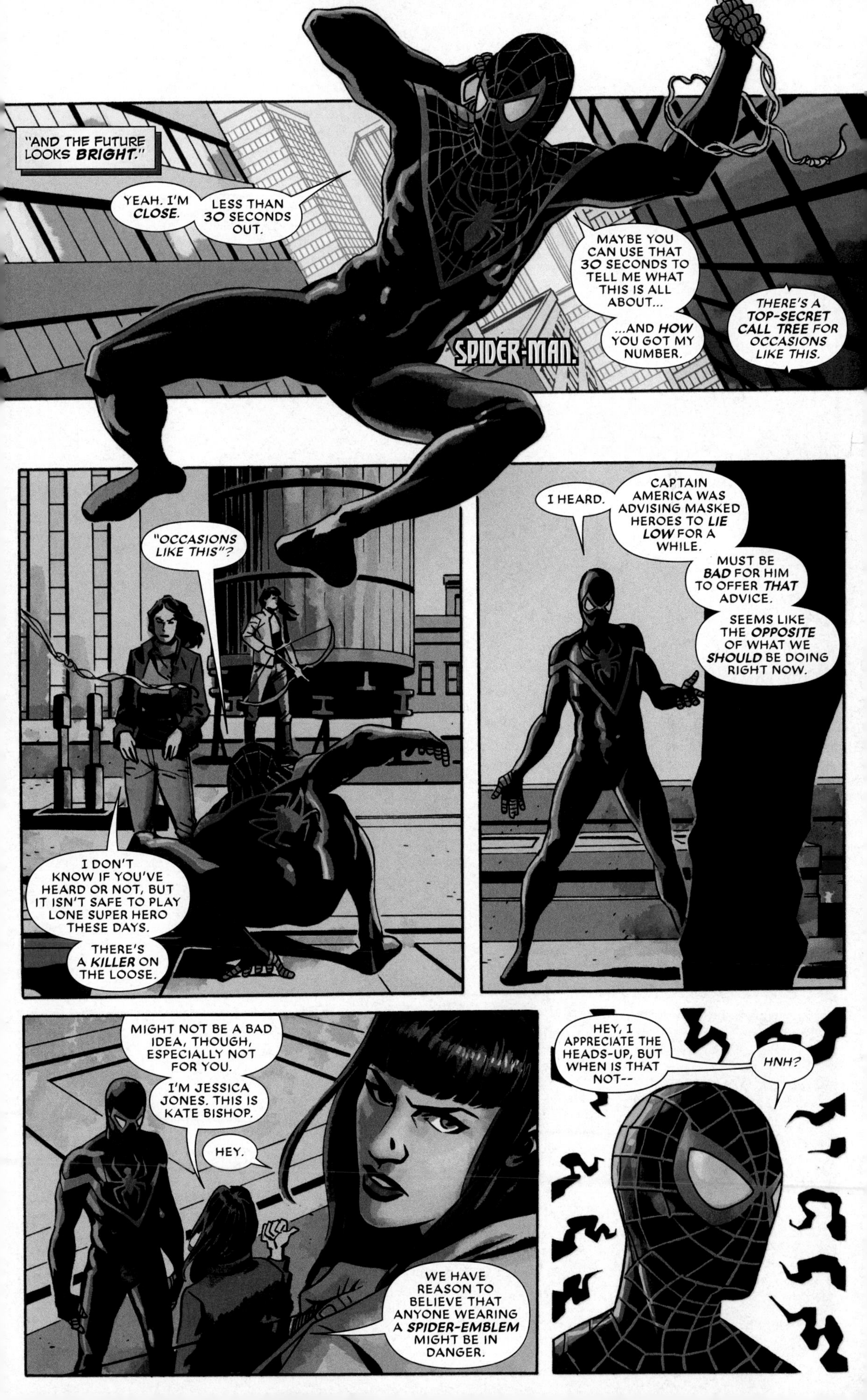
"AND THE FUTURE LOOKS BRIGHT."
YEAH. I'M CLOSE.
LESS THAN 30 SECONDS OUT.
MAYBE YOU CAN USE THAT 30 SECONDS TO TELL ME WHAT THIS IS ALL ABOUT...
...AND HOW YOU GOT MY NUMBER.
THERE'S A TOP-SECRET CALL TREE FOR OCCASIONS LIKE THIS.
SPIDER-MAN.
"OCCASIONS LIKE THIS"?
I DON'T KNOW IF YOU'VE HEARD OR NOT, BUT IT ISN'T SAFE TO PLAY LONE SUPER HERO THESE DAYS.
THERE'S A KILLER ON THE LOOSE.
I HEARD.
CAPTAIN AMERICA WAS ADVISING MASKED HEROES TO LIE LOW FOR A WHILE.
MUST BE BAD FOR HIM TO OFFER THAT ADVICE.
SEEMS LIKE THE OPPOSITE OF WHAT WE SHOULD BE DOING RIGHT NOW.
MIGHT NOT BE A BAD IDEA, THOUGH, ESPECIALLY NOT FOR YOU.
I'M JESSICA JONES. THIS IS KATE BISHOP.
HEY.
WE HAVE REASON TO BELIEVE THAT ANYONE WEARING A SPIDER-EMBLEM MIGHT BE IN DANGER.
HEY, I APPRECIATE THE HEADS-UP, BUT WHEN IS THAT NOT--
HNH?

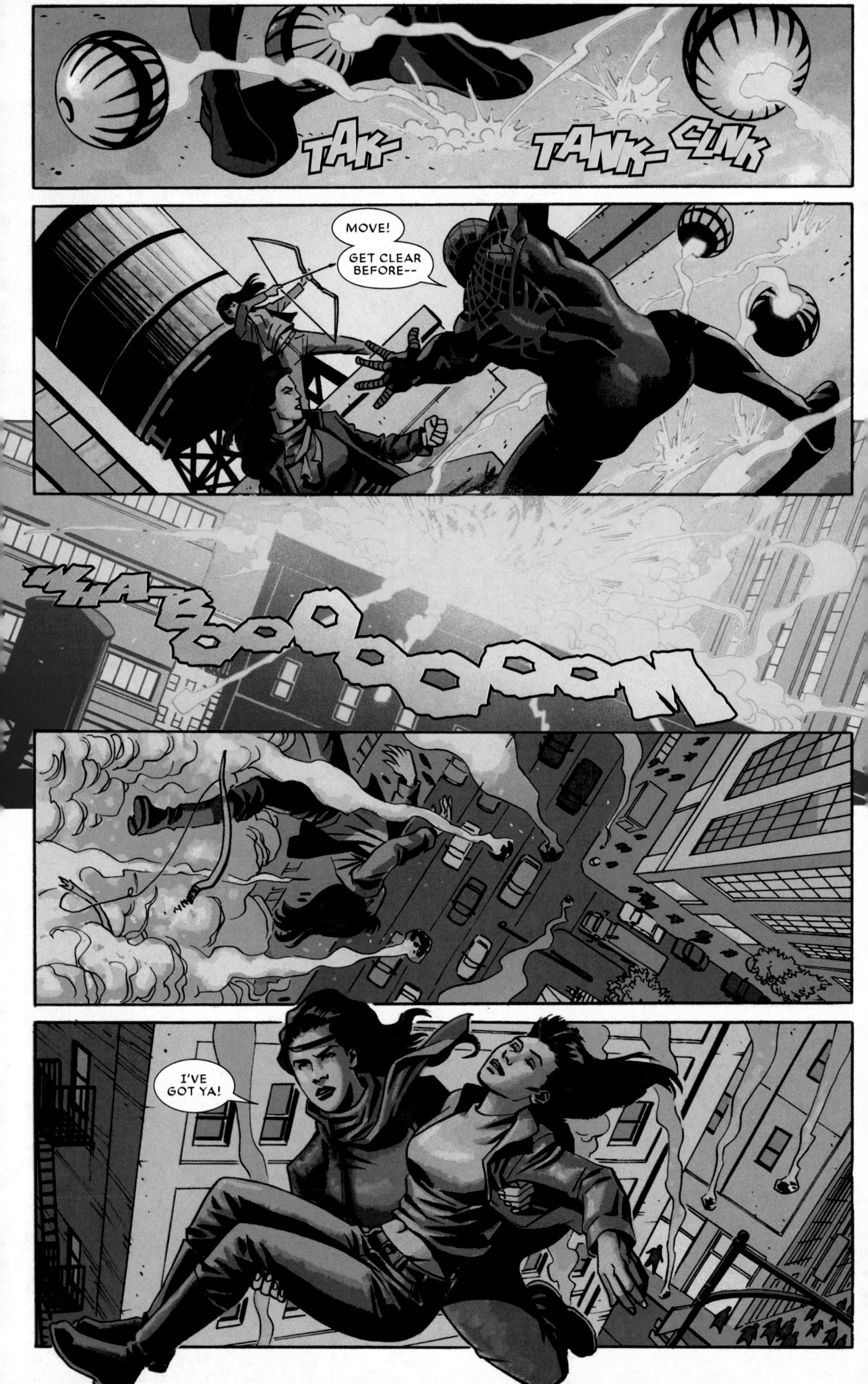
TAK
TANK
CLNK
MOVE!
GET CLEAR BEFORE--
WHA-BOOOOOOOOOM
I'VE GOT YA!

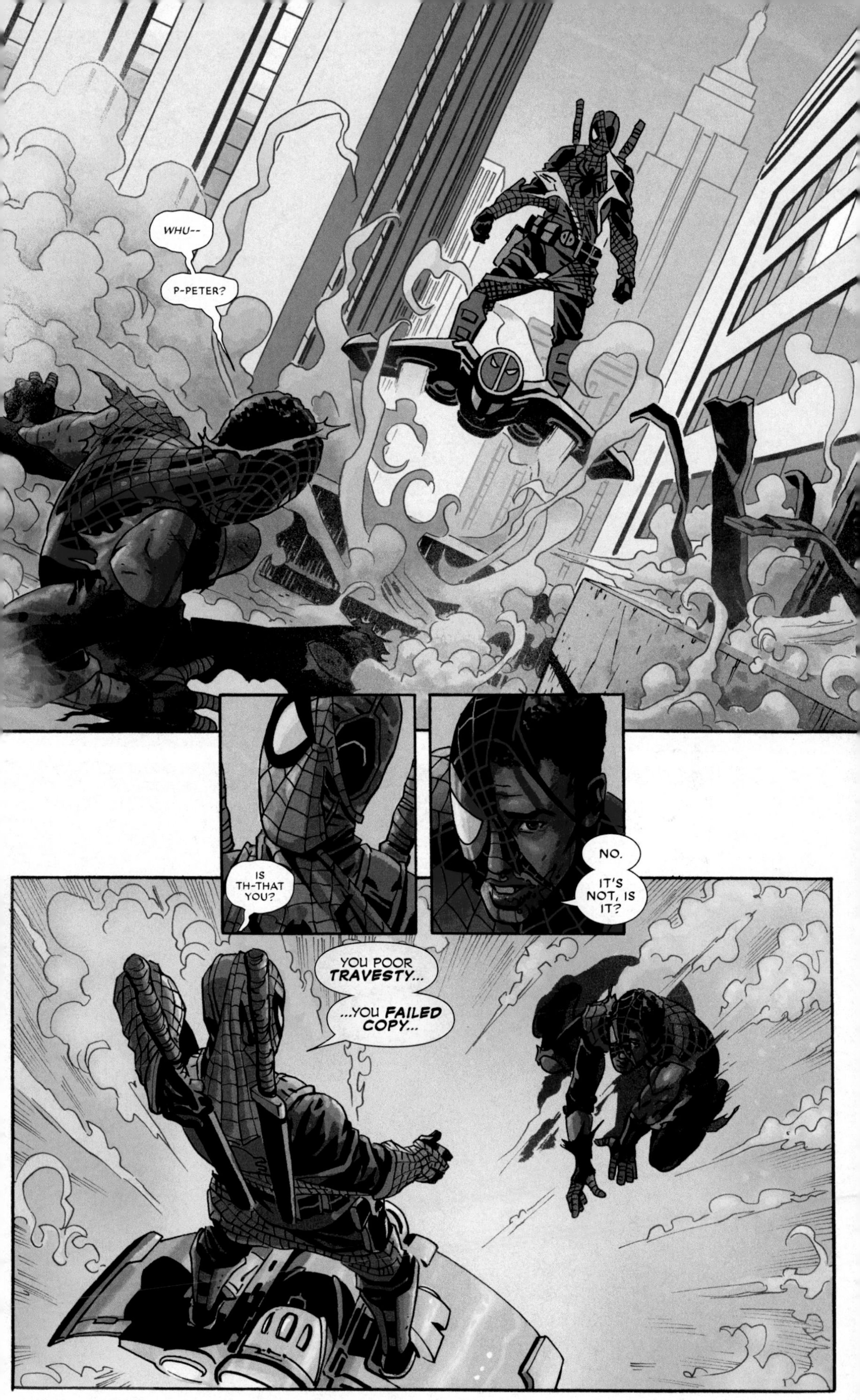
WHU--
P-PETER?
IS TH-THAT YOU?
NO.
IT'S NOT, IS IT?
YOU POOR TRAVESTY...
...YOU FAILED COPY...

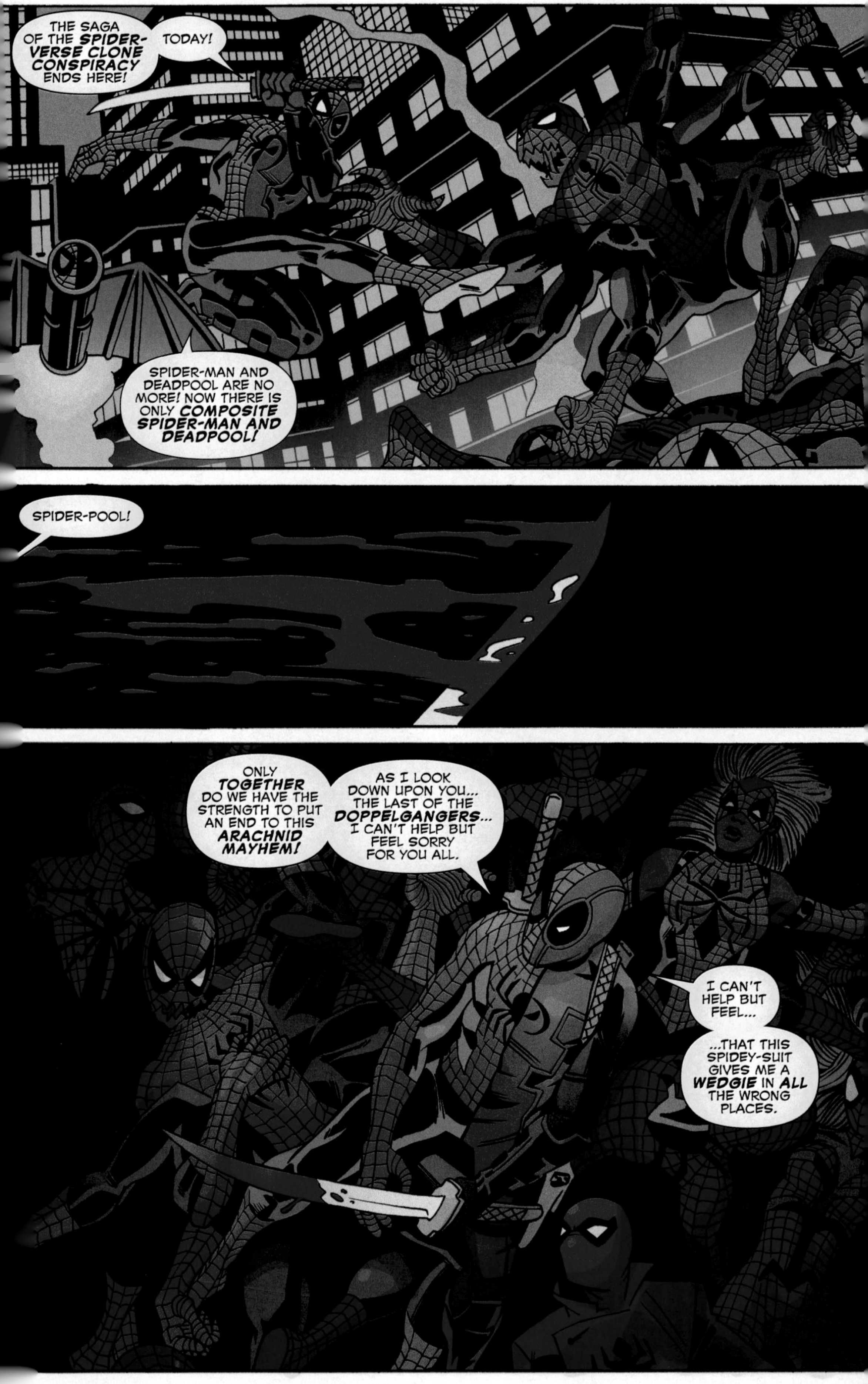
THE SAGA OF THE SPIDER-VERSE CLONE CONSPIRACY ENDS HERE!
TODAY!
SPIDER-MAN AND DEADPOOL ARE NO MORE! NOW THERE IS ONLY COMPOSITE SPIDER-MAN AND DEADPOOL!
SPIDER-POOL!
ONLY TOGETHER DO WE HAVE THE STRENGTH TO PUT AN END TO THIS ARACHNID MAYHEM!
AS I LOOK DOWN UPON YOU... THE LAST OF THE DOPPELGANGERS... I CAN'T HELP BUT FEEL SORRY FOR YOU ALL.
I CAN'T HELP BUT FEEL...
...THAT THIS SPIDEY-SUIT GIVES ME A WEDGIE IN ALL THE WRONG PLACES.

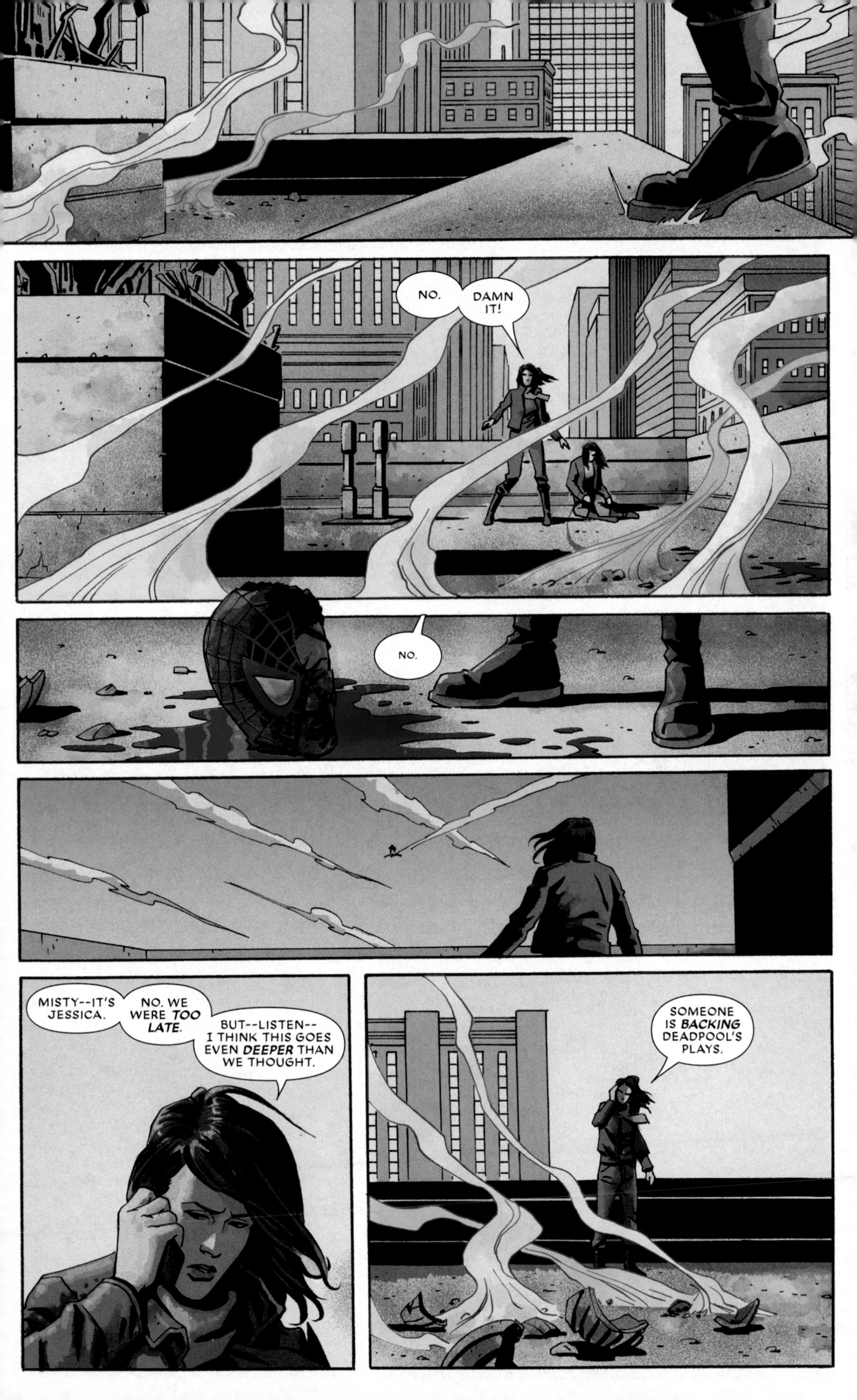
NO.
DAMN IT!
NO.
MISTY--IT'S JESSICA.
NO. WE WERE TOO LATE.
BUT--LISTEN-- I THINK THIS GOES EVEN DEEPER THAN WE THOUGHT.
SOMEONE IS BACKING DEADPOOL'S PLAYS.

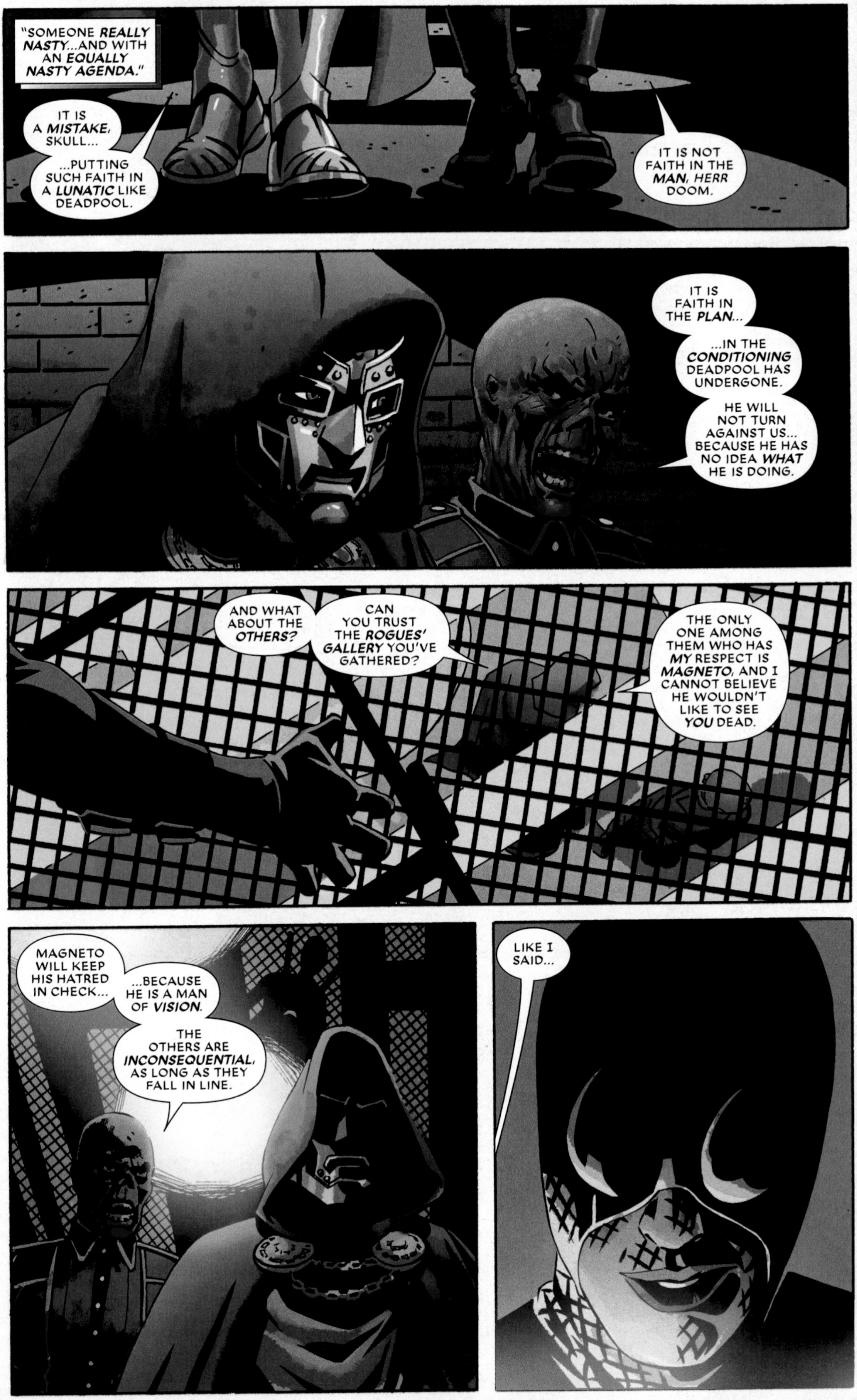
"SOMEONE REALLY NASTY...AND WITH AN EQUALLY NASTY AGENDA."
IT IS A MISTAKE, SKULL...
...PUTTING SUCH FAITH IN A LUNATIC LIKE DEADPOOL.
IT IS NOT FAITH IN THE MAN, HERR DOOM.
IT IS FAITH IN THE PLAN...
...IN THE CONDITIONING DEADPOOL HAS UNDERGONE.
HE WILL NOT TURN AGAINST US... BECAUSE HE HAS NO IDEA WHAT HE IS DOING.
AND WHAT ABOUT THE OTHERS?
CAN YOU TRUST THE ROGUES' GALLERY YOU'VE GATHERED?
THE ONLY ONE AMONG THEM WHO HAS MY RESPECT IS MAGNETO, AND I CANNOT BELIEVE HE WOULDN'T LIKE TO SEE YOU DEAD.
MAGNETO WILL KEEP HIS HATRED IN CHECK...
...BECAUSE HE IS A MAN OF VISION.
THE OTHERS ARE INCONSEQUENTIAL, AS LONG AS THEY FALL IN LINE.
LIKE I SAID...

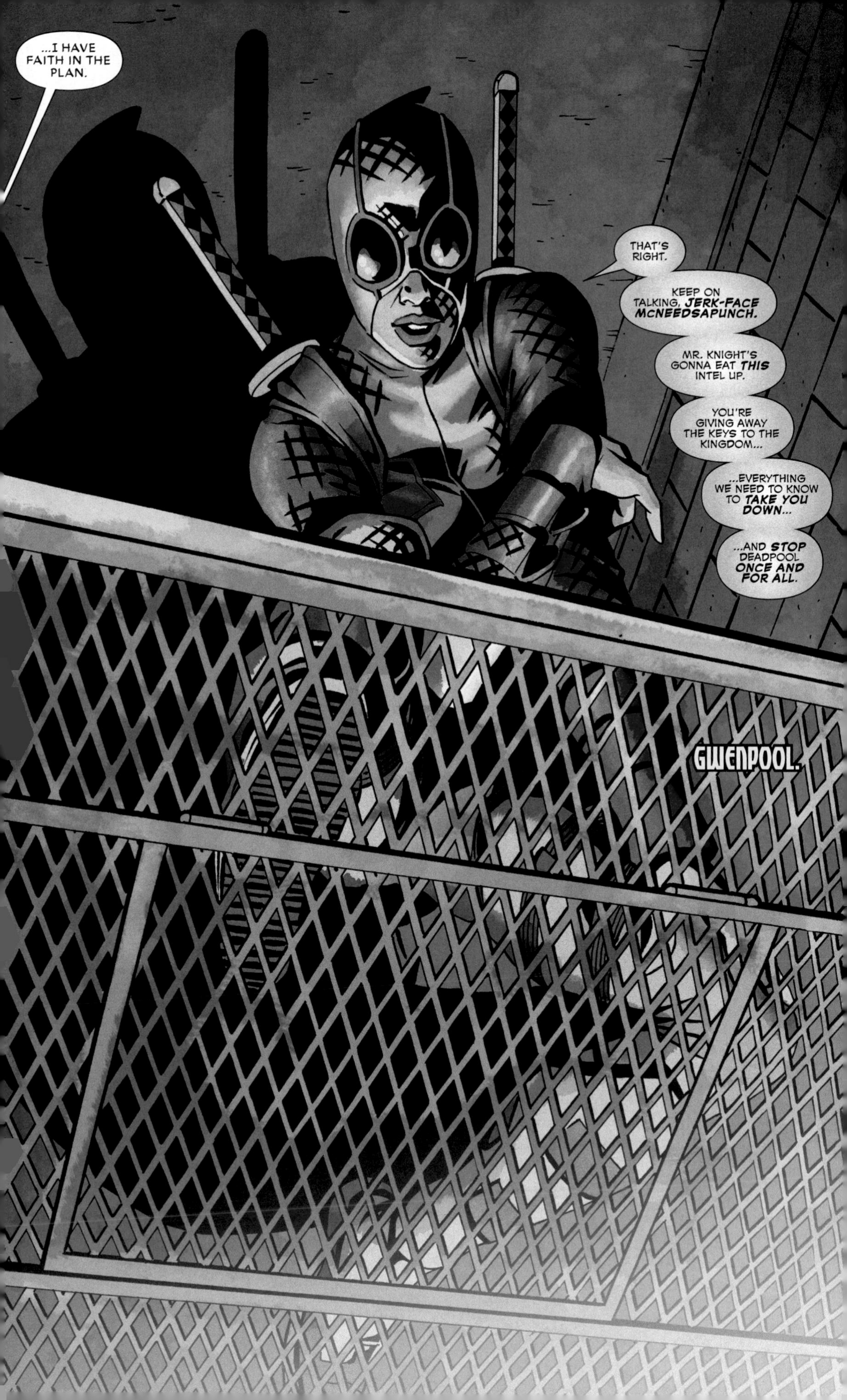
...I HAVE FAITH IN THE PLAN.
THAT'S RIGHT.
KEEP ON TALKING, JERK-FACE McNEEDSAPUNCH.
MR. KNIGHT'S GONNA EAT THIS INTEL UP.
YOU'RE GIVING AWAY THE KEYS TO THE KINGDOM...
...EVERYTHING WE NEED TO KNOW TO TAKE YOU DOWN...
...AND STOP DEADPOOL ONCE AND FOR ALL.
GWENPOOL.

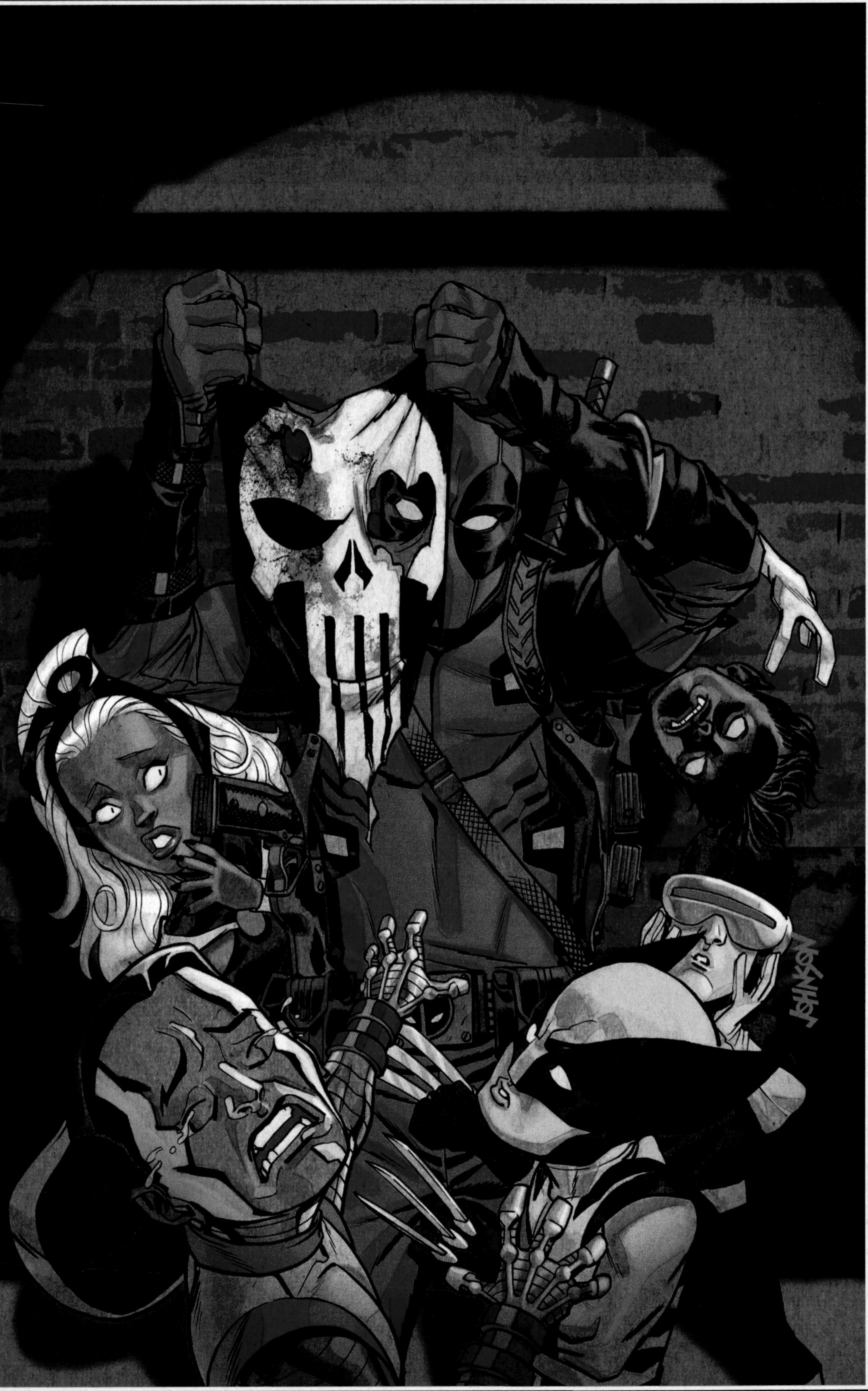
JOHNSON

3

YES.

I'M ABSATIVELY, POSILUTELY SURE.

100%.

YOU DIDN'T PUT ME ON THE CASE TO GET *SHODDY DEETS.*

HOLD ON--

I'M SENDING YOU SOME PICS RIGHT NOW.

YEESH!

YOU DETECTIVE TYPES AND YOUR NEED FOR *PROOF.*

HAVE A LITTLE *FAITH*, HUH?

SEE?

WHU--

WHAT DO YOU MEAN?

OF *COURSE* YOU CAN TELL WHO IT IS BY LOOKING AT THE BACK OF THEIR HEADS!

NO ONE ELSE HAS BACKS OF HEADS THAT LOOK LIKE *THAT!*

FINE. WHATEVER.

I'LL GET YOU A BETTER PICTURE.

JUST HOLD ON A SEC.

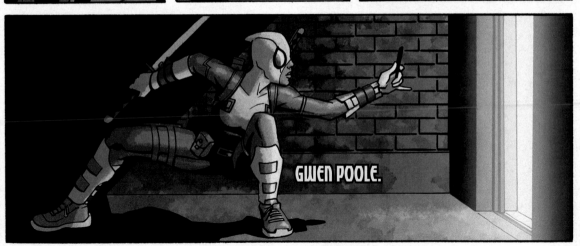

GWEN POOLE.

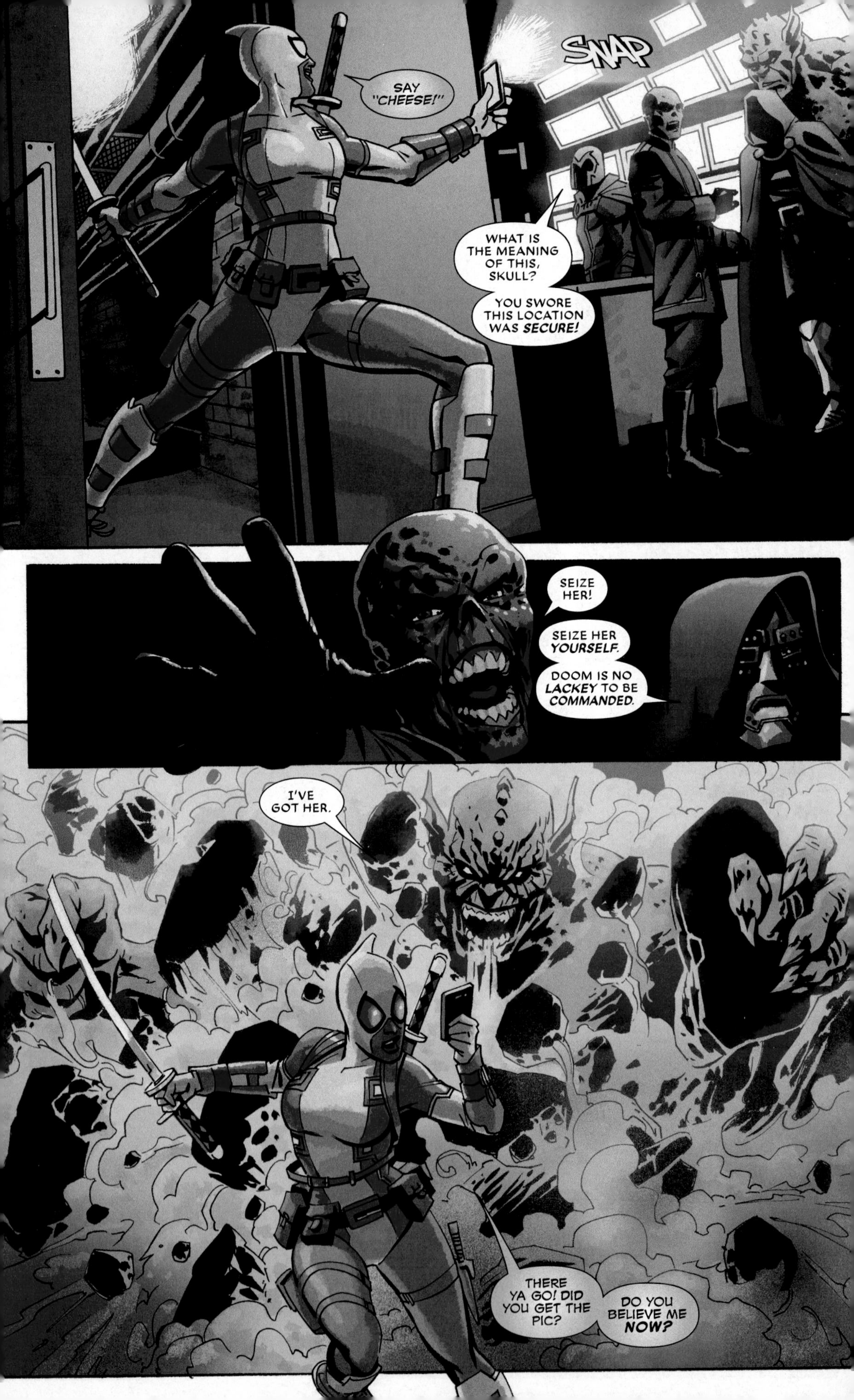
SNAP
SAY "CHEESE!"
WHAT IS THE MEANING OF THIS, SKULL?
YOU SWORE THIS LOCATION WAS SECURE!
SEIZE HER!
SEIZE HER YOURSELF.
DOOM IS NO LACKEY TO BE COMMANDED.
I'VE GOT HER.
THERE YA GO! DID YOU GET THE PIC?
DO YOU BELIEVE ME NOW?

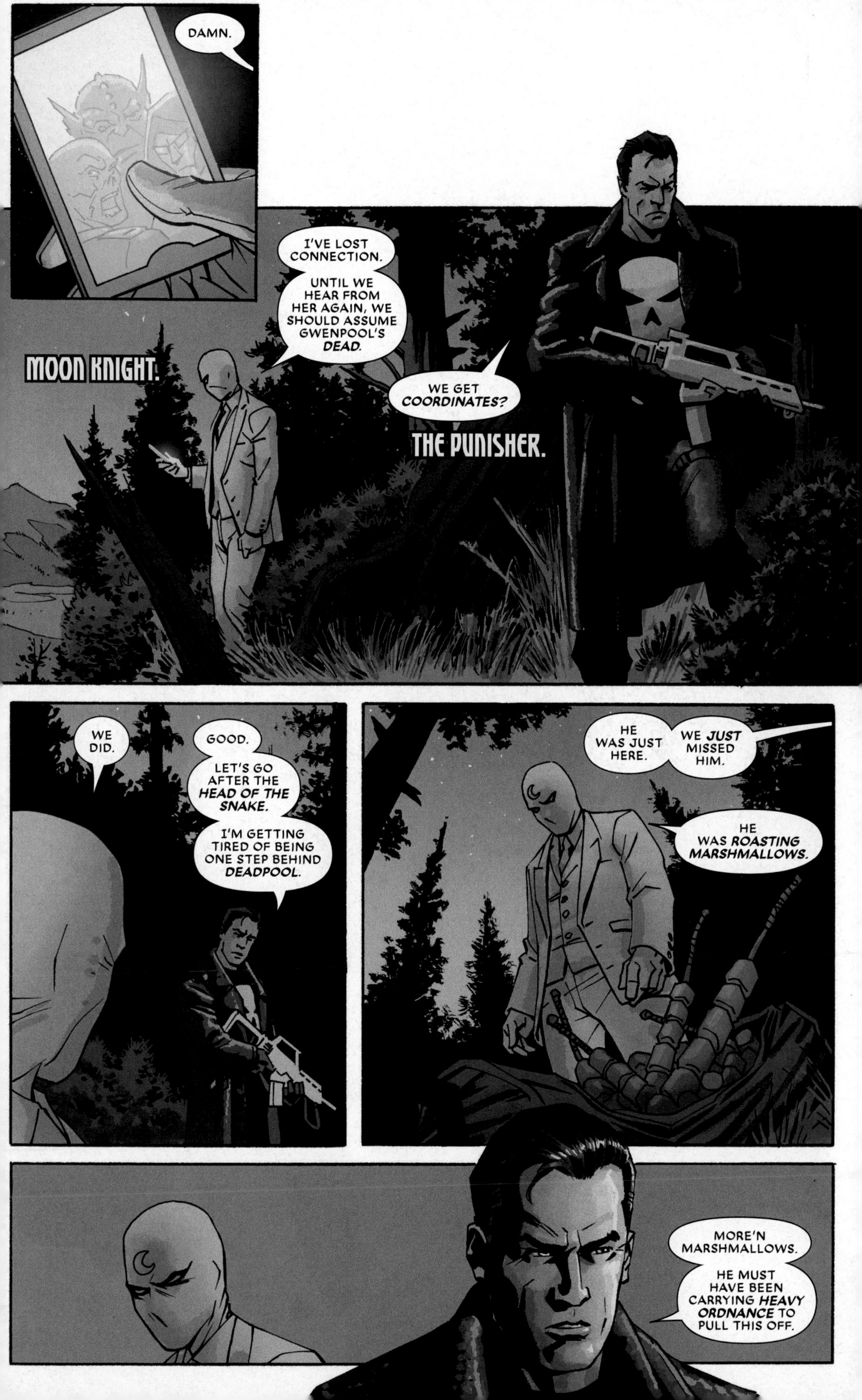
DAMN.
I'VE LOST CONNECTION.
UNTIL WE HEAR FROM HER AGAIN, WE SHOULD ASSUME GWENPOOL'S DEAD.
MOON KNIGHT.
WE GET COORDINATES?
THE PUNISHER.
WE DID.
GOOD.
LET'S GO AFTER THE HEAD OF THE SNAKE.
I'M GETTING TIRED OF BEING ONE STEP BEHIND DEADPOOL.
HE WAS JUST HERE.
WE JUST MISSED HIM.
HE WAS ROASTING MARSHMALLOWS.
MORE'N MARSHMALLOWS.
HE MUST HAVE BEEN CARRYING HEAVY ORDNANCE TO PULL THIS OFF.

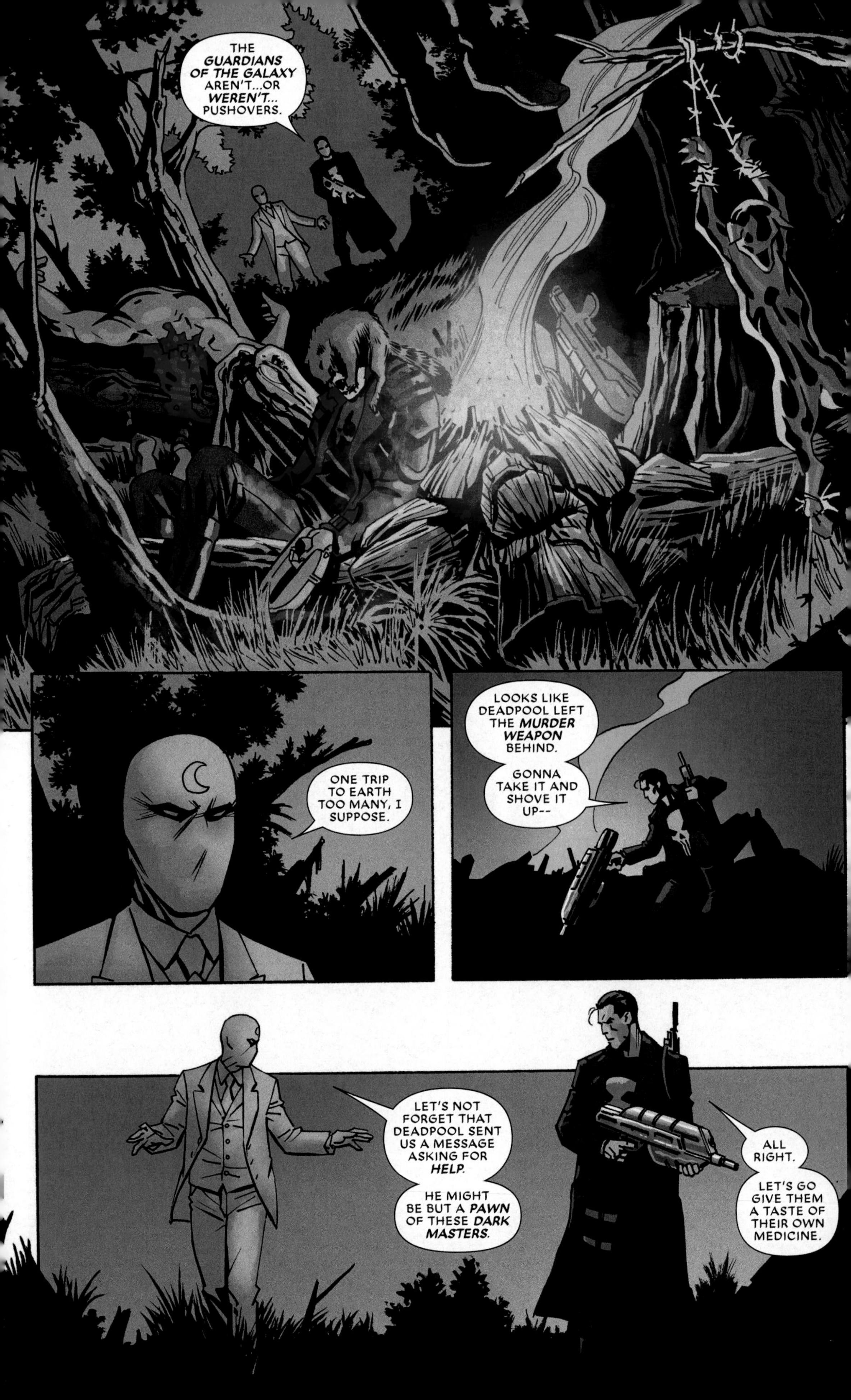
THE GUARDIANS OF THE GALAXY AREN'T...OR WEREN'T... PUSHOVERS.
ONE TRIP TO EARTH TOO MANY, I SUPPOSE.
LOOKS LIKE DEADPOOL LEFT THE MURDER WEAPON BEHIND.
GONNA TAKE IT AND SHOVE IT UP--
LET'S NOT FORGET THAT DEADPOOL SENT US A MESSAGE ASKING FOR HELP.
HE MIGHT BE BUT A PAWN OF THESE DARK MASTERS.
ALL RIGHT.
LET'S GO GIVE THEM A TASTE OF THEIR OWN MEDICINE.

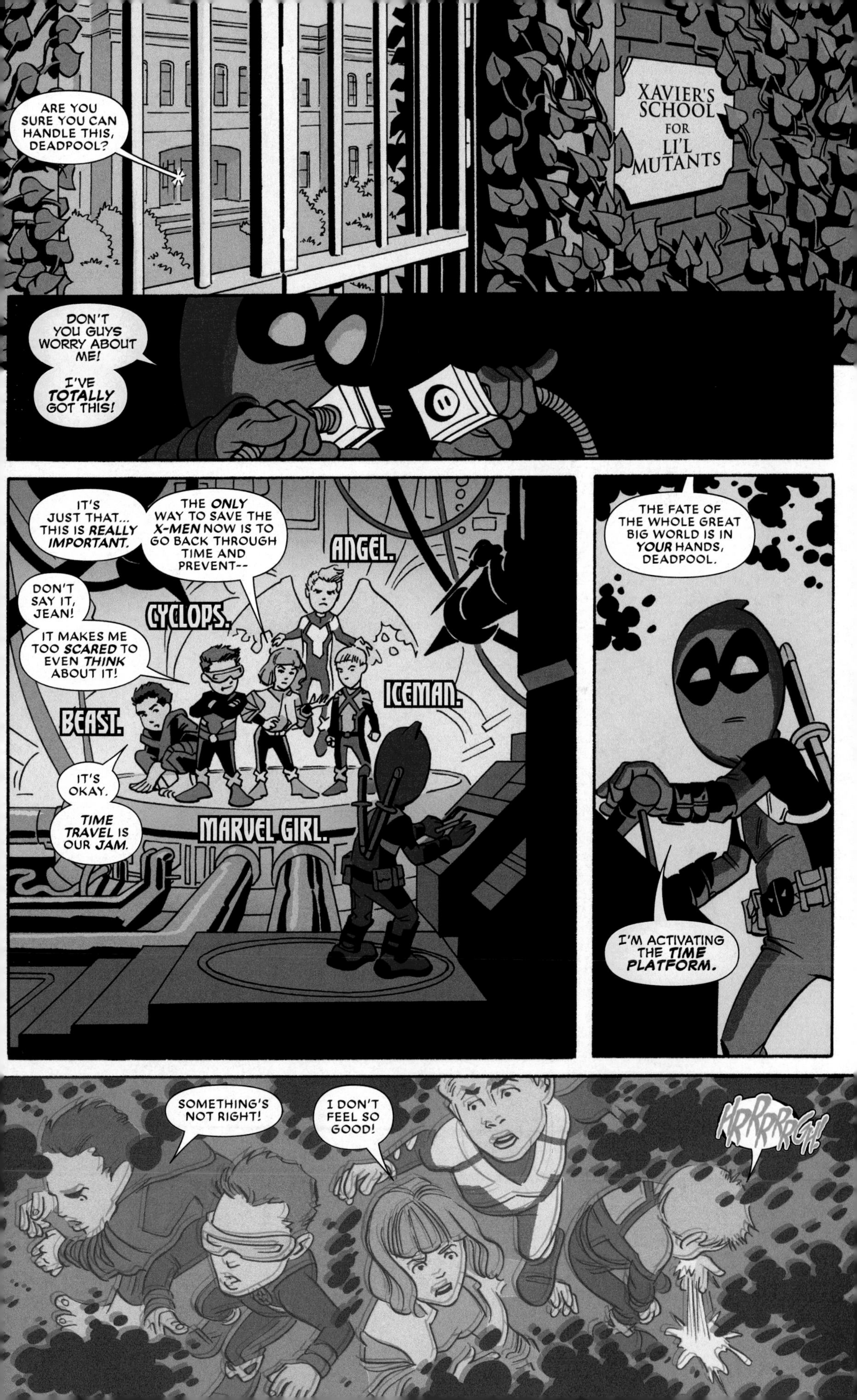
ARE YOU SURE YOU CAN HANDLE THIS, DEADPOOL?
XAVIER'S SCHOOL FOR LI'L MUTANTS
DON'T YOU GUYS WORRY ABOUT ME!
I'VE TOTALLY GOT THIS!
IT'S JUST THAT... THIS IS REALLY IMPORTANT.
THE ONLY WAY TO SAVE THE X-MEN NOW IS TO GO BACK THROUGH TIME AND PREVENT--
ANGEL.
DON'T SAY IT, JEAN!
IT MAKES ME TOO SCARED TO EVEN THINK ABOUT IT!
CYCLOPS.
ICEMAN.
BEAST.
IT'S OKAY.
TIME TRAVEL IS OUR JAM.
MARVEL GIRL.
THE FATE OF THE WHOLE GREAT BIG WORLD IS IN YOUR HANDS, DEADPOOL.
I'M ACTIVATING THE TIME PLATFORM.
SOMETHING'S NOT RIGHT!
I DON'T FEEL SO GOOD!
KRRRRRGH!

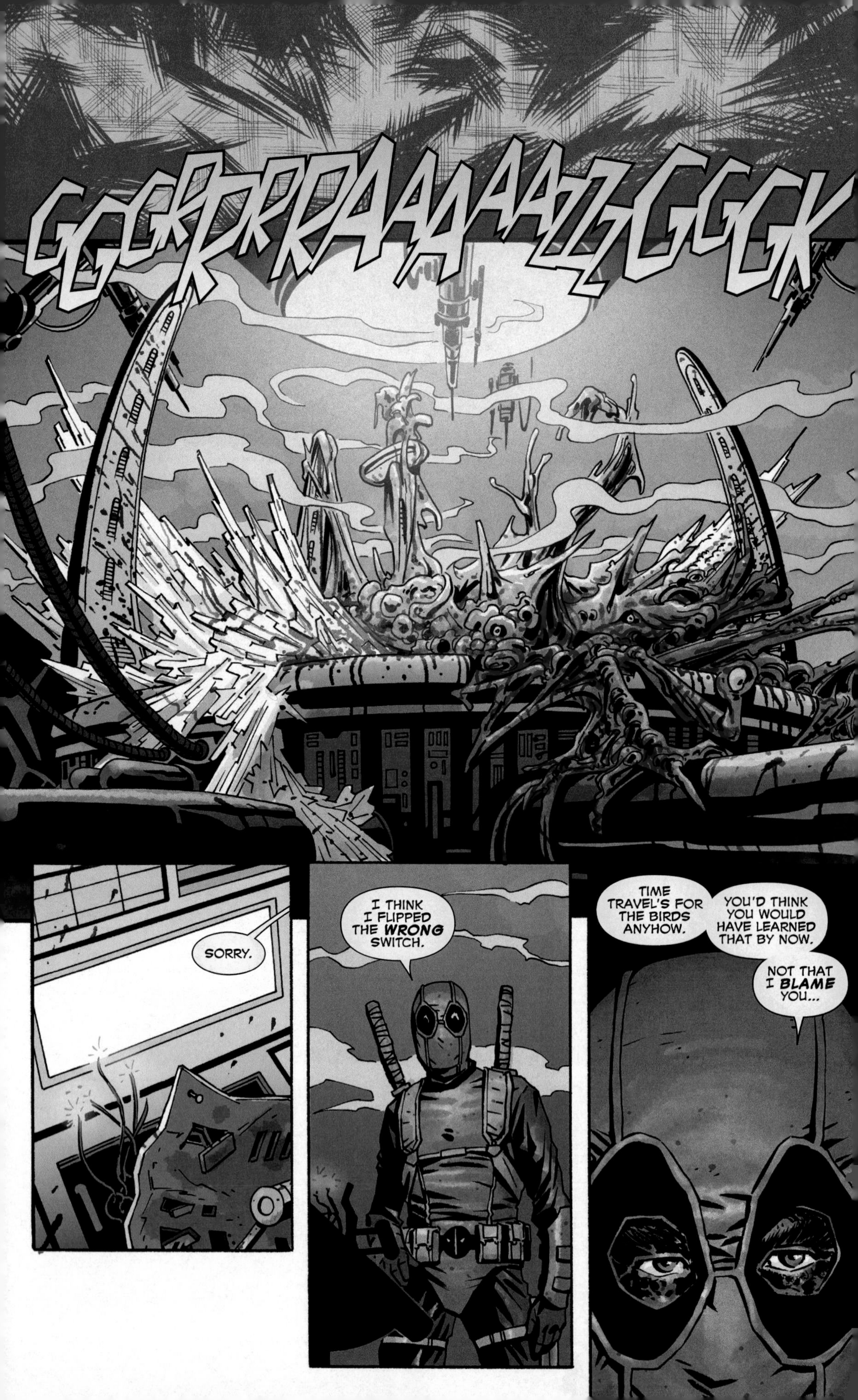
GGGRRRRAAAAAAZZZGGGK
SORRY.
I THINK I FLIPPED THE WRONG SWITCH.
TIME TRAVEL'S FOR THE BIRDS ANYHOW.
YOU'D THINK YOU WOULD HAVE LEARNED THAT BY NOW.
NOT THAT I BLAME YOU...

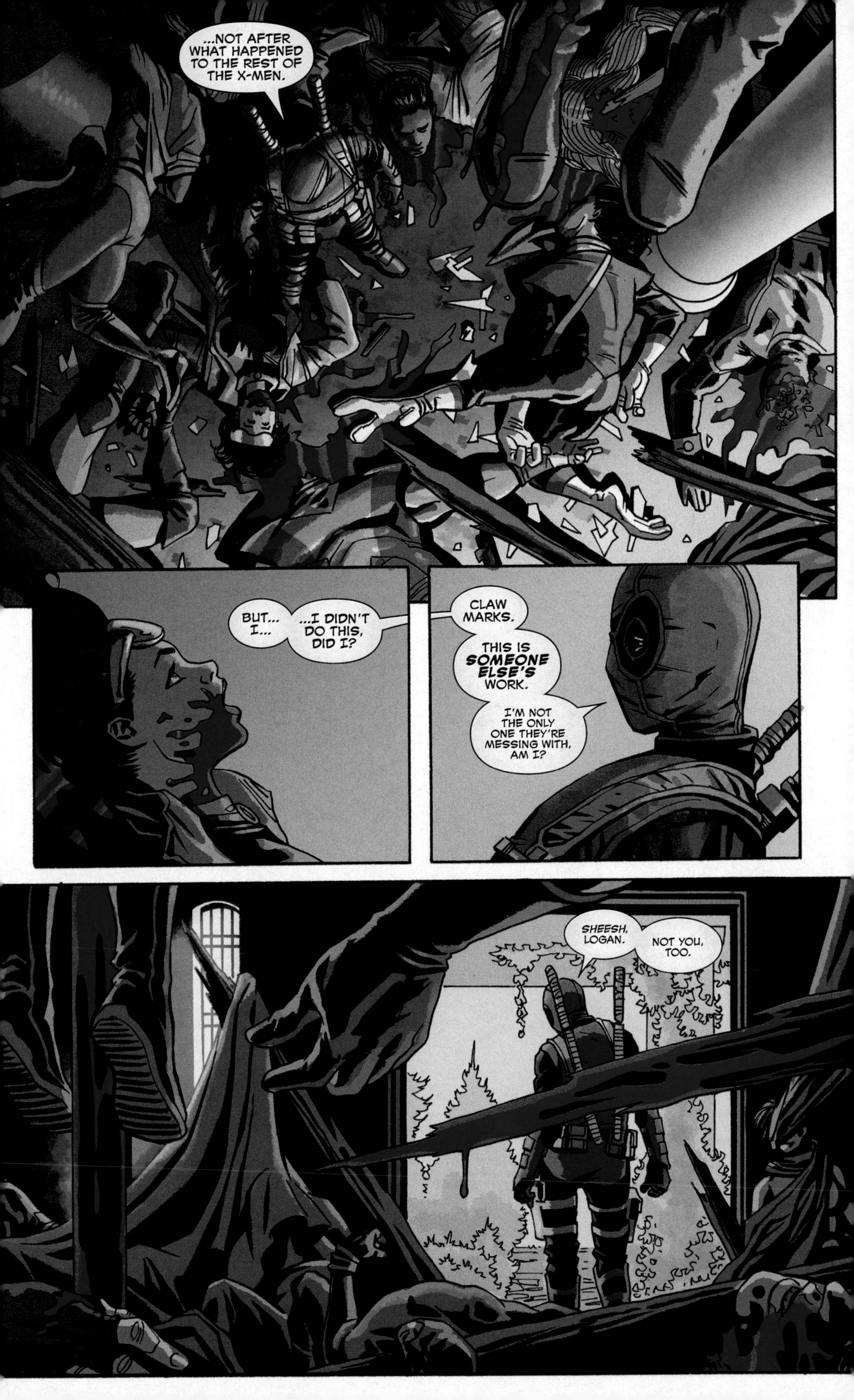
...NOT AFTER WHAT HAPPENED TO THE REST OF THE X-MEN.
BUT... I...
...I DIDN'T DO THIS, DID I?
CLAW MARKS.
THIS IS SOMEONE ELSE'S WORK.
I'M NOT THE ONLY ONE THEY'RE MESSING WITH, AM I?
SHEESH, LOGAN.
NOT YOU, TOO.

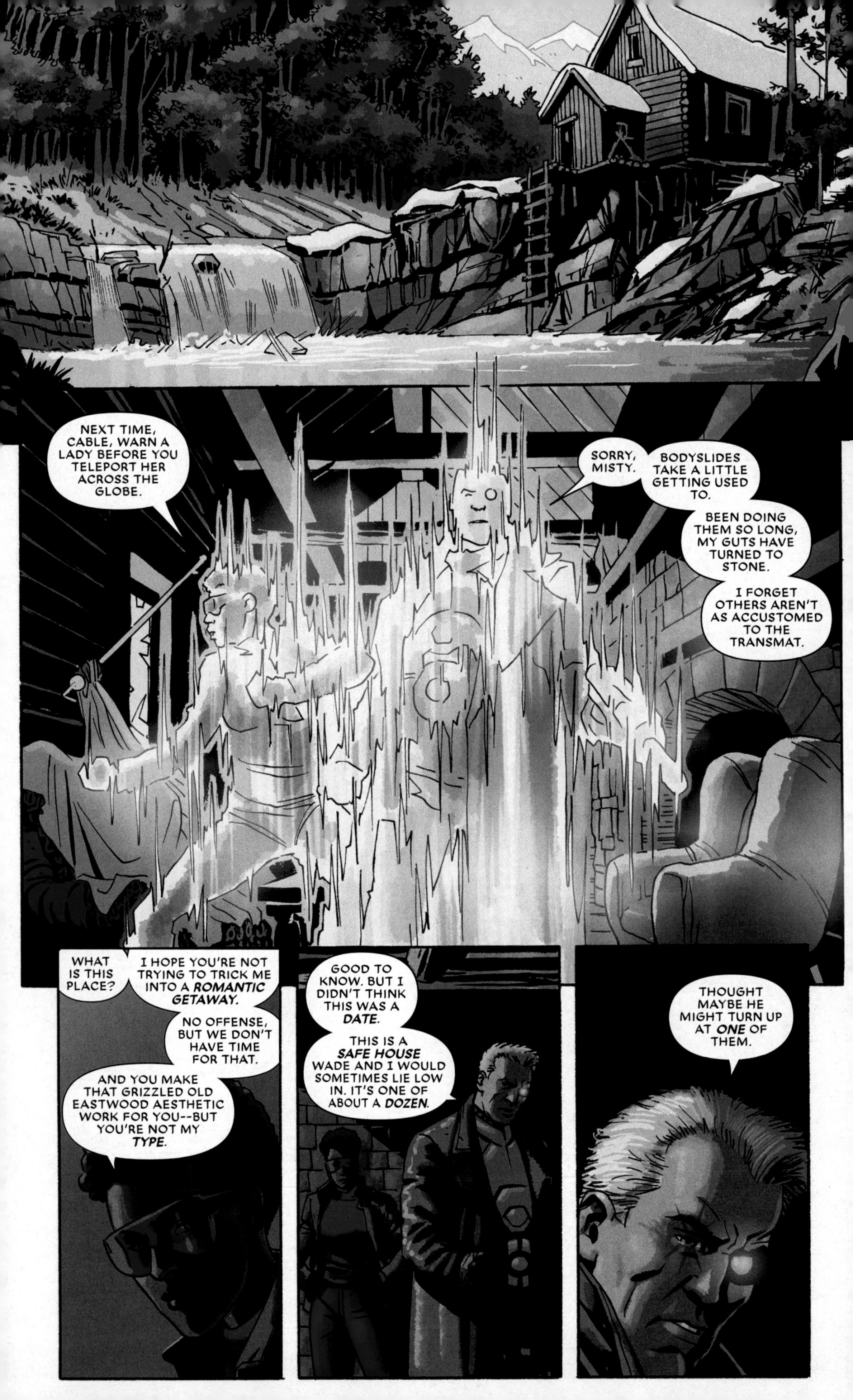
NEXT TIME, CABLE, WARN A LADY BEFORE YOU TELEPORT HER ACROSS THE GLOBE.
SORRY, MISTY.
BODYSLIDES TAKE A LITTLE GETTING USED TO.
BEEN DOING THEM SO LONG, MY GUTS HAVE TURNED TO STONE.
I FORGET OTHERS AREN'T AS ACCUSTOMED TO THE TRANSMAT.
WHAT IS THIS PLACE?
I HOPE YOU'RE NOT TRYING TO TRICK ME INTO A *ROMANTIC GETAWAY.*
NO OFFENSE, BUT WE DON'T HAVE TIME FOR THAT.
AND YOU MAKE THAT GRIZZLED OLD EASTWOOD AESTHETIC WORK FOR YOU--BUT YOU'RE NOT MY *TYPE*.
GOOD TO KNOW. BUT I DIDN'T THINK THIS WAS A *DATE*.
THIS IS A *SAFE HOUSE* WADE AND I WOULD SOMETIMES LIE LOW IN. IT'S ONE OF ABOUT A *DOZEN*.
THOUGHT MAYBE HE MIGHT TURN UP AT *ONE* OF THEM.

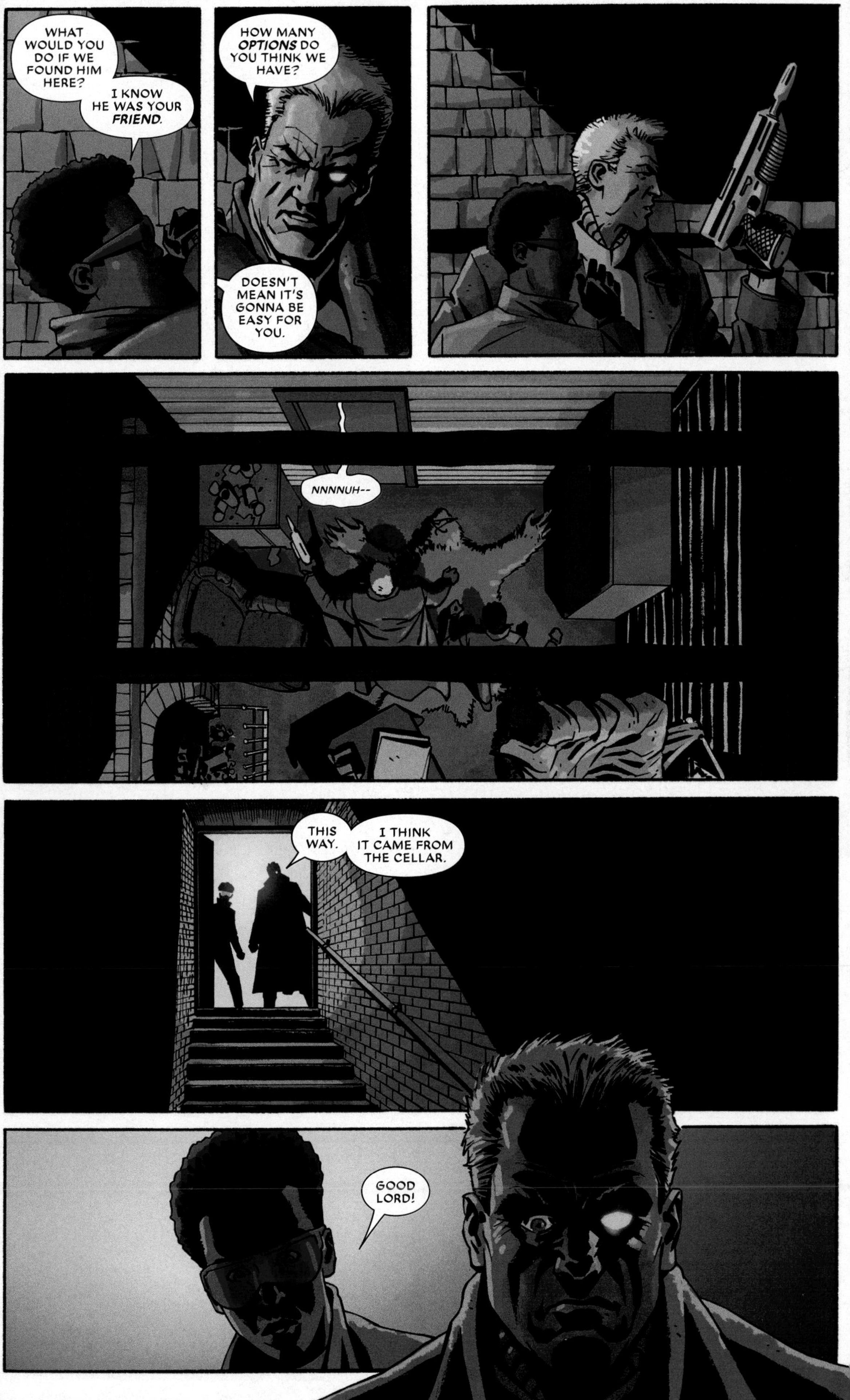
WHAT WOULD YOU DO IF WE FOUND HIM HERE?
I KNOW HE WAS YOUR FRIEND.
HOW MANY OPTIONS DO YOU THINK WE HAVE?
DOESN'T MEAN IT'S GONNA BE EASY FOR YOU.
NNNNUH--
THIS WAY.
I THINK IT CAME FROM THE CELLAR.
GOOD LORD!

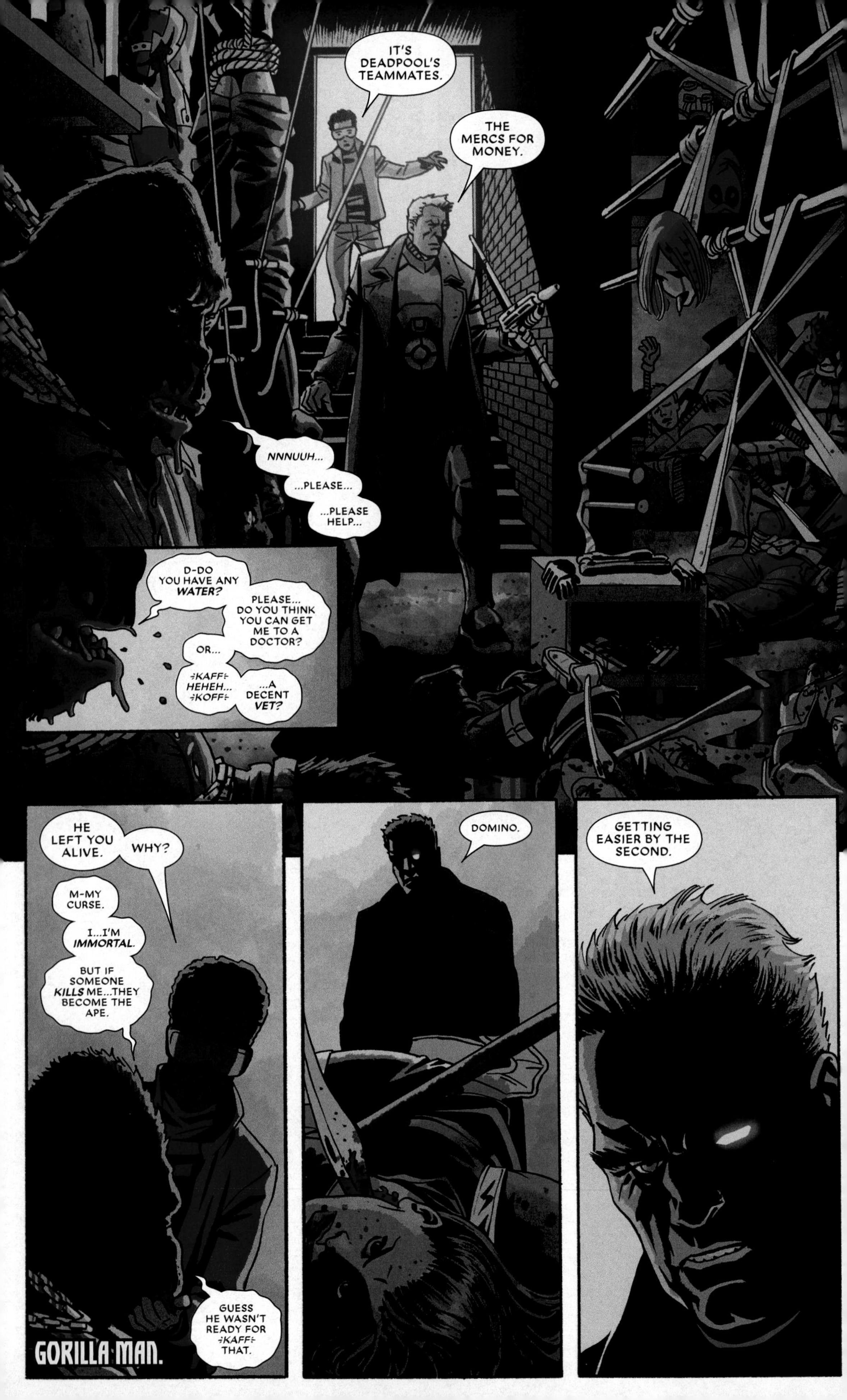
IT'S DEADPOOL'S TEAMMATES.
THE MERCS FOR MONEY.
NNNUUH...
...PLEASE...
...PLEASE HELP...
D-DO YOU HAVE ANY WATER?
PLEASE... DO YOU THINK YOU CAN GET ME TO A DOCTOR?
OR...
=KAFF= HEHEH... =KOFF=
...A DECENT VET?
HE LEFT YOU ALIVE.
WHY?
M-MY CURSE.
I...I'M IMMORTAL.
BUT IF SOMEONE KILLS ME...THEY BECOME THE APE.
GUESS HE WASN'T READY FOR =KAFF= THAT.
GORILLA MAN.
DOMINO.
GETTING EASIER BY THE SECOND.

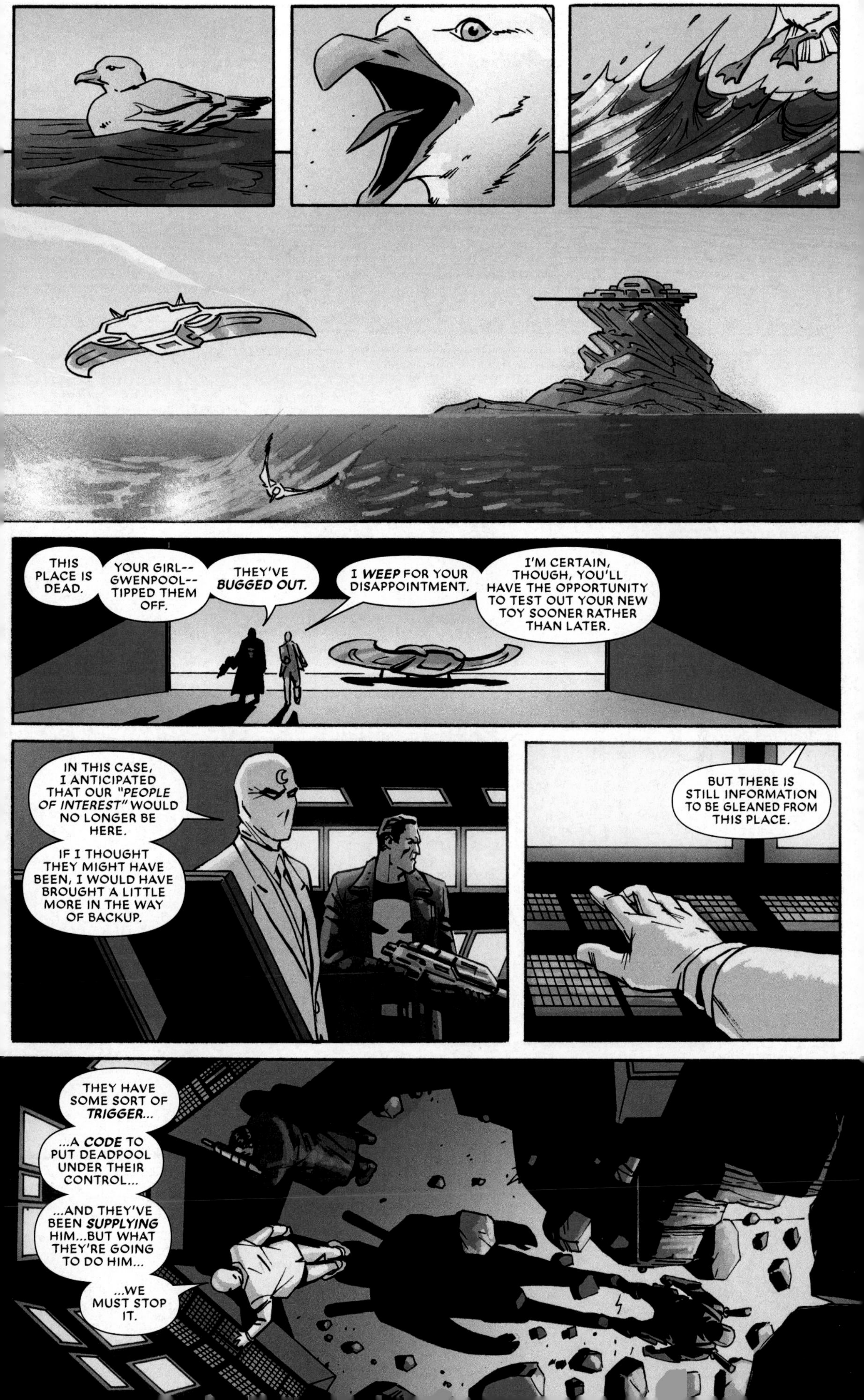
THIS PLACE IS DEAD.
YOUR GIRL-- GWENPOOL-- TIPPED THEM OFF.
THEY'VE BUGGED OUT.
I WEEP FOR YOUR DISAPPOINTMENT.
I'M CERTAIN, THOUGH, YOU'LL HAVE THE OPPORTUNITY TO TEST OUT YOUR NEW TOY SOONER RATHER THAN LATER.
IN THIS CASE, I ANTICIPATED THAT OUR "PEOPLE OF INTEREST" WOULD NO LONGER BE HERE.
IF I THOUGHT THEY MIGHT HAVE BEEN, I WOULD HAVE BROUGHT A LITTLE MORE IN THE WAY OF BACKUP.
BUT THERE IS STILL INFORMATION TO BE GLEANED FROM THIS PLACE.
THEY HAVE SOME SORT OF TRIGGER...
...A CODE TO PUT DEADPOOL UNDER THEIR CONTROL...
...AND THEY'VE BEEN SUPPLYING HIM...BUT WHAT THEY'RE GOING TO DO HIM...
...WE MUST STOP IT.

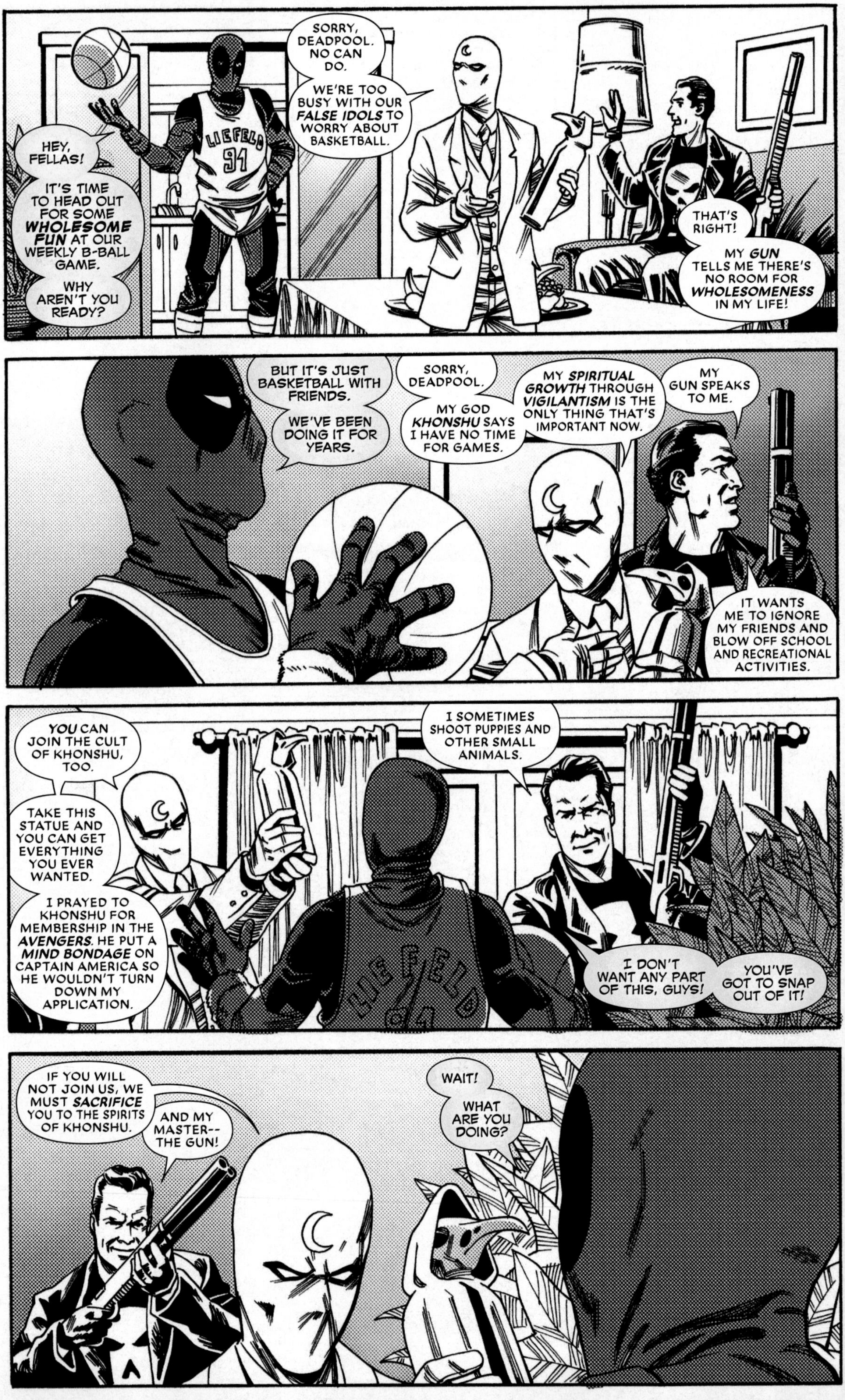
HEY, FELLAS!
IT'S TIME TO HEAD OUT FOR SOME WHOLESOME FUN AT OUR WEEKLY B-BALL GAME.
WHY AREN'T YOU READY?
LIEFELD 91
SORRY, DEADPOOL. NO CAN DO.
WE'RE TOO BUSY WITH OUR FALSE IDOLS TO WORRY ABOUT BASKETBALL.
THAT'S RIGHT!
MY GUN TELLS ME THERE'S NO ROOM FOR WHOLESOMENESS IN MY LIFE!
BUT IT'S JUST BASKETBALL WITH FRIENDS.
WE'VE BEEN DOING IT FOR YEARS.
SORRY, DEADPOOL.
MY GOD KHONSHU SAYS I HAVE NO TIME FOR GAMES.
MY SPIRITUAL GROWTH THROUGH VIGILANTISM IS THE ONLY THING THAT'S IMPORTANT NOW.
MY GUN SPEAKS TO ME.
IT WANTS ME TO IGNORE MY FRIENDS AND BLOW OFF SCHOOL AND RECREATIONAL ACTIVITIES.
YOU CAN JOIN THE CULT OF KHONSHU, TOO.
TAKE THIS STATUE AND YOU CAN GET EVERYTHING YOU EVER WANTED.
I PRAYED TO KHONSHU FOR MEMBERSHIP IN THE AVENGERS. HE PUT A MIND BONDAGE ON CAPTAIN AMERICA SO HE WOULDN'T TURN DOWN MY APPLICATION.
I SOMETIMES SHOOT PUPPIES AND OTHER SMALL ANIMALS.
I DON'T WANT ANY PART OF THIS, GUYS!
YOU'VE GOT TO SNAP OUT OF IT!
IF YOU WILL NOT JOIN US, WE MUST SACRIFICE YOU TO THE SPIRITS OF KHONSHU.
AND MY MASTER-- THE GUN!
WAIT!
WHAT ARE YOU DOING?

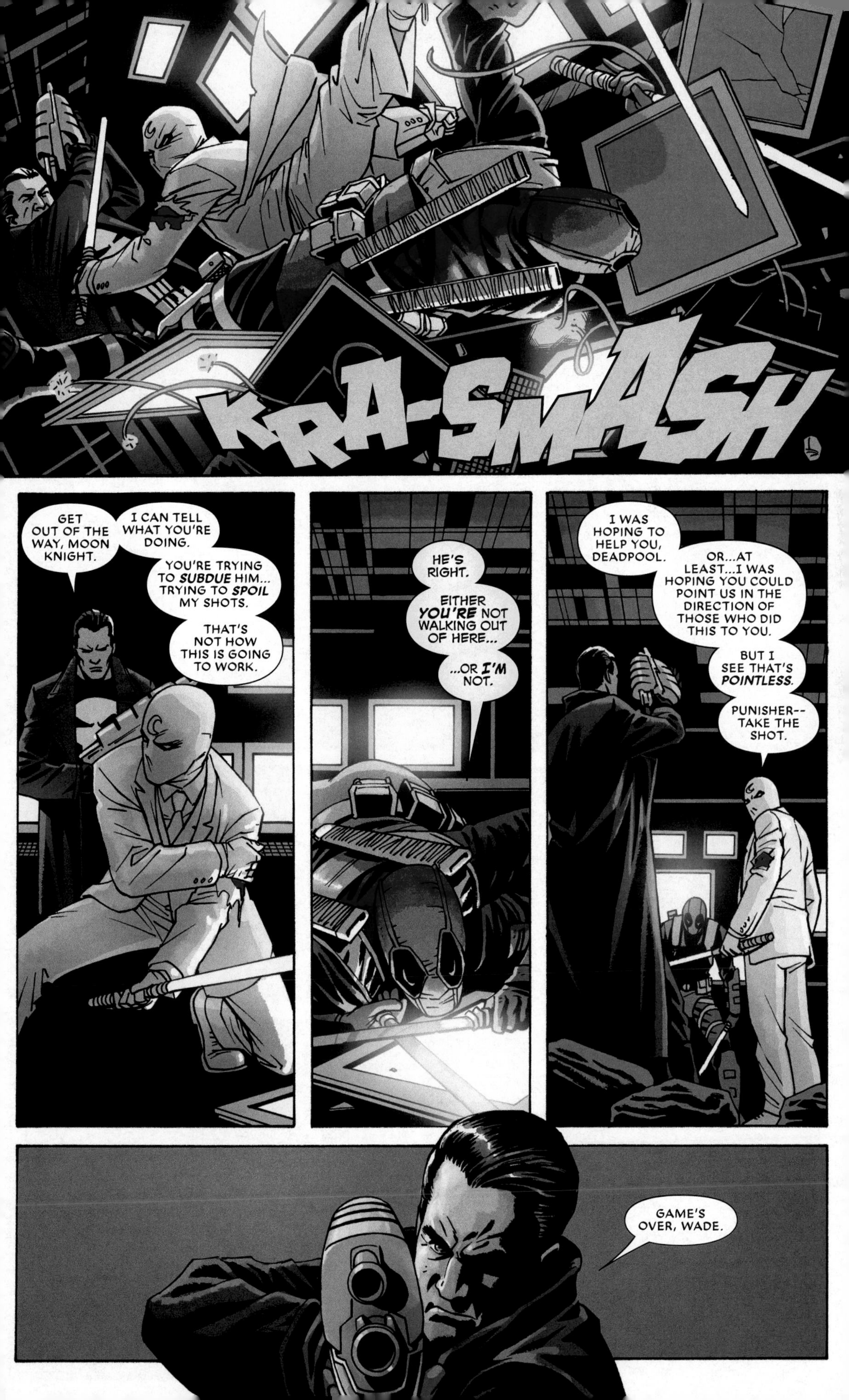
KRA-SMASH
GET OUT OF THE WAY, MOON KNIGHT.
I CAN TELL WHAT YOU'RE DOING.
YOU'RE TRYING TO SUBDUE HIM... TRYING TO SPOIL MY SHOTS.
THAT'S NOT HOW THIS IS GOING TO WORK.
HE'S RIGHT.
EITHER YOU'RE NOT WALKING OUT OF HERE...
...OR I'M NOT.
I WAS HOPING TO HELP YOU, DEADPOOL.
OR...AT LEAST...I WAS HOPING YOU COULD POINT US IN THE DIRECTION OF THOSE WHO DID THIS TO YOU.
BUT I SEE THAT'S POINTLESS.
PUNISHER-- TAKE THE SHOT.
GAME'S OVER, WADE.

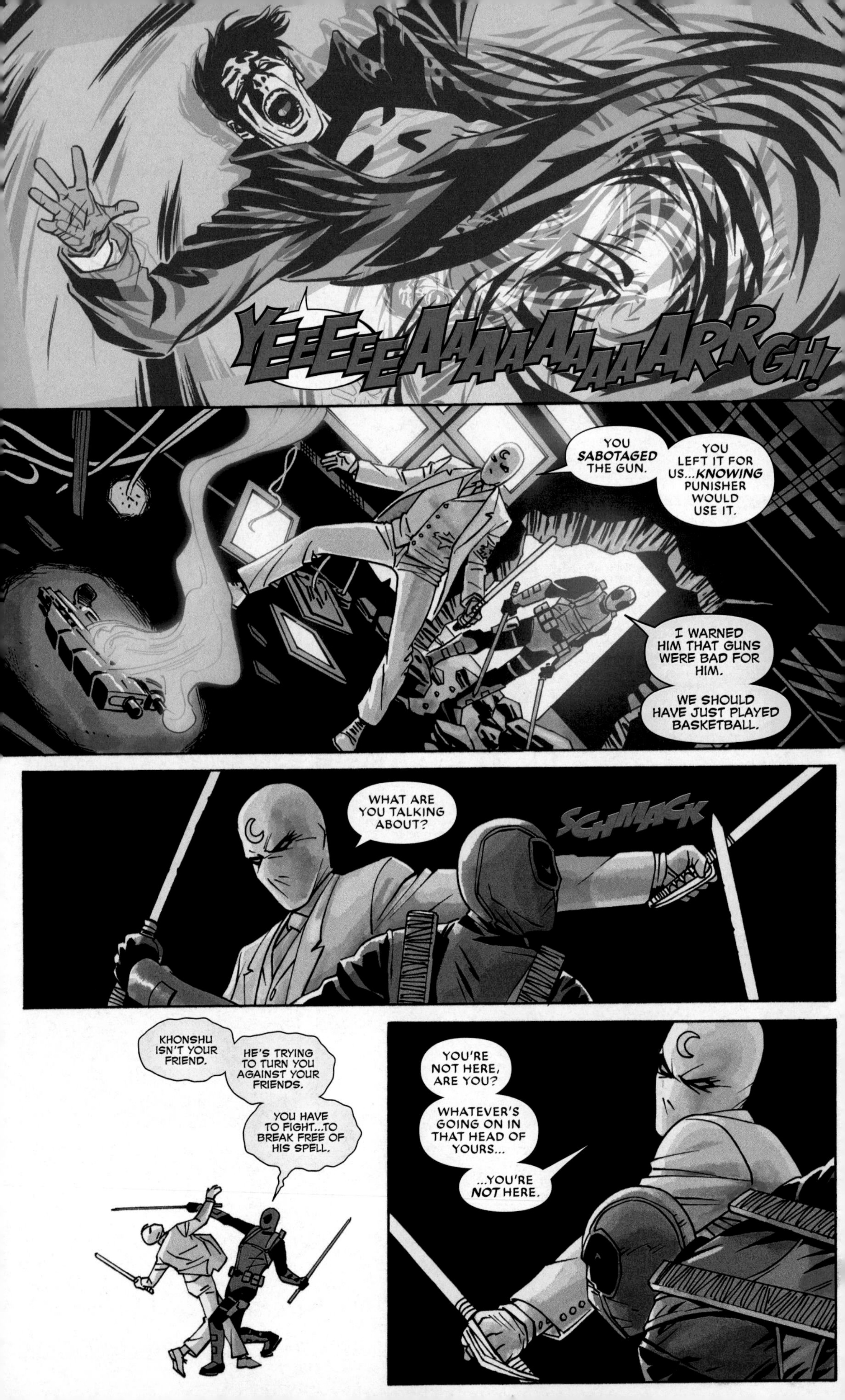
YEEEEEEAAAAAAAAAARRRGH!
YOU SABOTAGED THE GUN.
YOU LEFT IT FOR US...KNOWING PUNISHER WOULD USE IT.
I WARNED HIM THAT GUNS WERE BAD FOR HIM.
WE SHOULD HAVE JUST PLAYED BASKETBALL.
WHAT ARE YOU TALKING ABOUT?
SCHMACK
KHONSHU ISN'T YOUR FRIEND.
HE'S TRYING TO TURN YOU AGAINST YOUR FRIENDS.
YOU HAVE TO FIGHT...TO BREAK FREE OF HIS SPELL.
YOU'RE NOT HERE, ARE YOU?
WHATEVER'S GOING ON IN THAT HEAD OF YOURS...
...YOU'RE NOT HERE.

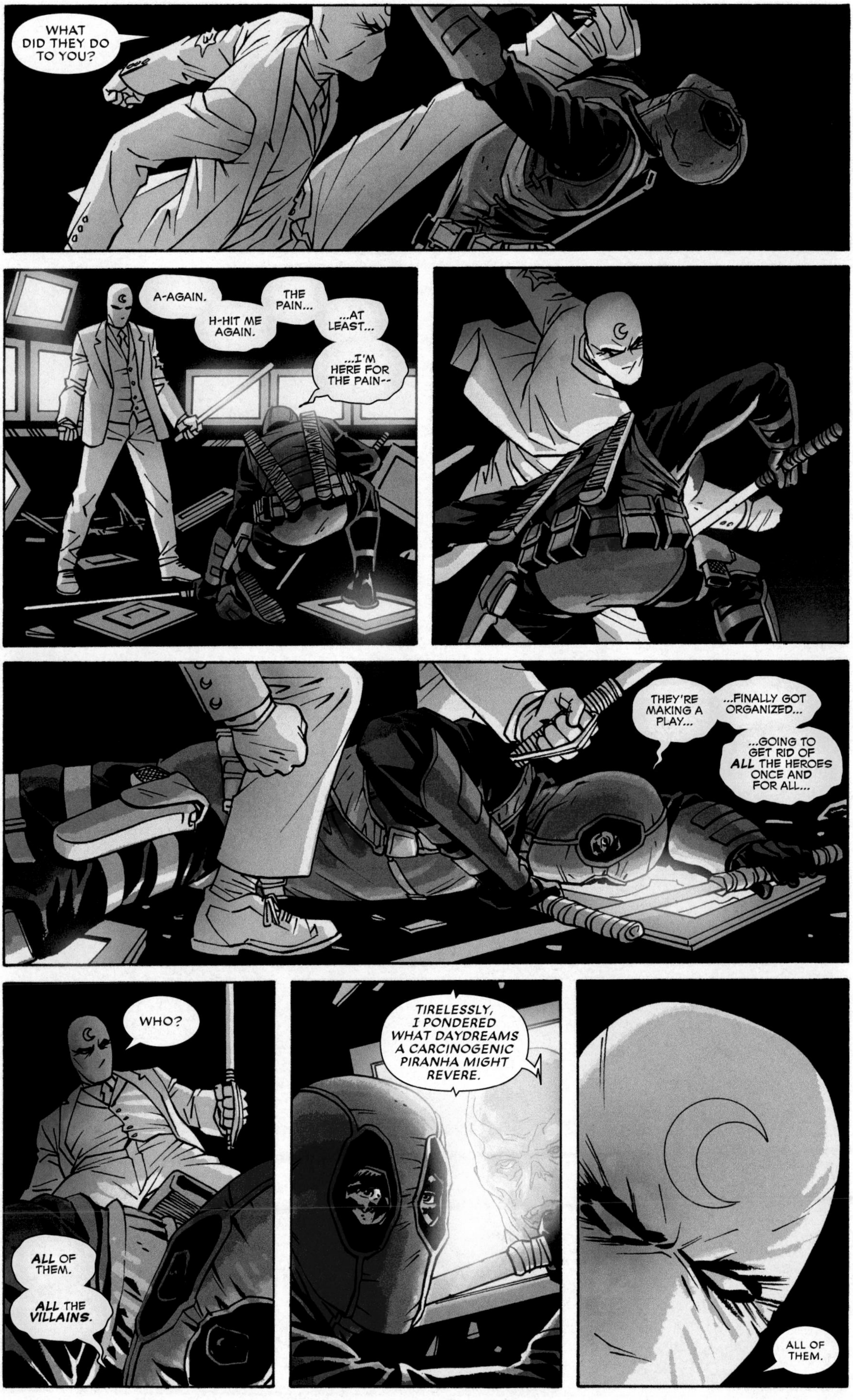
WHAT DID THEY DO TO YOU?
A-AGAIN.
H-HIT ME AGAIN.
THE PAIN...
...AT LEAST...
...I'M HERE FOR THE PAIN--
THEY'RE MAKING A PLAY...
...FINALLY GOT ORGANIZED...
...GOING TO GET RID OF ALL THE HEROES ONCE AND FOR ALL...
WHO?
ALL OF THEM.
ALL THE VILLAINS.
TIRELESSLY, I PONDERED WHAT DAYDREAMS A CARCINOGENIC PIRANHA MIGHT REVERE.
ALL OF THEM.

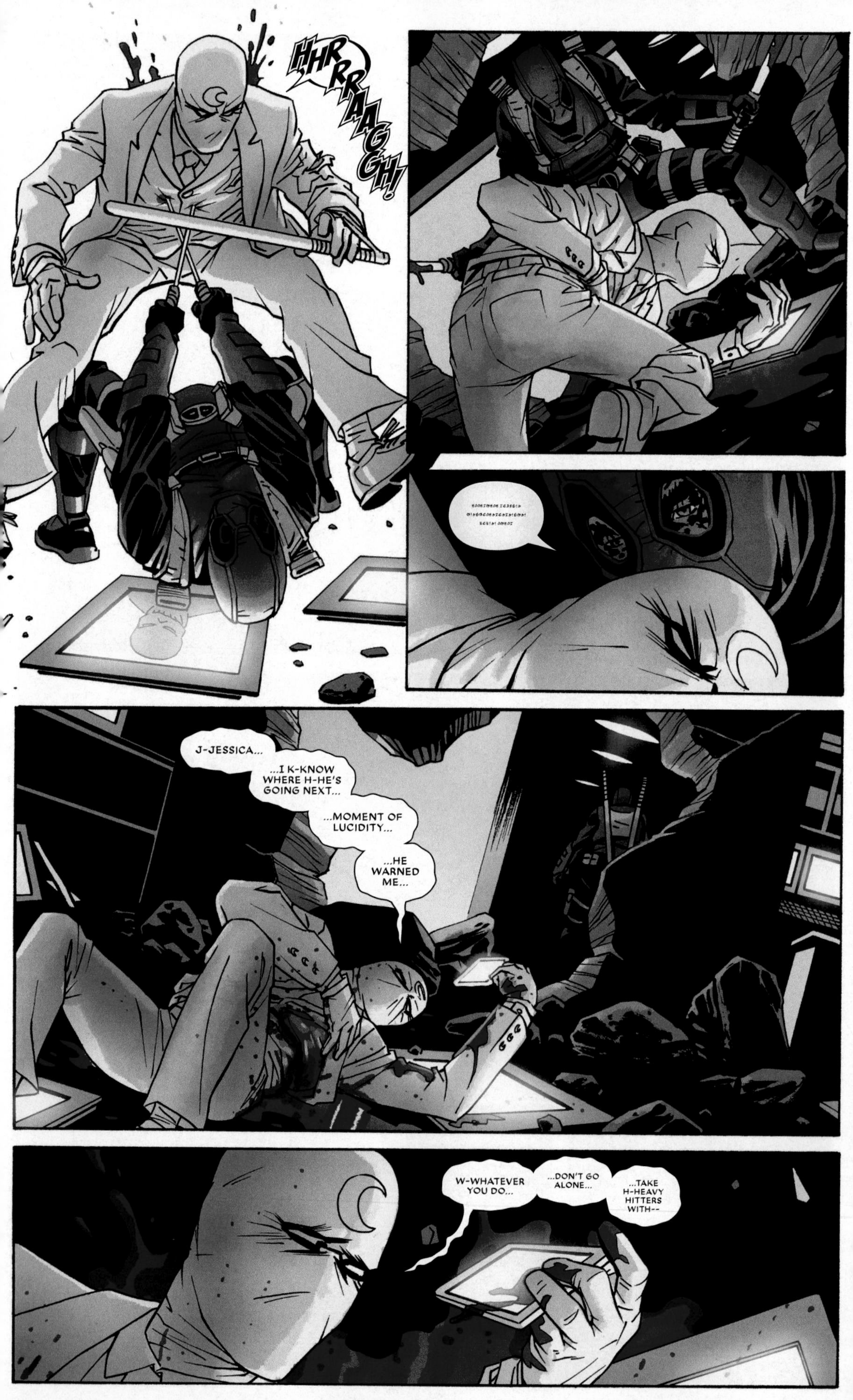
HHRRAAGGH!
J-JESSICA...
...I K-KNOW WHERE H-HE'S GOING NEXT...
...MOMENT OF LUCIDITY...
...HE WARNED ME...
W-WHATEVER YOU DO...
...DON'T GO ALONE...
...TAKE H-HEAVY HITTERS WITH--

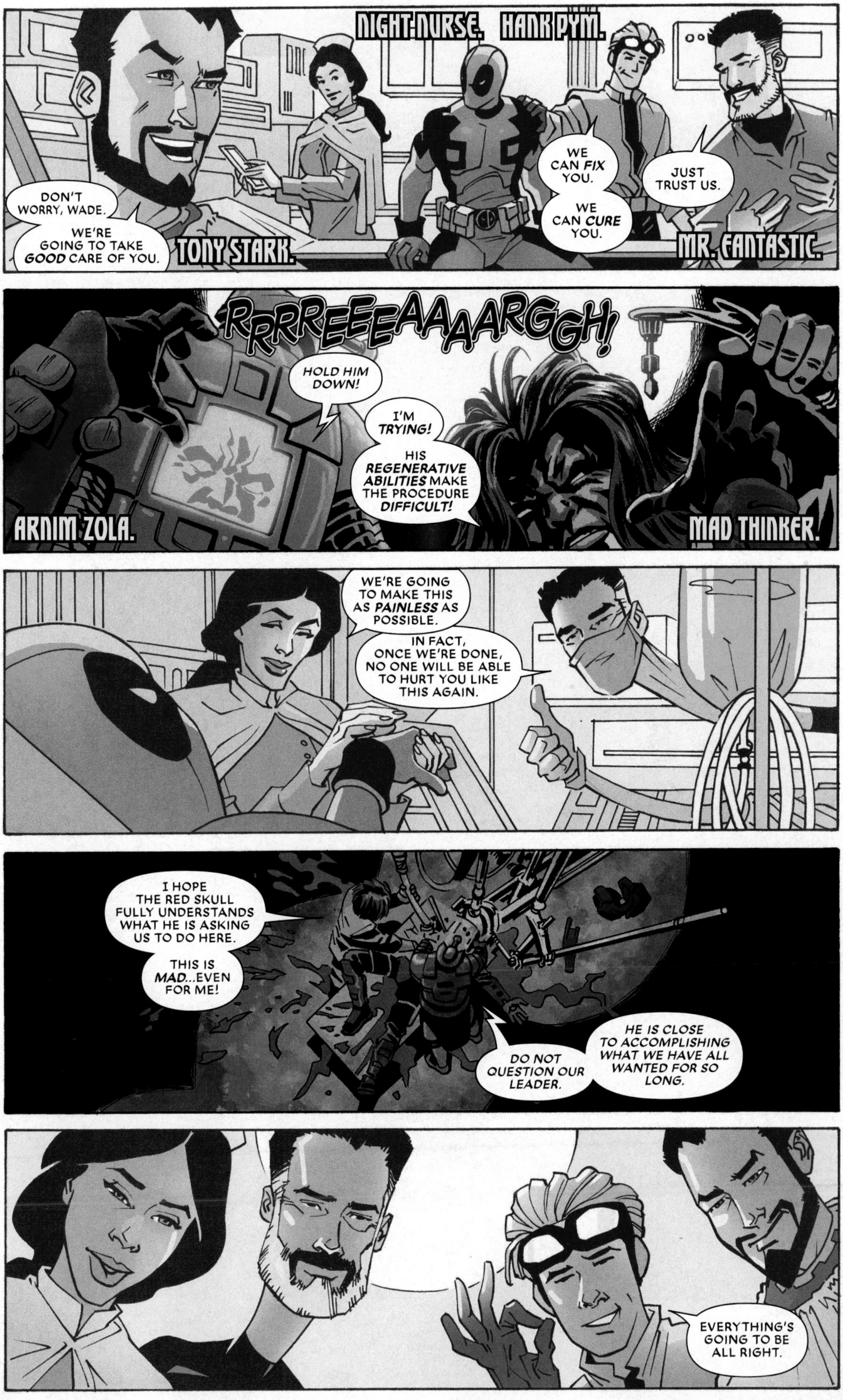
NIGHT NURSE.
HANK PYM.
DON'T WORRY, WADE.
WE'RE GOING TO TAKE *GOOD* CARE OF YOU.
TONY STARK.
WE CAN *FIX* YOU.
WE CAN *CURE* YOU.
JUST TRUST US.
MR. FANTASTIC.
RRRREEEEAAAAARGGH!
HOLD HIM DOWN!
I'M *TRYING!*
HIS *REGENERATIVE ABILITIES* MAKE THE PROCEDURE *DIFFICULT!*
ARNIM ZOLA.
MAD THINKER.
WE'RE GOING TO MAKE THIS AS *PAINLESS* AS POSSIBLE.
IN FACT, ONCE WE'RE DONE, NO ONE WILL BE ABLE TO HURT YOU LIKE THIS AGAIN.
I HOPE THE RED SKULL FULLY UNDERSTANDS WHAT HE IS ASKING US TO DO HERE.
THIS IS *MAD*...EVEN FOR ME!
DO NOT QUESTION OUR LEADER.
HE IS CLOSE TO ACCOMPLISHING WHAT WE HAVE ALL WANTED FOR SO LONG.
EVERYTHING'S GOING TO BE ALL RIGHT.

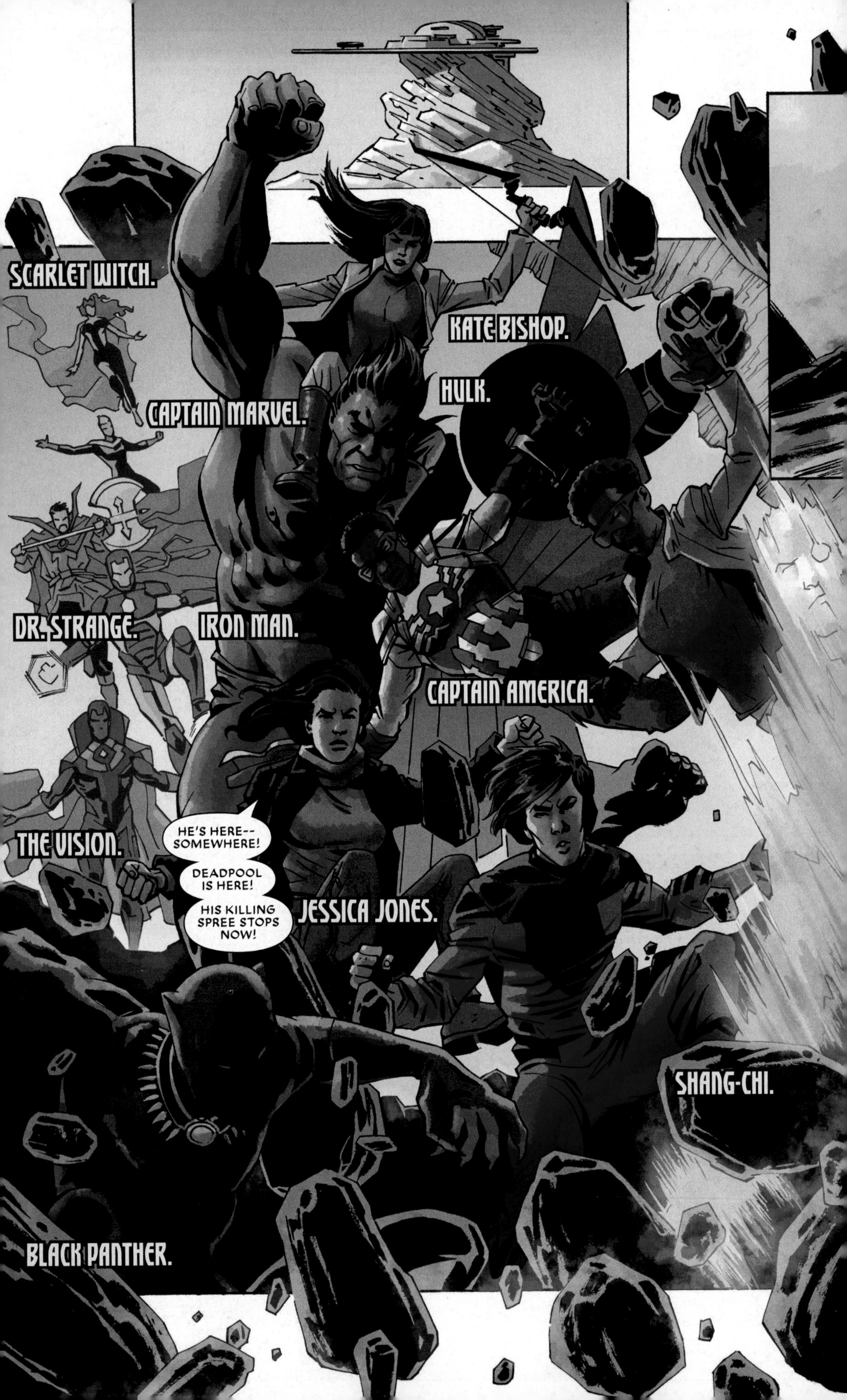
SCARLET WITCH.
KATE BISHOP.
HULK.
CAPTAIN MARVEL.
DR. STRANGE.
IRON MAN.
CAPTAIN AMERICA.
THE VISION.
HE'S HERE-- SOMEWHERE!
DEADPOOL IS HERE!
HIS KILLING SPREE STOPS NOW!
JESSICA JONES.
SHANG-CHI.
BLACK PANTHER.

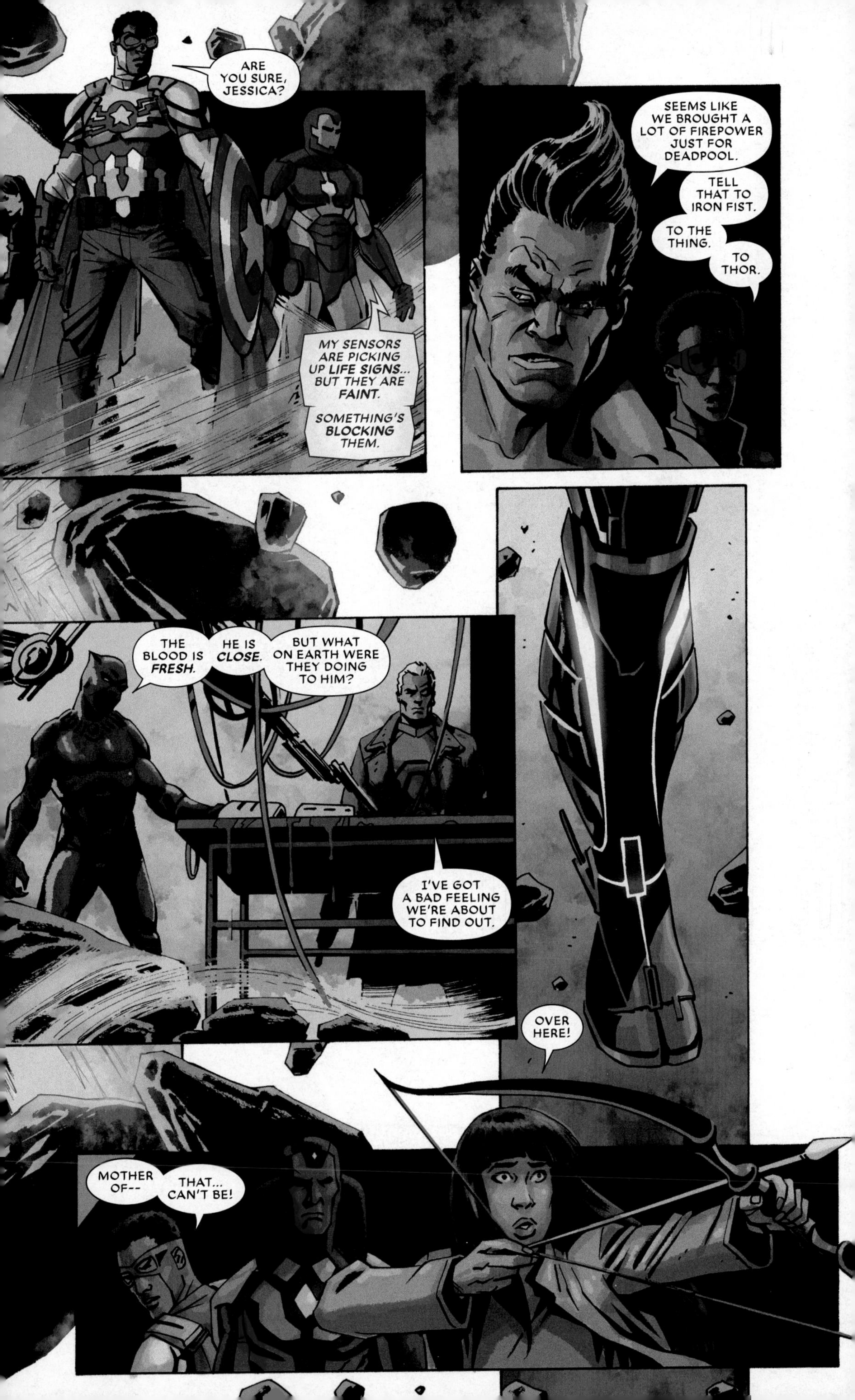
ARE YOU SURE, JESSICA?
MY SENSORS ARE PICKING UP LIFE SIGNS... BUT THEY ARE FAINT.
SOMETHING'S BLOCKING THEM.
SEEMS LIKE WE BROUGHT A LOT OF FIREPOWER JUST FOR DEADPOOL.
TELL THAT TO IRON FIST.
TO THE THING.
TO THOR.
THE BLOOD IS FRESH.
HE IS CLOSE.
BUT WHAT ON EARTH WERE THEY DOING TO HIM?
I'VE GOT A BAD FEELING WE'RE ABOUT TO FIND OUT.
OVER HERE!
MOTHER OF--
THAT... CAN'T BE!

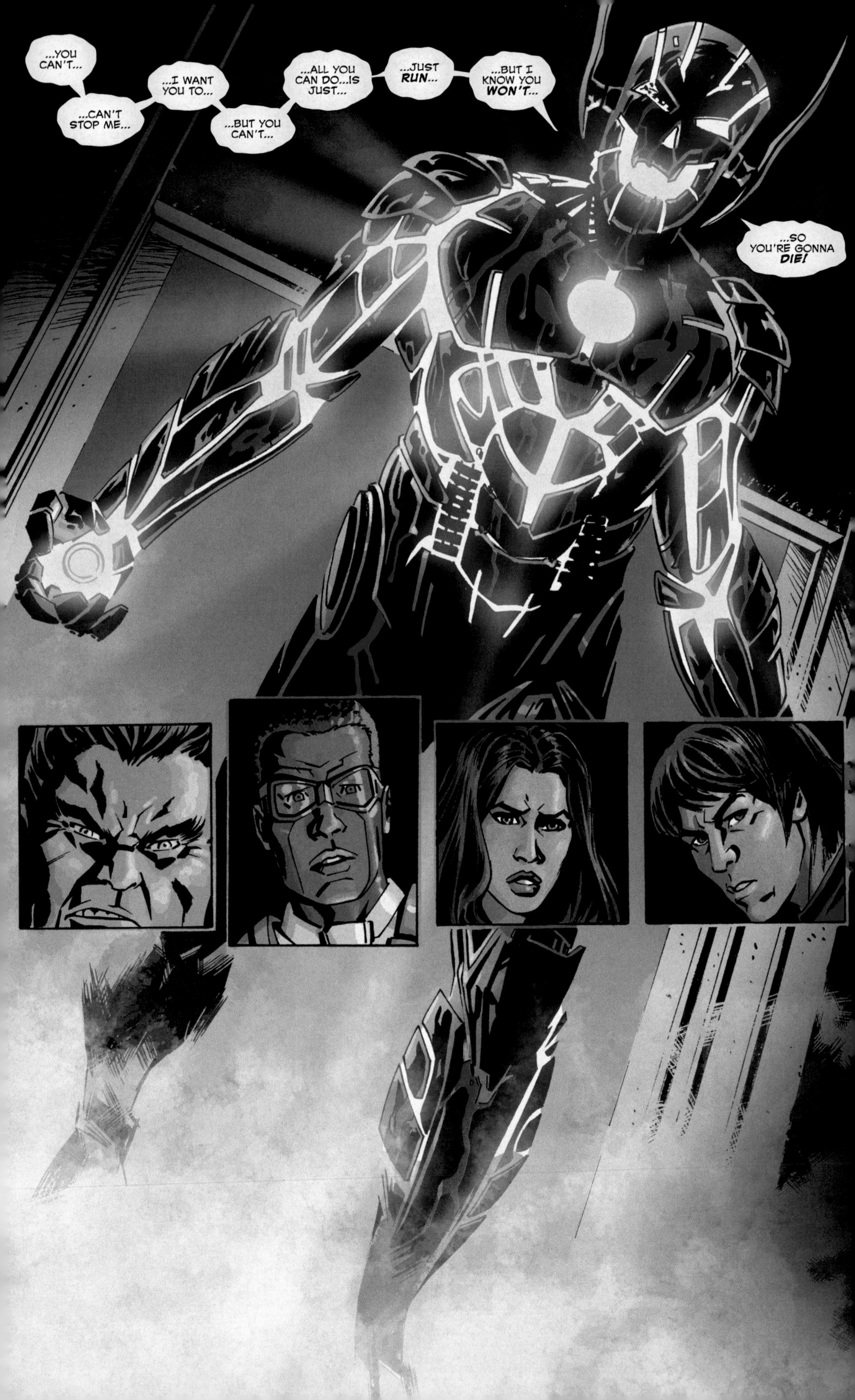
...YOU CAN'T...
...CAN'T STOP ME...
...I WANT YOU TO...
...BUT YOU CAN'T...
...ALL YOU CAN DO...IS JUST...
...JUST RUN...
...BUT I KNOW YOU WON'T...
...SO YOU'RE GONNA DIE!

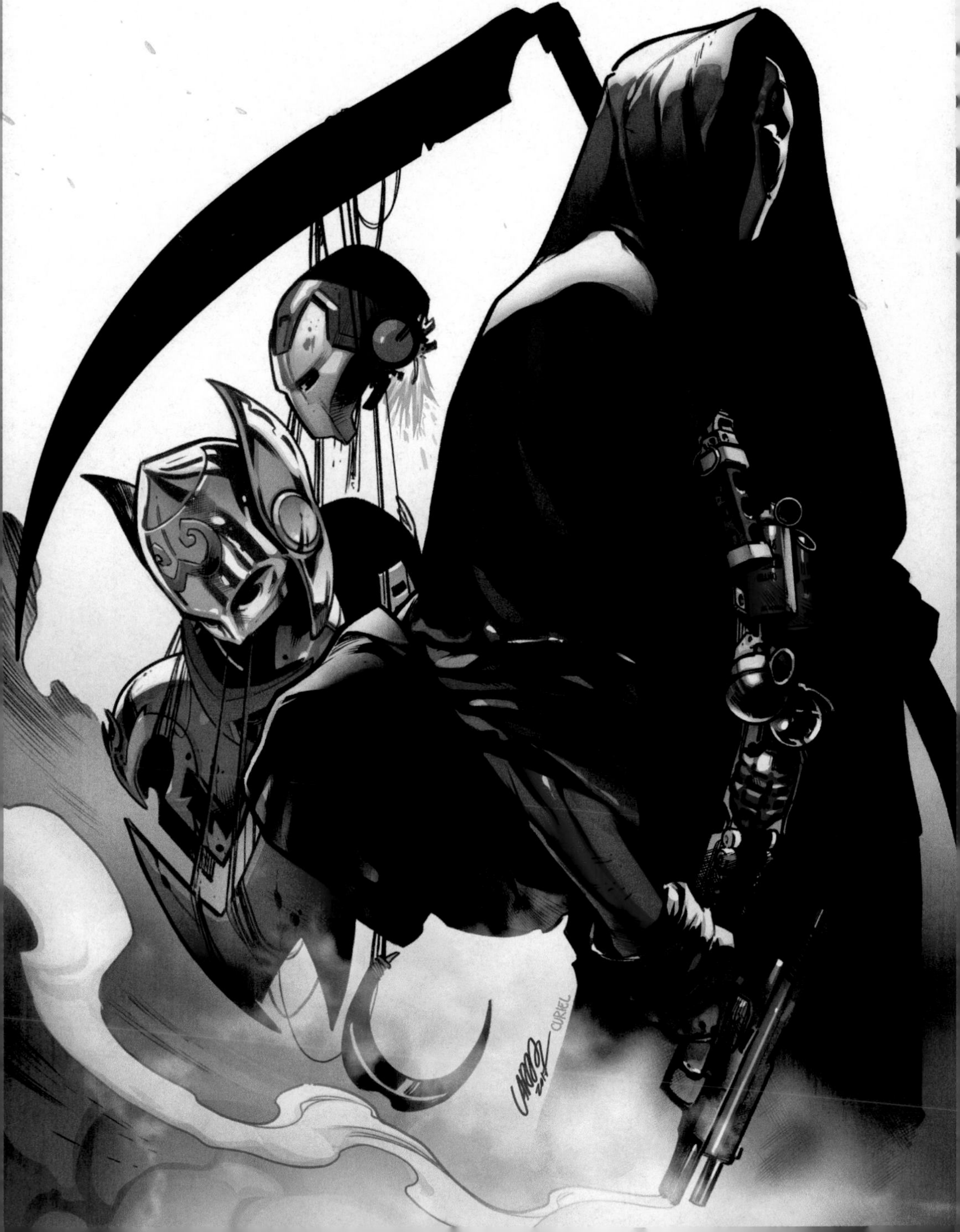
CURIEL

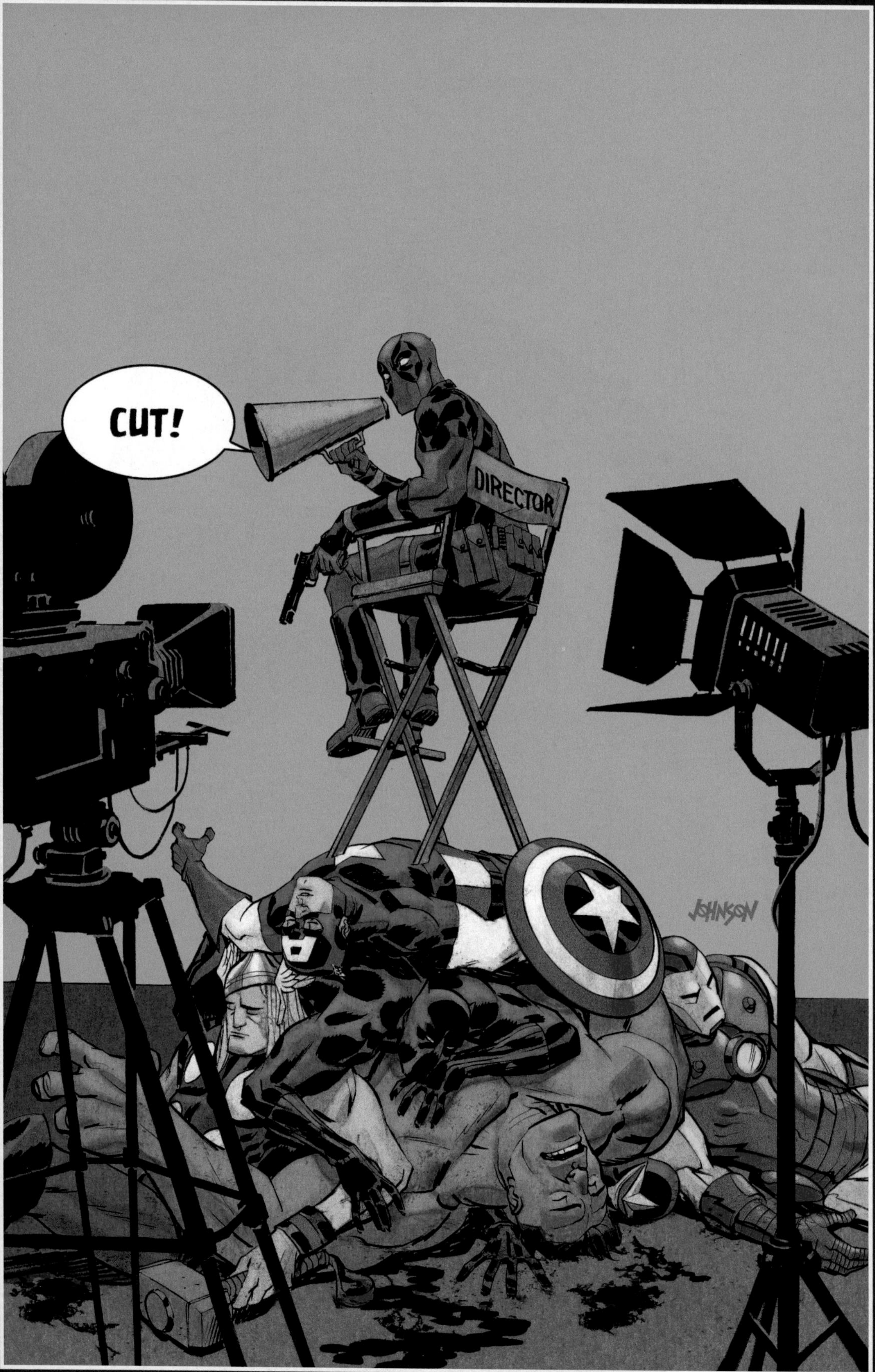
CUT!
DIRECTOR
JOHNSON

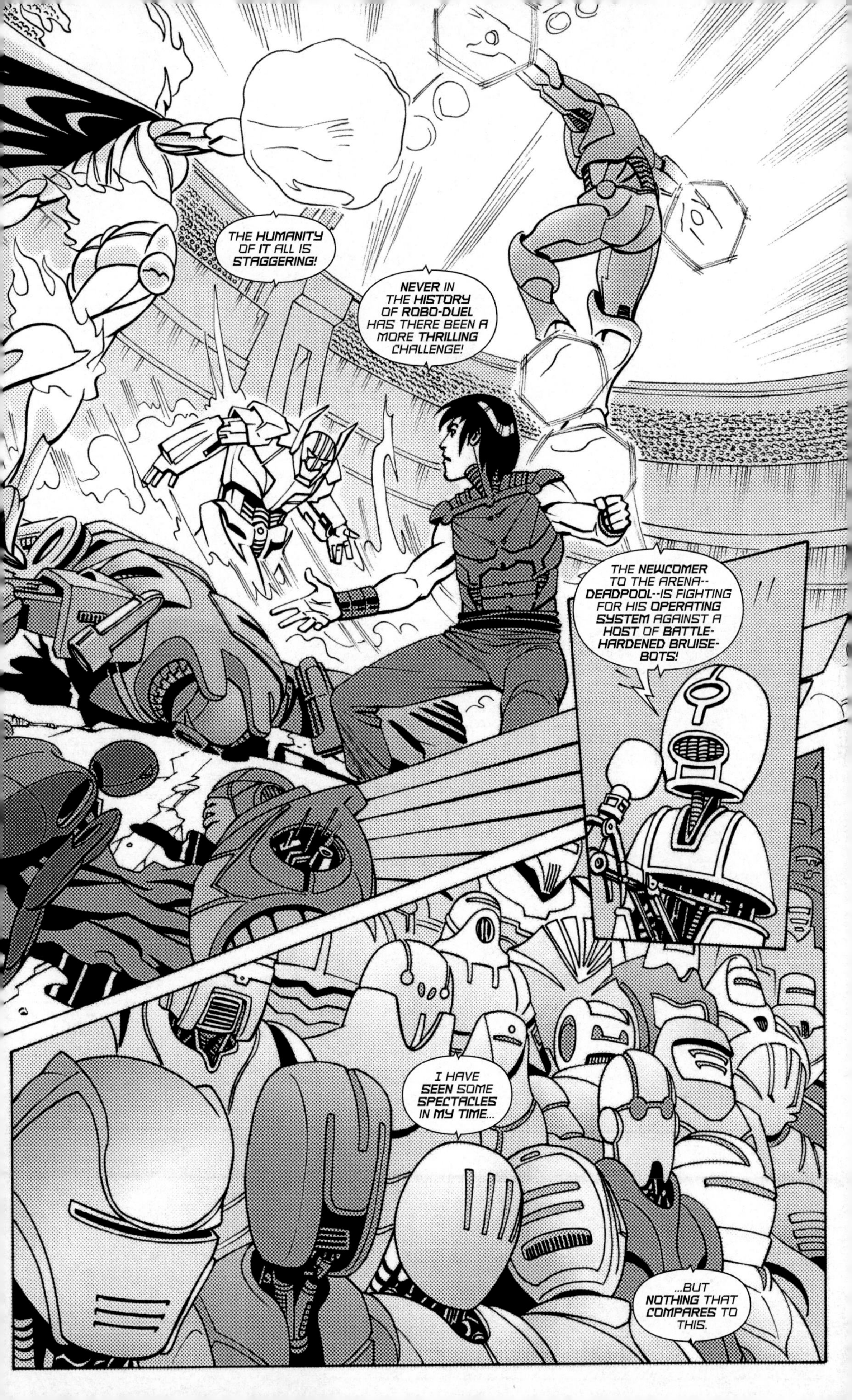
THE HUMANITY OF IT ALL IS STAGGERING!
NEVER IN THE HISTORY OF ROBO-DUEL HAS THERE BEEN A MORE THRILLING CHALLENGE!
THE NEWCOMER TO THE ARENA--DEADPOOL--IS FIGHTING FOR HIS OPERATING SYSTEM AGAINST A HOST OF BATTLE-HARDENED BRUISE-BOTS!
I HAVE SEEN SOME SPECTACLES IN MY TIME...
...BUT NOTHING THAT COMPARES TO THIS.

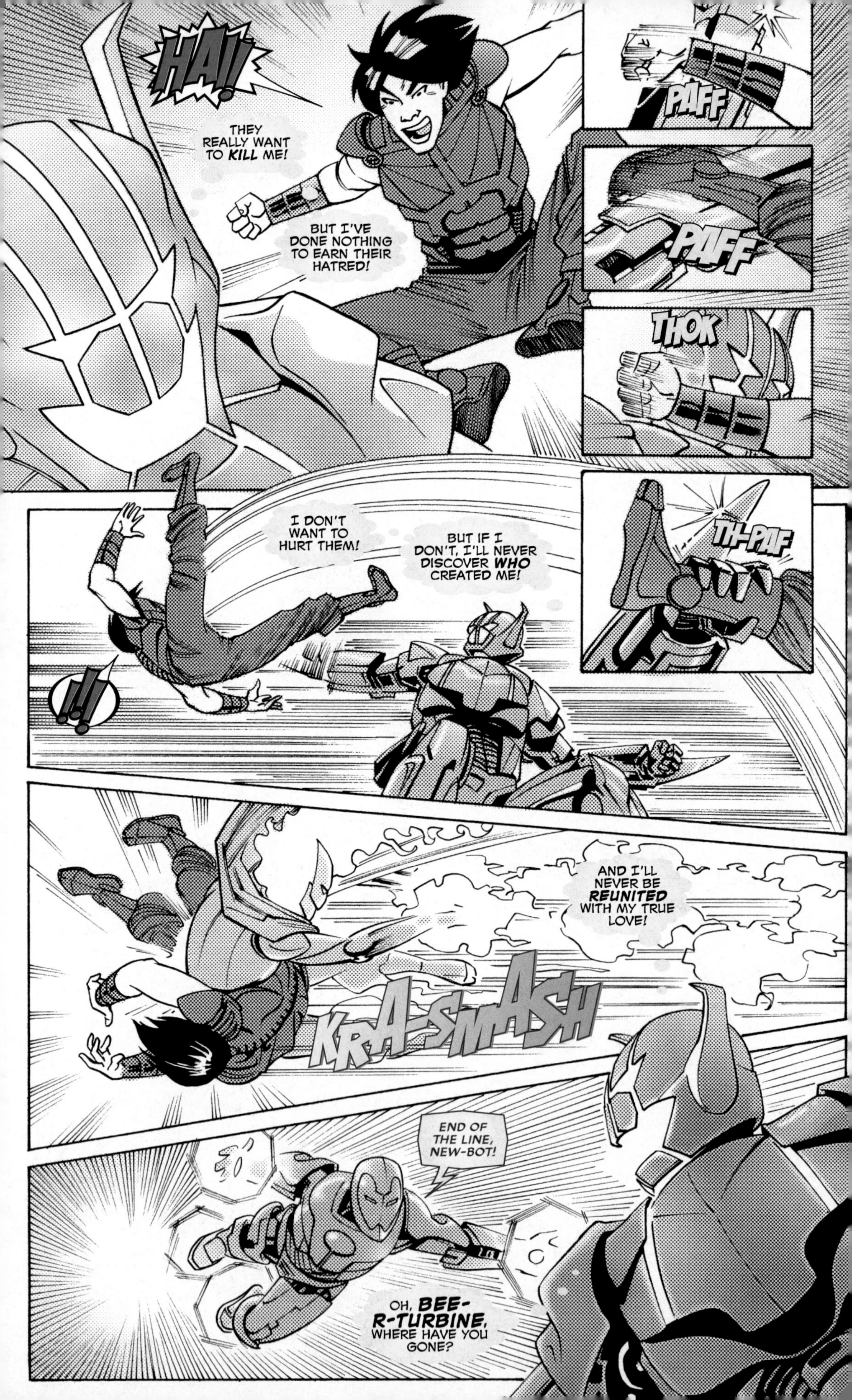
HAI!
THEY REALLY WANT TO KILL ME!
BUT I'VE DONE NOTHING TO EARN THEIR HATRED!
PAFF
PAFF
THOK
TH-PAF
I DON'T WANT TO HURT THEM!
BUT IF I DON'T, I'LL NEVER DISCOVER WHO CREATED ME!
!!
AND I'LL NEVER BE REUNITED WITH MY TRUE LOVE!
KRA-SMASH
END OF THE LINE, NEW-BOT!
OH, BEE-R-TURBINE, WHERE HAVE YOU GONE?

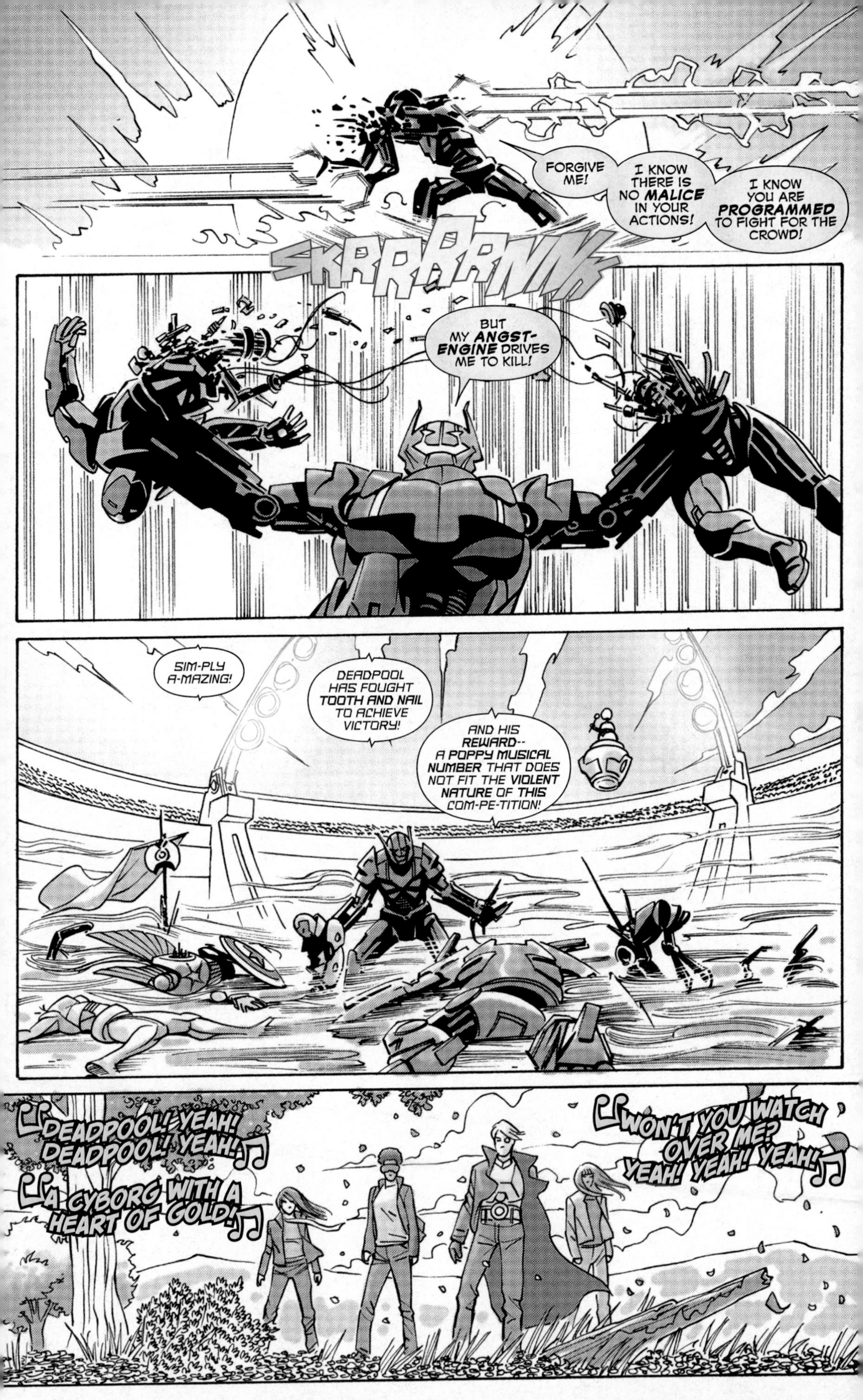
FORGIVE ME!
I KNOW THERE IS NO MALICE IN YOUR ACTIONS!
I KNOW YOU ARE PROGRAMMED TO FIGHT FOR THE CROWD!
SKRRAAANK
BUT MY ANGST-ENGINE DRIVES ME TO KILL!
SIM-PLY A-MAZING!
DEADPOOL HAS FOUGHT TOOTH AND NAIL TO ACHIEVE VICTORY!
AND HIS REWARD-- A POPPY MUSICAL NUMBER THAT DOES NOT FIT THE VIOLENT NATURE OF THIS COM-PE-TITION!
DEADPOOL! YEAH! DEADPOOL! YEAH!
A CYBORG WITH A HEART OF GOLD!
WON'T YOU WATCH OVER ME? YEAH! YEAH! YEAH!

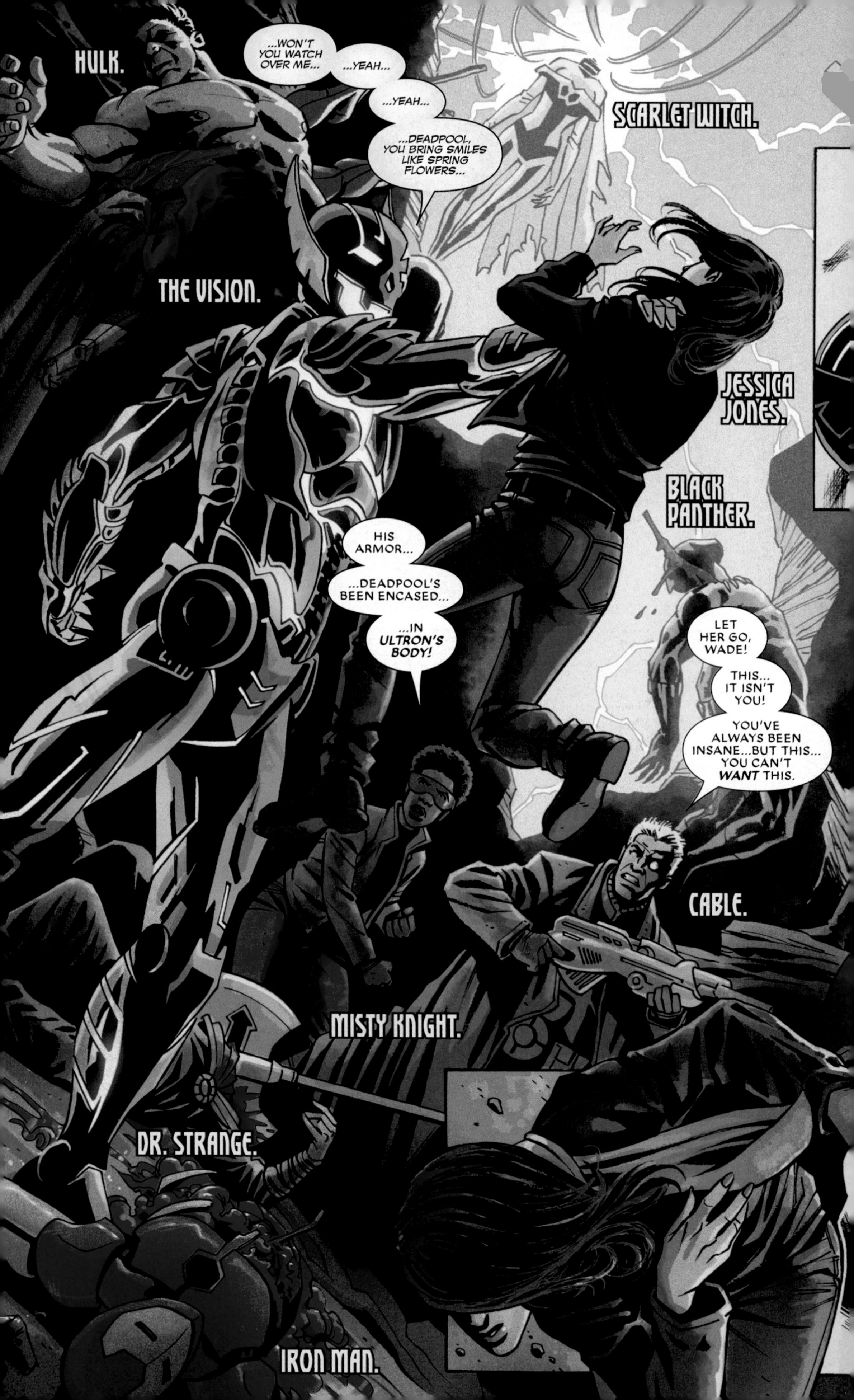
HULK.
...WON'T YOU WATCH OVER ME...
...YEAH...
...YEAH...
...DEADPOOL, YOU BRING SMILES LIKE SPRING FLOWERS...
SCARLET WITCH.
THE VISION.
JESSICA JONES.
BLACK PANTHER.
HIS ARMOR...
...DEADPOOL'S BEEN ENCASED...
...IN ULTRON'S BODY!
LET HER GO, WADE!
THIS... IT ISN'T YOU!
YOU'VE ALWAYS BEEN INSANE...BUT THIS... YOU CAN'T WANT THIS.
CABLE.
MISTY KNIGHT.
DR. STRANGE.
IRON MAN.

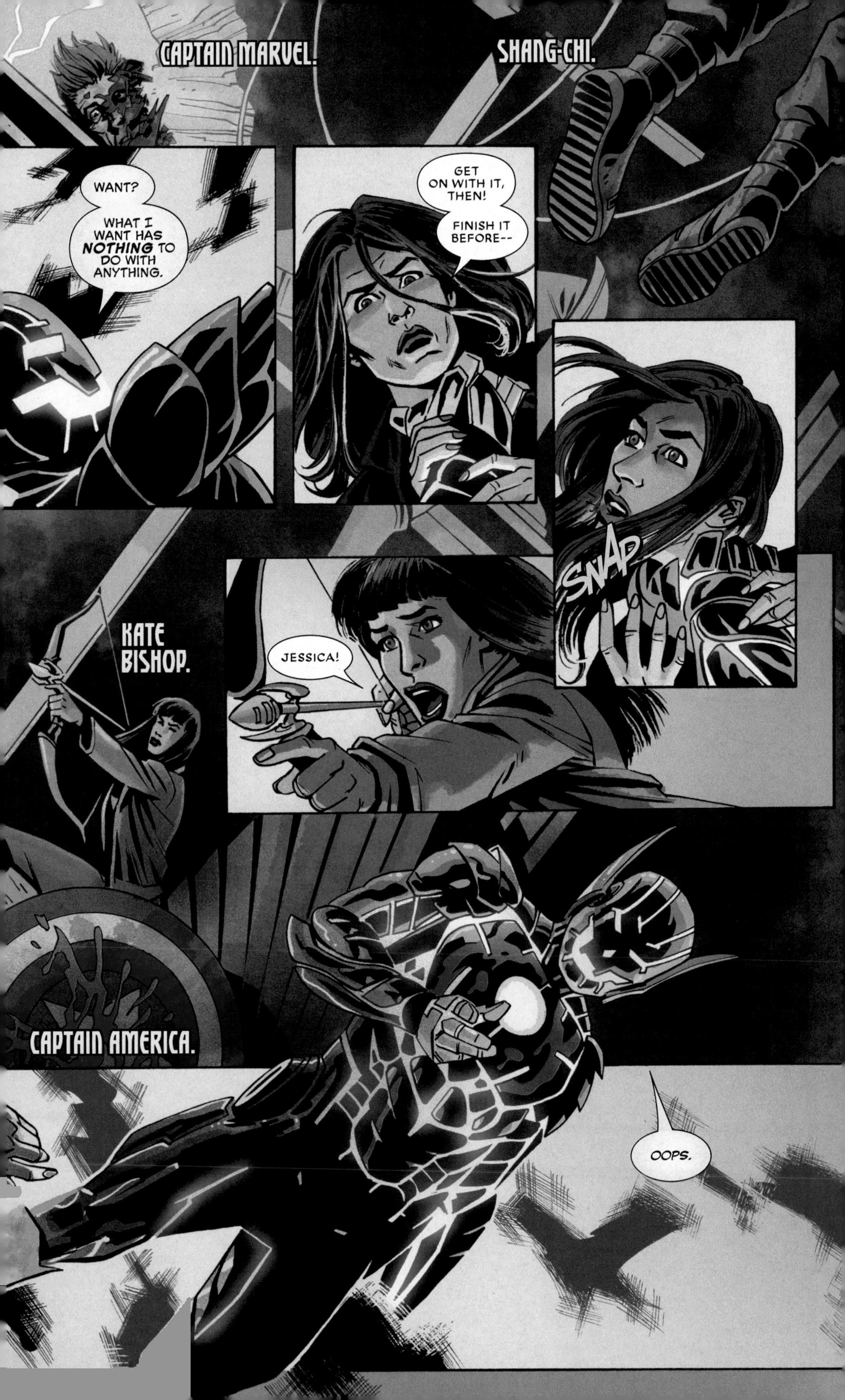

CAPTAIN MARVEL.
SHANG-CHI.
WANT?
WHAT I WANT HAS NOTHING TO DO WITH ANYTHING.
GET ON WITH IT, THEN!
FINISH IT BEFORE--
SNAP
KATE BISHOP.
JESSICA!
CAPTAIN AMERICA.
OOPS.

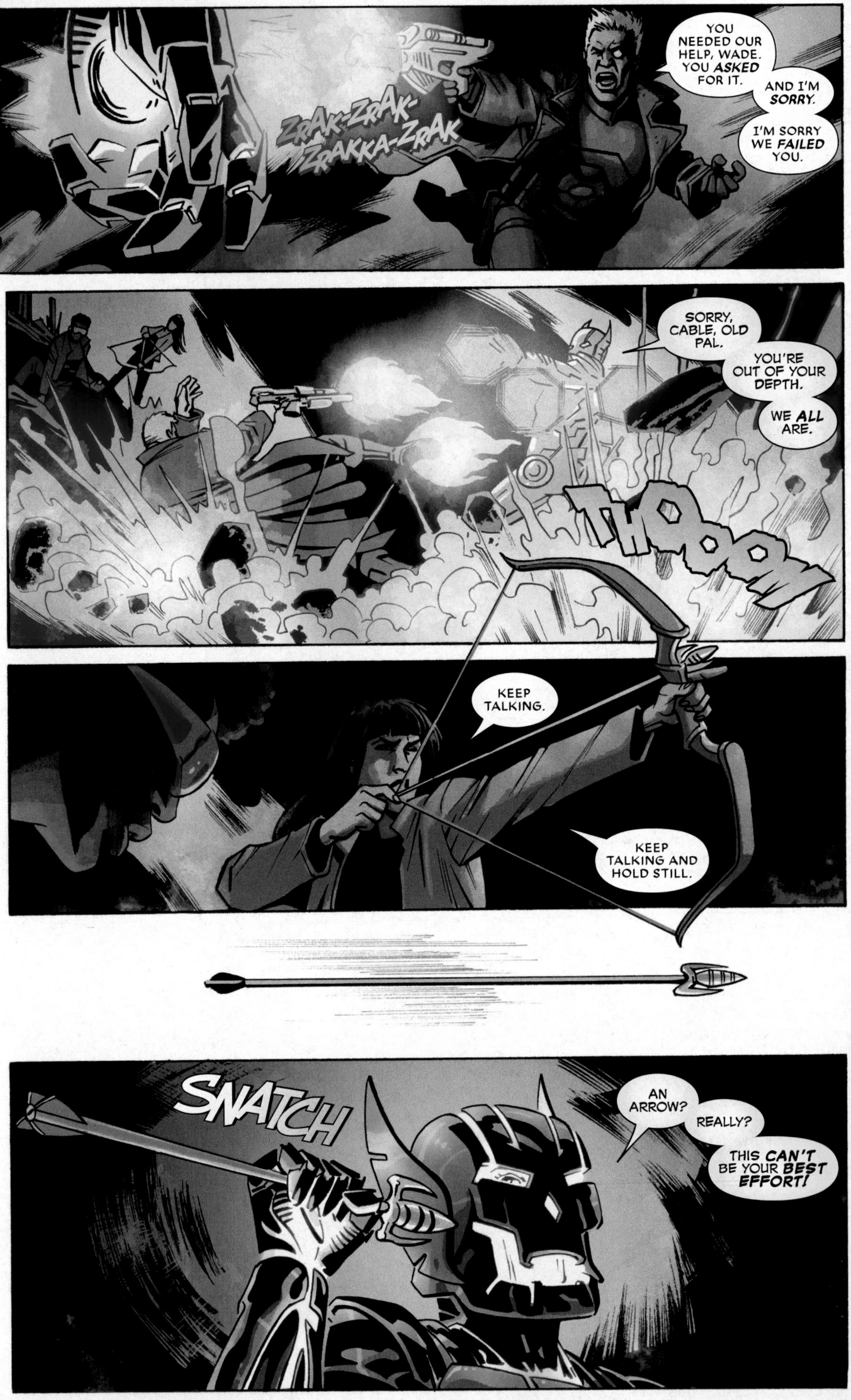
YOU NEEDED OUR HELP, WADE. YOU ASKED FOR IT.
ZRAK-ZRAK-ZRAKKA-ZRAK
AND I'M SORRY.
I'M SORRY WE FAILED YOU.
SORRY, CABLE, OLD PAL.
YOU'RE OUT OF YOUR DEPTH.
WE ALL ARE.
THOOOM
KEEP TALKING.
KEEP TALKING AND HOLD STILL.
SNATCH
AN ARROW?
REALLY?
THIS CAN'T BE YOUR BEST EFFORT!

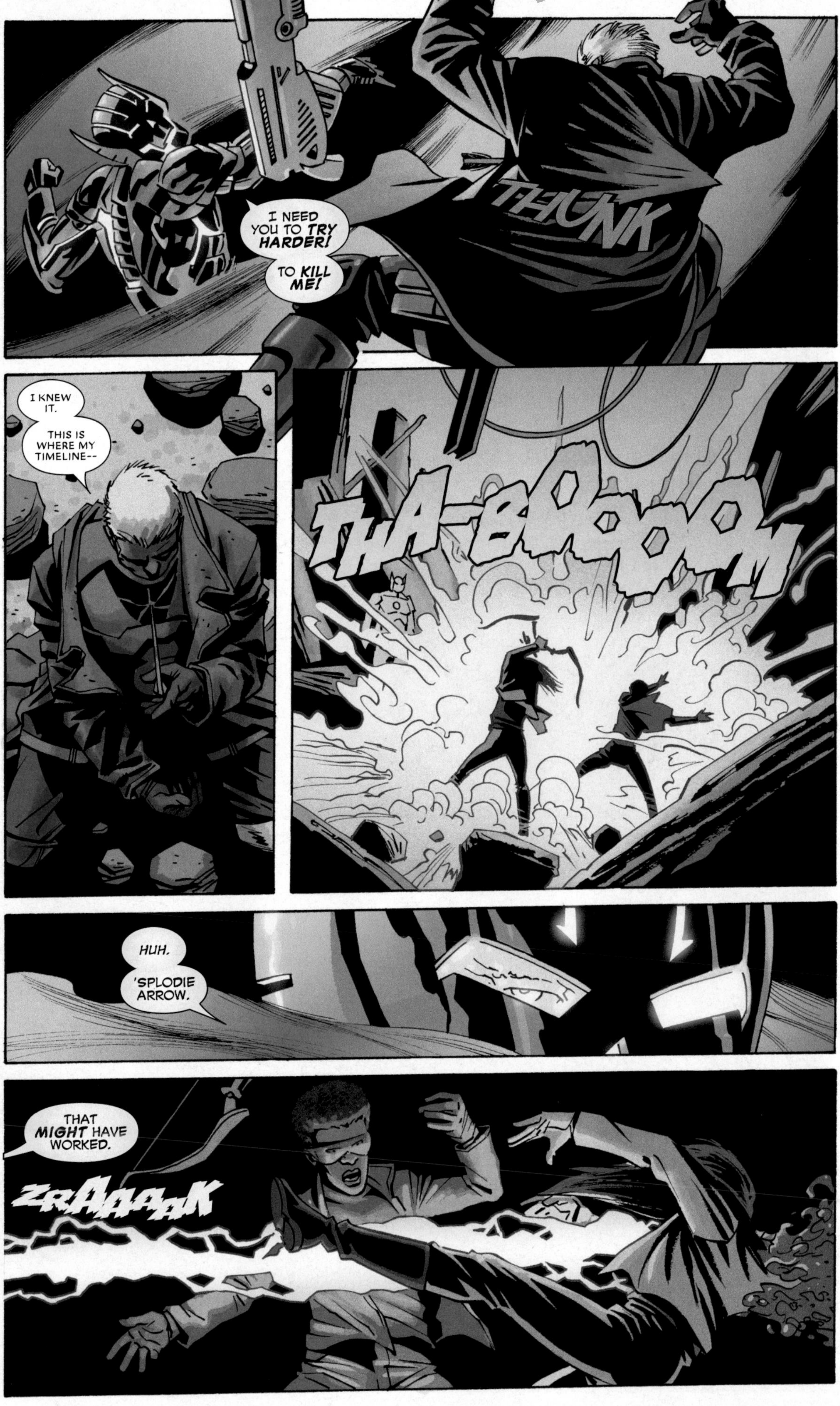
I NEED YOU TO TRY HARDER!
TO KILL ME!
THUNK
I KNEW IT.
THIS IS WHERE MY TIMELINE--
THA-BOOOOM
HUH.
'SPLODIE ARROW.
THAT MIGHT HAVE WORKED.
ZRAAAAK

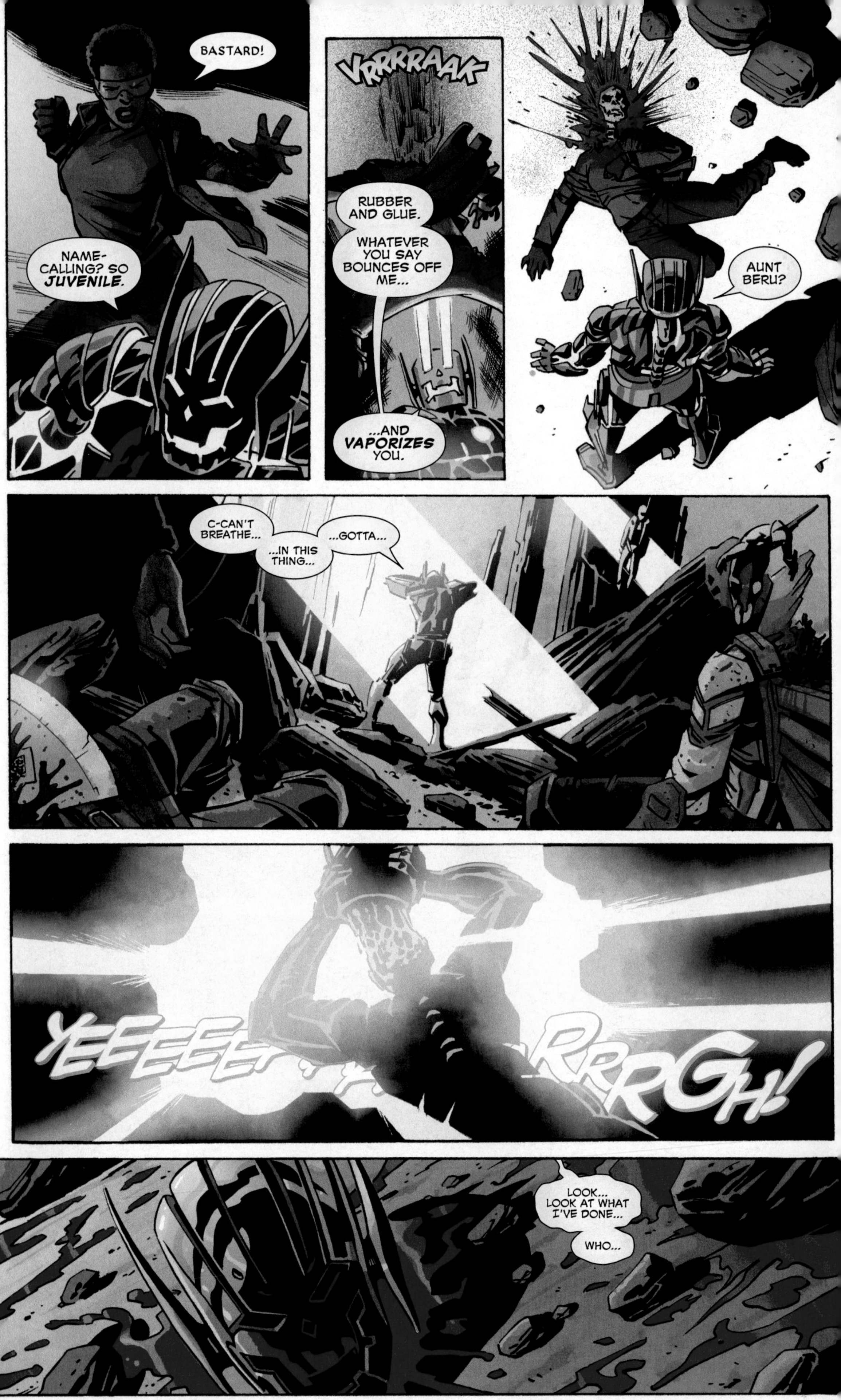
BASTARD!
NAME-CALLING? SO JUVENILE.
VRRRRAAK
RUBBER AND GLUE.
WHATEVER YOU SAY BOUNCES OFF ME...
...AND VAPORIZES YOU.
AUNT BERU?
C-CAN'T BREATHE...
...IN THIS THING...
...GOTTA...
LOOK... LOOK AT WHAT I'VE DONE...
WHO...

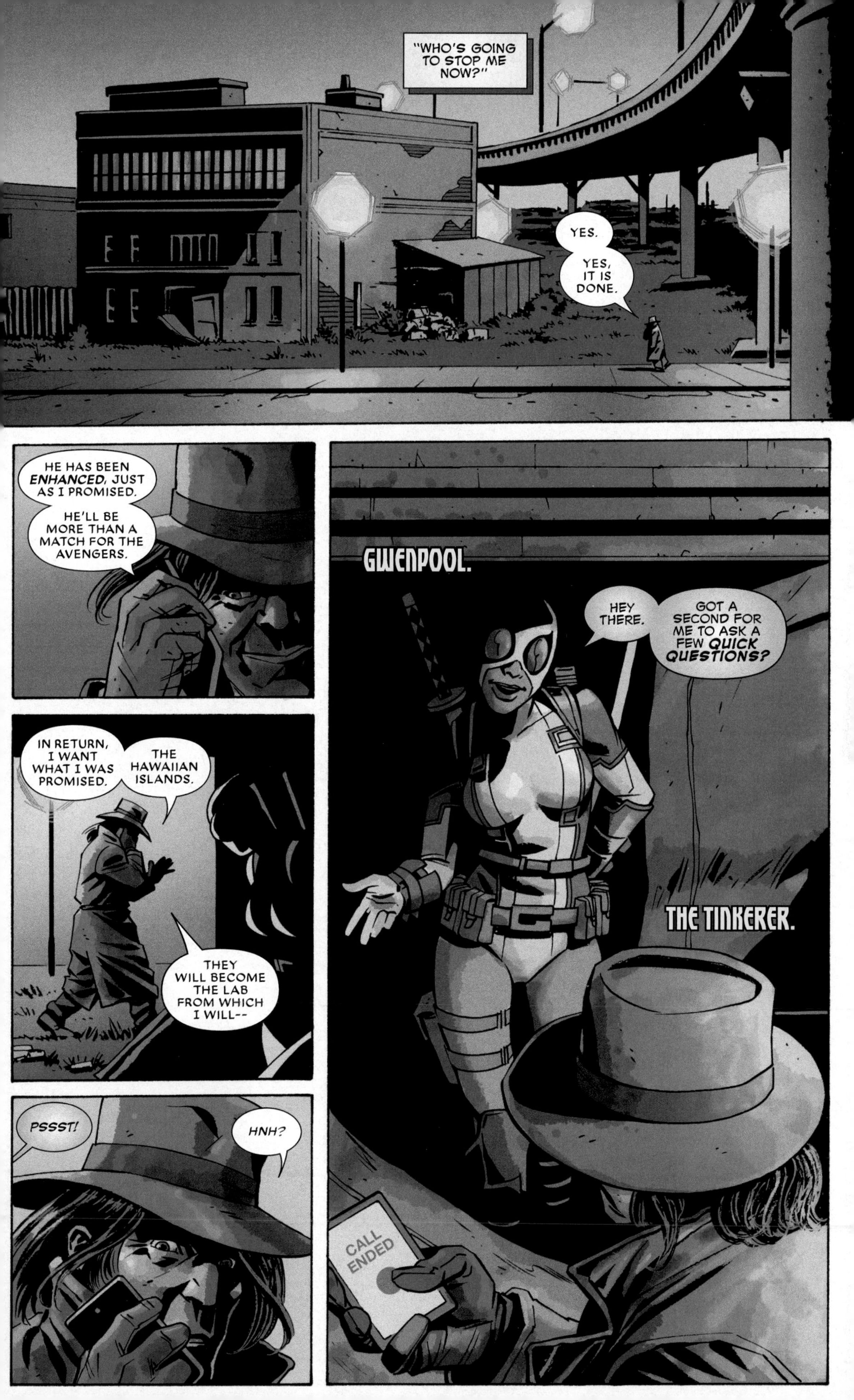

"WHO'S GOING TO STOP ME NOW?"
YES.
YES, IT IS DONE.
HE HAS BEEN ENHANCED, JUST AS I PROMISED.
HE'LL BE MORE THAN A MATCH FOR THE AVENGERS.
IN RETURN, I WANT WHAT I WAS PROMISED.
THE HAWAIIAN ISLANDS.
THEY WILL BECOME THE LAB FROM WHICH I WILL--
PSSST!
HNH?
GWENPOOL.
HEY THERE.
GOT A SECOND FOR ME TO ASK A FEW QUICK QUESTIONS?
THE TINKERER.
CALL ENDED

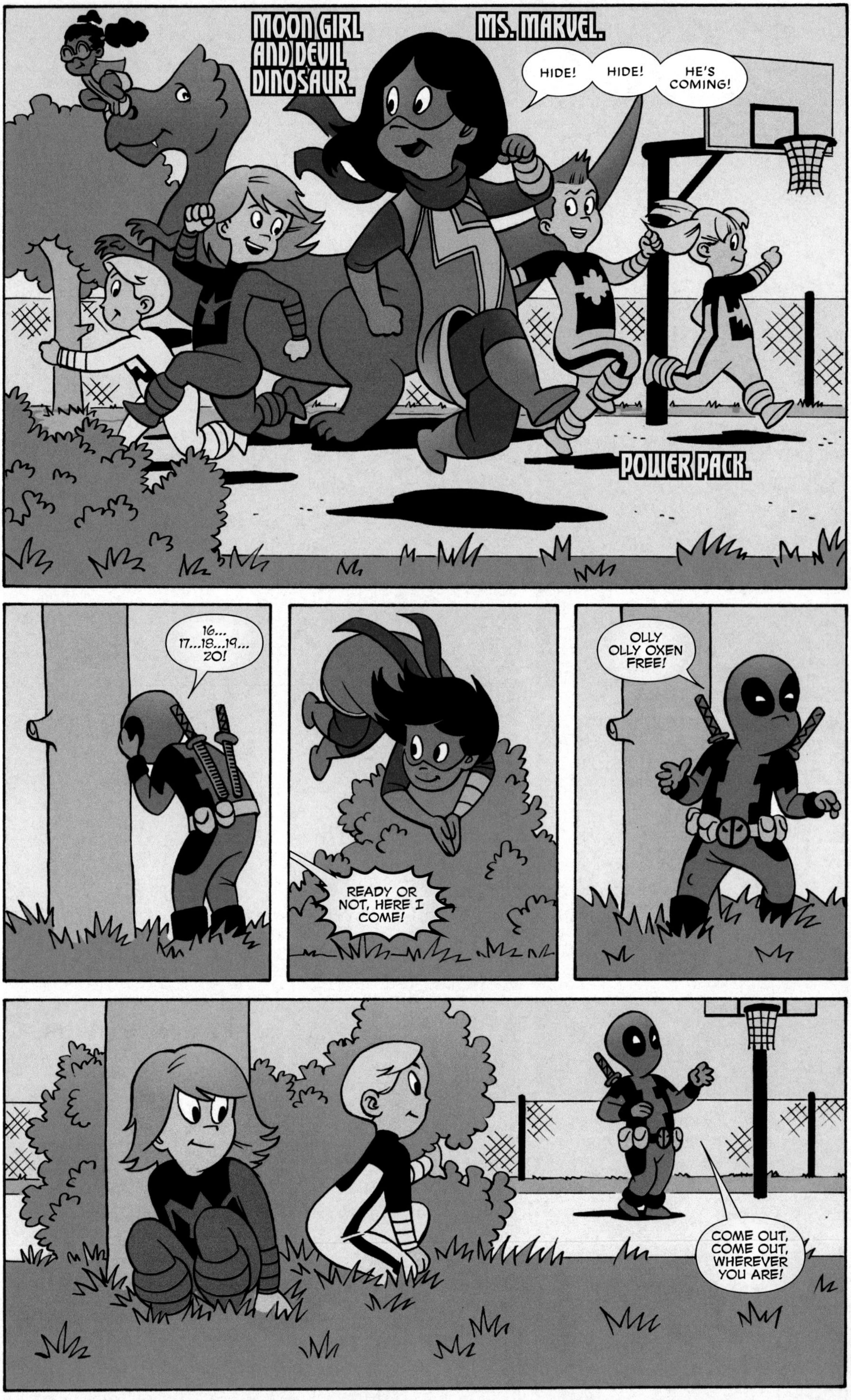
MOON GIRL AND DEVIL DINOSAUR.
MS. MARVEL.
HIDE!
HIDE!
HE'S COMING!
POWER PACK.
16... 17...18...19... 20!
READY OR NOT, HERE I COME!
OLLY OLLY OXEN FREE!
COME OUT, COME OUT, WHEREVER YOU ARE!

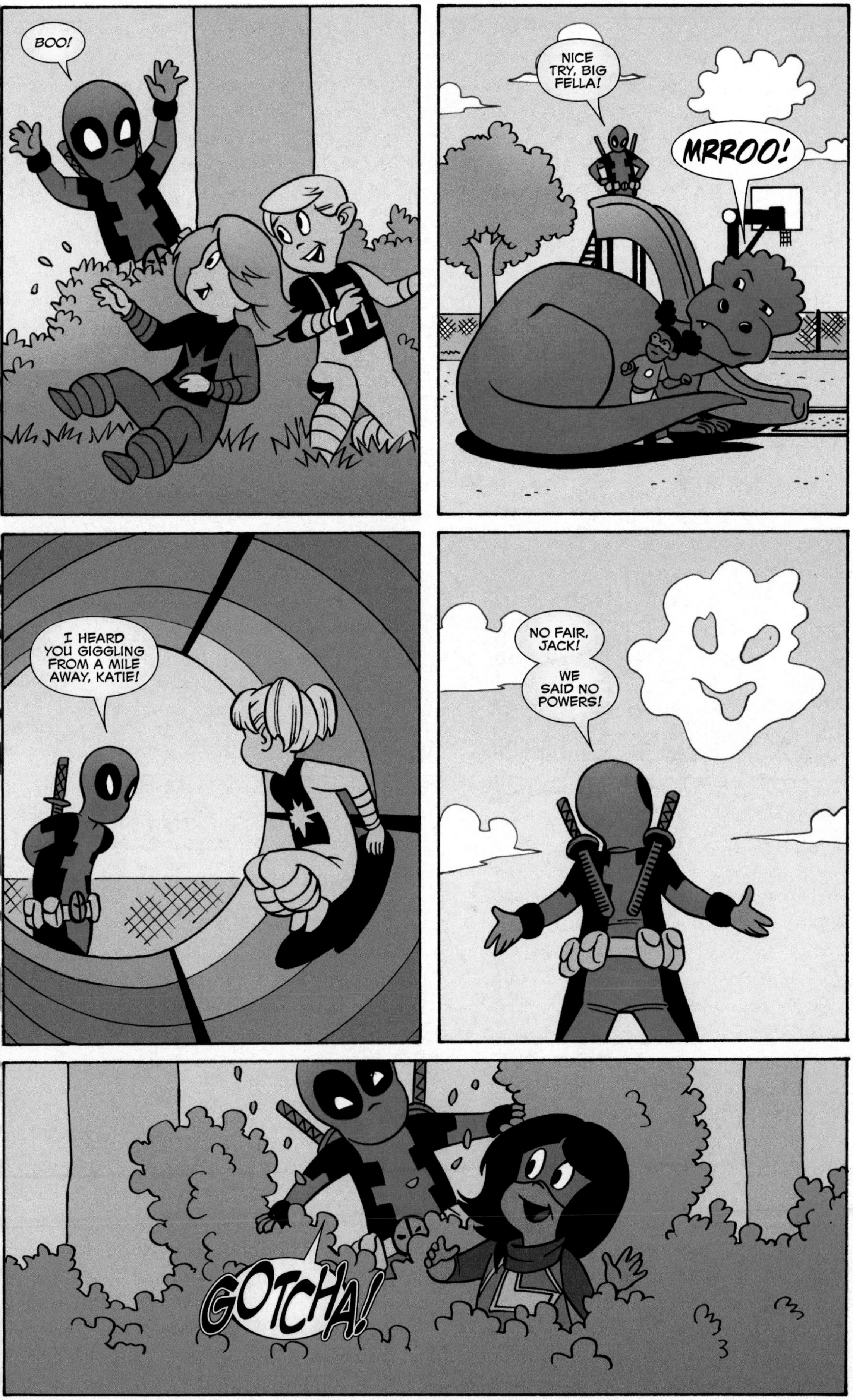
BOO!
NICE TRY, BIG FELLA!
MRROO!
I HEARD YOU GIGGLING FROM A MILE AWAY, KATIE!
NO FAIR, JACK!
WE SAID NO POWERS!
GOTCHA!

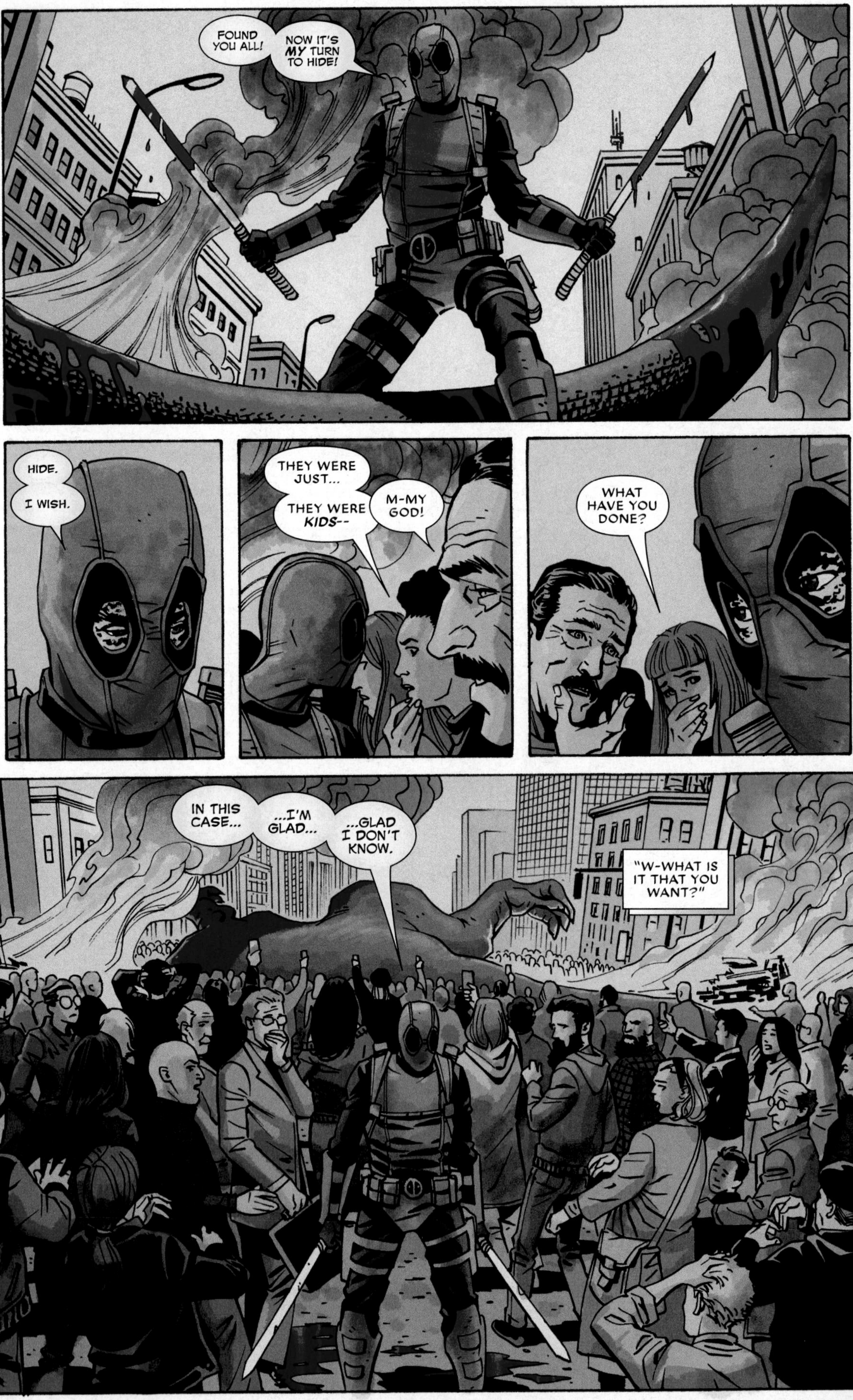
FOUND YOU ALL!
NOW IT'S MY TURN TO HIDE!
HIDE.
I WISH.
THEY WERE JUST...
THEY WERE KIDS--
M-MY GOD!
WHAT HAVE YOU DONE?
IN THIS CASE...
...I'M GLAD...
...GLAD I DON'T KNOW.
"W-WHAT IS IT THAT YOU WANT?"

WHAT ARE YOU GOING TO DO TO ME?

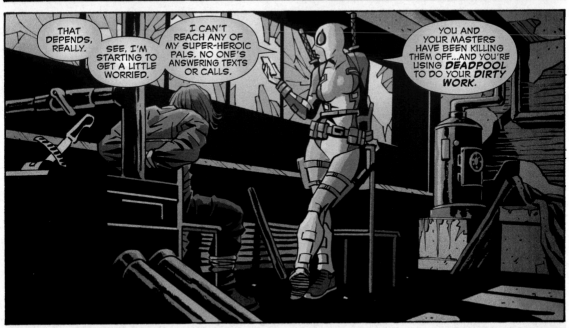

THAT DEPENDS, REALLY.

SEE, I'M STARTING TO GET A LITTLE WORRIED.

I CAN'T REACH ANY OF MY SUPER-HEROIC PALS. NO ONE'S ANSWERING TEXTS OR CALLS.

YOU AND YOUR MASTERS HAVE BEEN KILLING THEM OFF...AND YOU'RE USING *DEADPOOL* TO DO YOUR *DIRTY WORK.*

IT... WASN'T *MY* PLAN.

THE OTHERS... THE RED SKULL, DOOM, MAGNETO, AND ABOMINATION... IT WAS *THEIR* IDEA.

OH, I KNOW ALL THAT ALREADY.

WHAT I DON'T KNOW IS HOW THEY'RE CONTROLLING DEADPOOL.

THEY HAVE A CONTROL PHRASE...

...POST-HYPNOTIC SUGGESTION...

...ADVANCED BRAINWASHING TECHNIQUES.

WE'VE MADE IT SO HE DOESN'T EVEN *REALIZE* WHAT HE IS DOING.

I NEED YOU TO TELL ME HOW TO BREAK THAT CONTROL PHRASE.

AND THEN I'M GONNA HURT YOU... *REAL BAD.*

BUT IF YOU DON'T TELL ME WHAT I NEED TO KNOW, I'M GONNA HURT YOU *EVEN WORSE.*

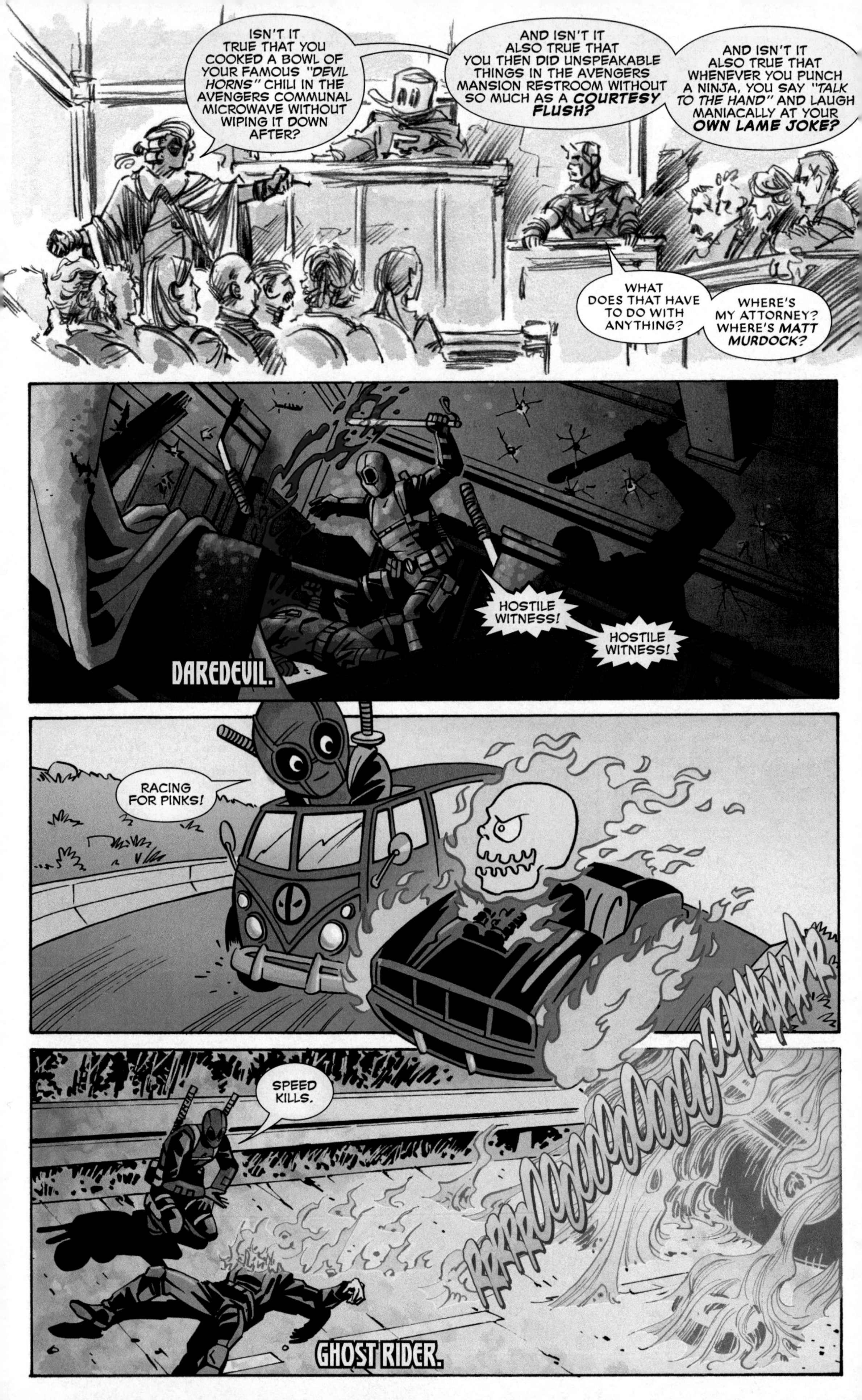
ISN'T IT TRUE THAT YOU COOKED A BOWL OF YOUR FAMOUS "DEVIL HORNS" CHILI IN THE AVENGERS COMMUNAL MICROWAVE WITHOUT WIPING IT DOWN AFTER?
AND ISN'T IT ALSO TRUE THAT YOU THEN DID UNSPEAKABLE THINGS IN THE AVENGERS MANSION RESTROOM WITHOUT SO MUCH AS A COURTESY FLUSH?
AND ISN'T IT ALSO TRUE THAT WHENEVER YOU PUNCH A NINJA, YOU SAY "TALK TO THE HAND" AND LAUGH MANIACALLY AT YOUR OWN LAME JOKE?
WHAT DOES THAT HAVE TO DO WITH ANYTHING?
WHERE'S MY ATTORNEY? WHERE'S MATT MURDOCK?
HOSTILE WITNESS!
HOSTILE WITNESS!
DAREDEVIL.
RACING FOR PINKS!
RRRRROOOOOOOOOOOOOOOOOOOAAAAAAAR
SPEED KILLS.
GHOST RIDER.

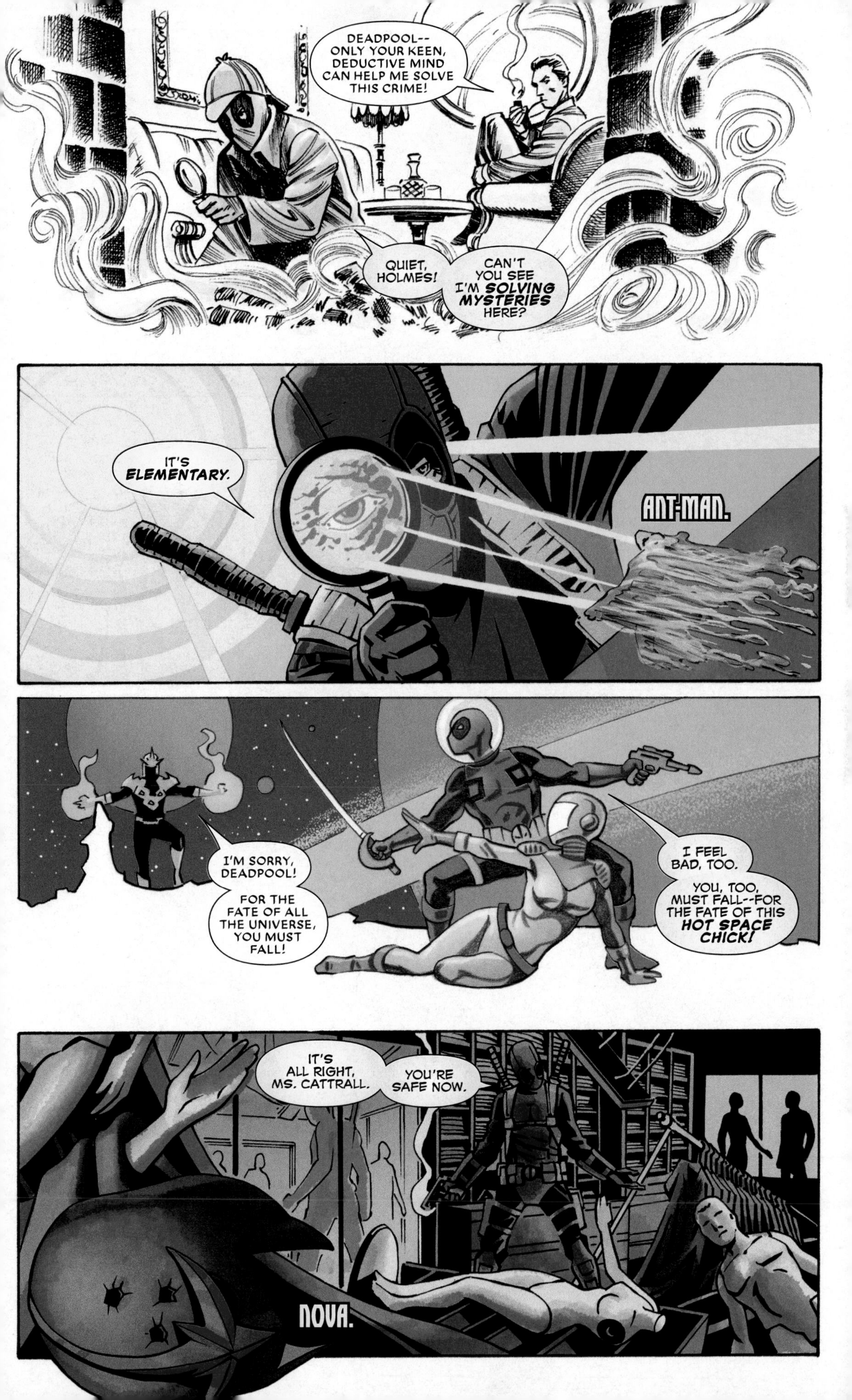

DEADPOOL-- ONLY YOUR KEEN, DEDUCTIVE MIND CAN HELP ME SOLVE THIS CRIME!
QUIET, HOLMES!
CAN'T YOU SEE I'M SOLVING MYSTERIES HERE?
IT'S ELEMENTARY.
ANT-MAN.
I'M SORRY, DEADPOOL!
FOR THE FATE OF ALL THE UNIVERSE, YOU MUST FALL!
I FEEL BAD, TOO.
YOU, TOO, MUST FALL--FOR THE FATE OF THIS HOT SPACE CHICK!
IT'S ALL RIGHT, MS. CATTRALL.
YOU'RE SAFE NOW.
NOVA.

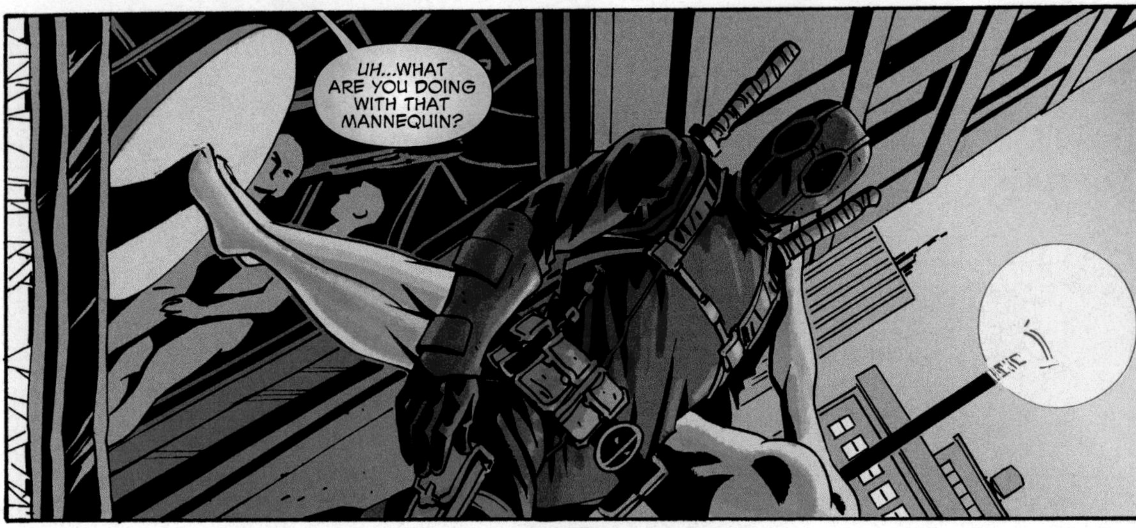
UH...WHAT ARE YOU DOING WITH THAT MANNEQUIN?

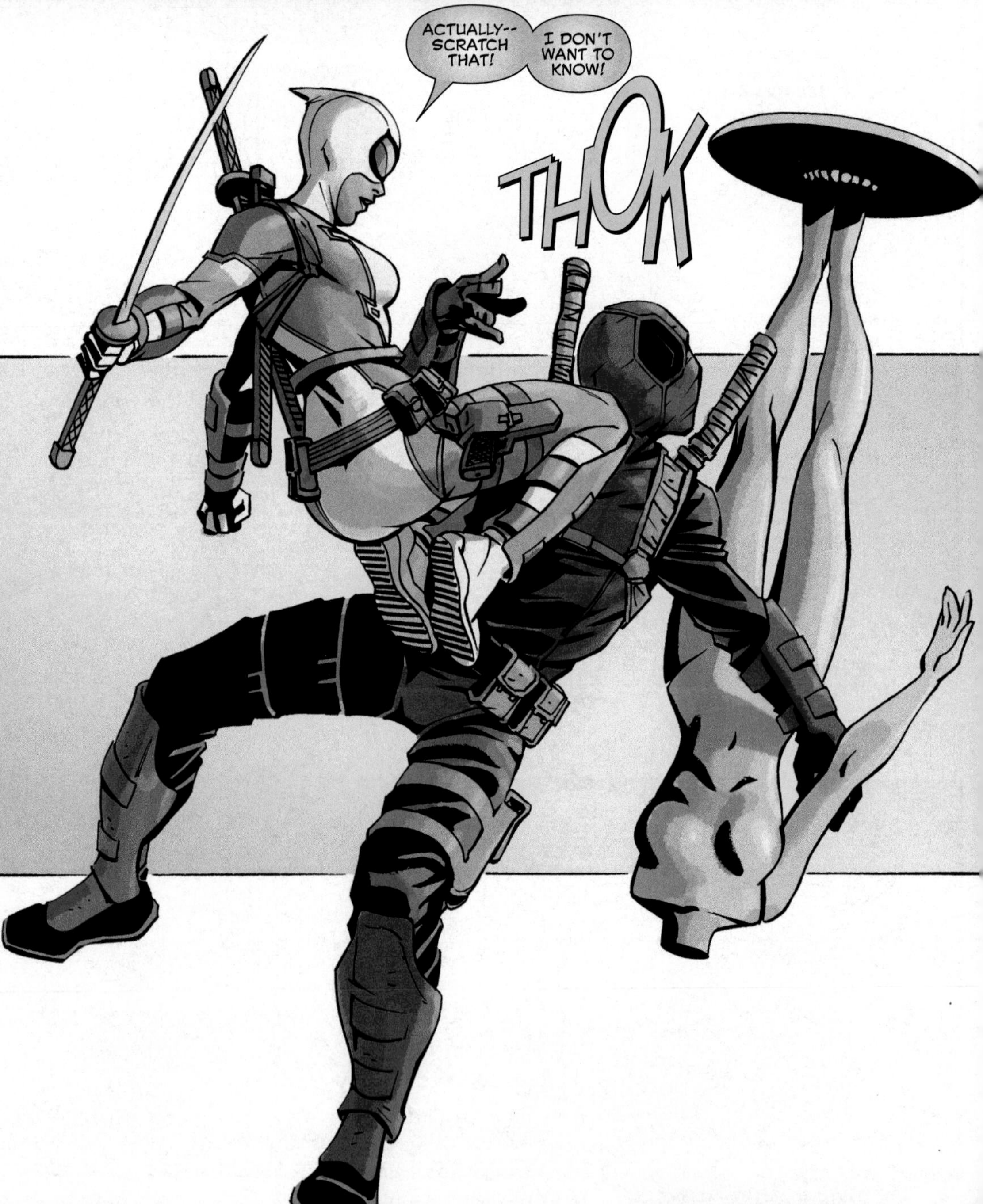
ACTUALLY-- SCRATCH THAT!
I DON'T WANT TO KNOW!
THOK

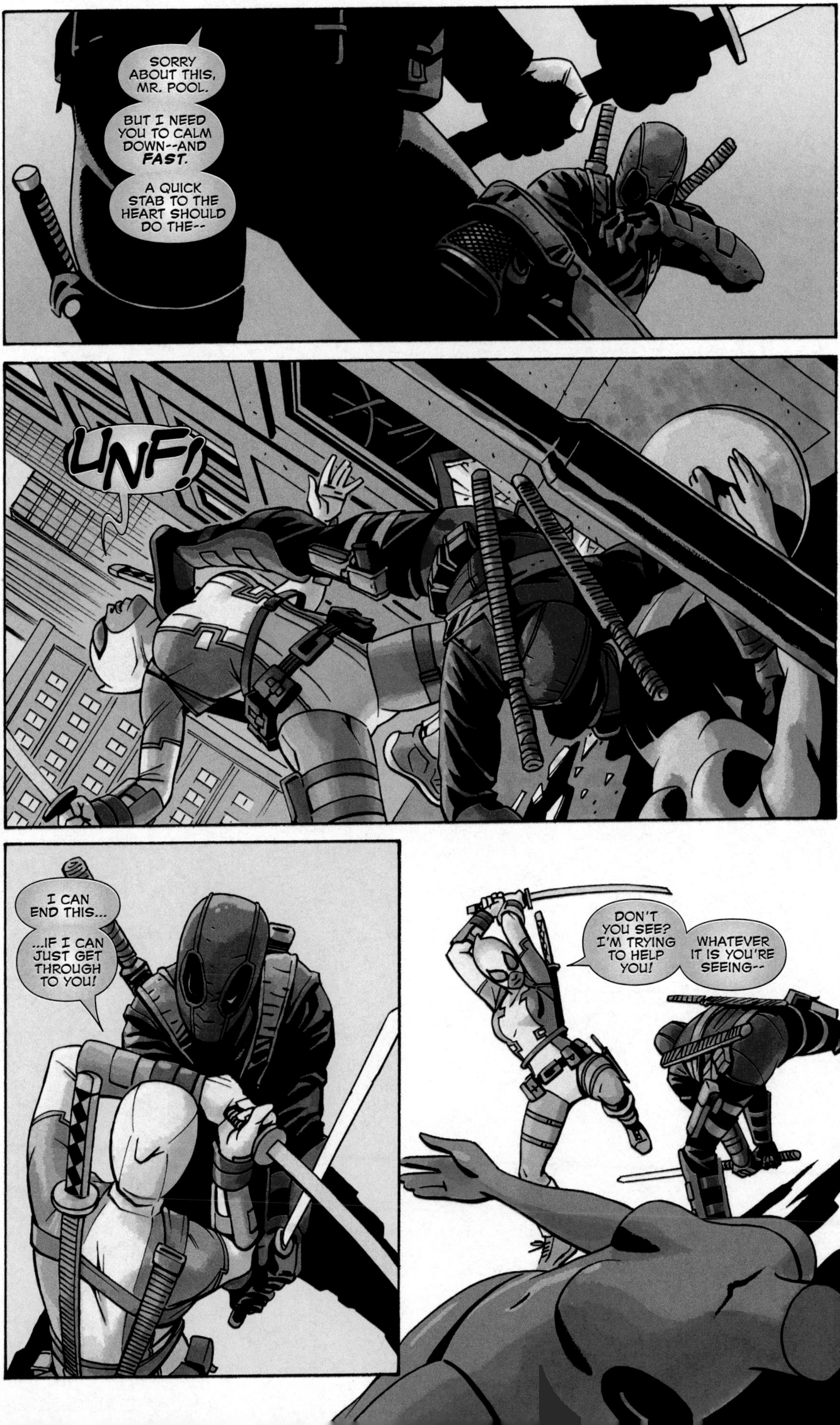
SORRY ABOUT THIS, MR. POOL.
BUT I NEED YOU TO CALM DOWN--AND **FAST**.
A QUICK STAB TO THE HEART SHOULD DO THE--
UNF!
I CAN END THIS...
...IF I CAN JUST GET THROUGH TO YOU!
DON'T YOU SEE? I'M TRYING TO HELP YOU!
WHATEVER IT IS YOU'RE SEEING--

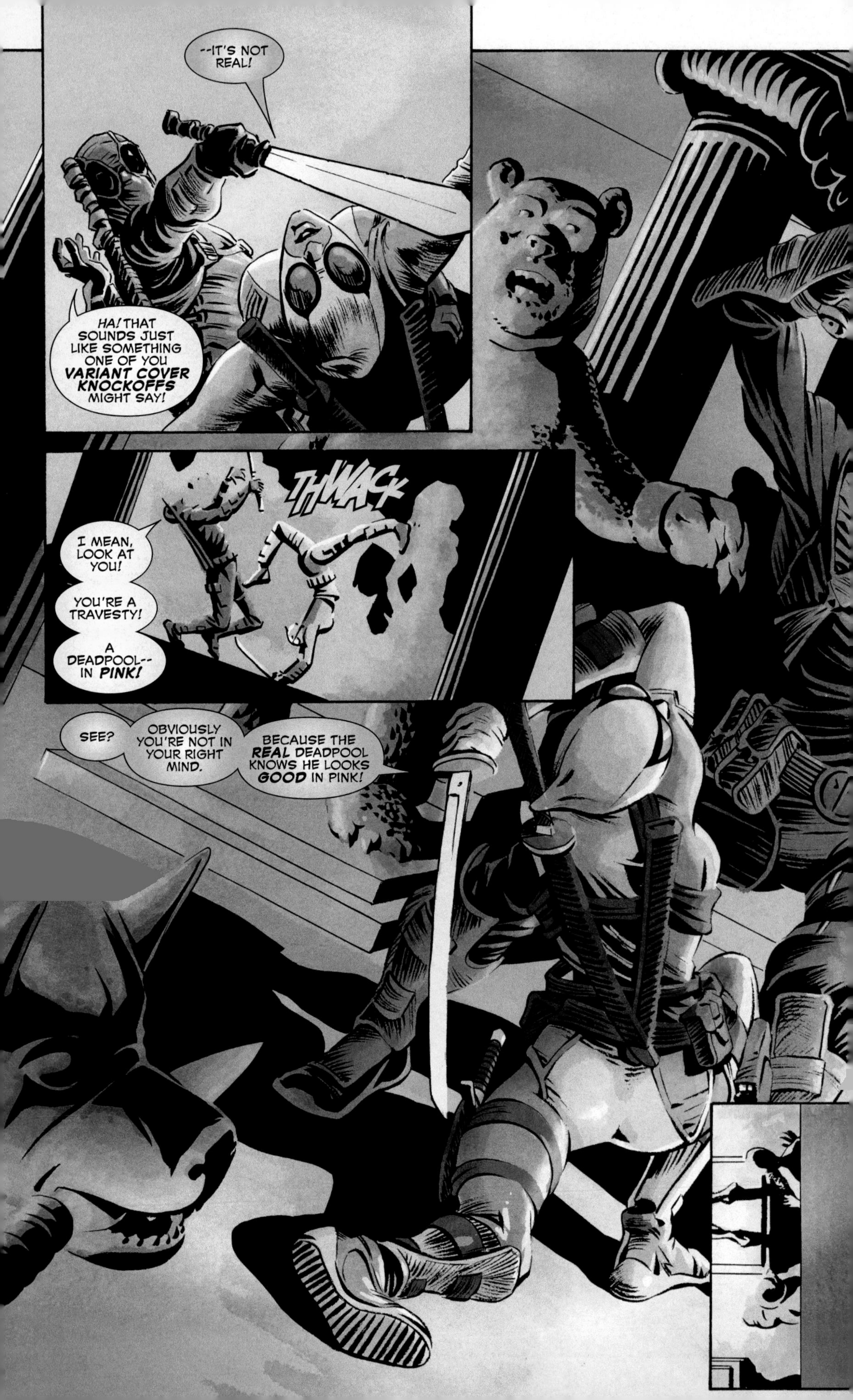
--IT'S NOT REAL!
HA! THAT SOUNDS JUST LIKE SOMETHING ONE OF YOU **VARIANT COVER KNOCKOFFS** MIGHT SAY!
THWACK
I MEAN, LOOK AT YOU!
YOU'RE A TRAVESTY!
A DEADPOOL-- IN **PINK!**
SEE?
OBVIOUSLY YOU'RE NOT IN YOUR RIGHT MIND.
BECAUSE THE **REAL** DEADPOOL KNOWS HE LOOKS **GOOD** IN PINK!

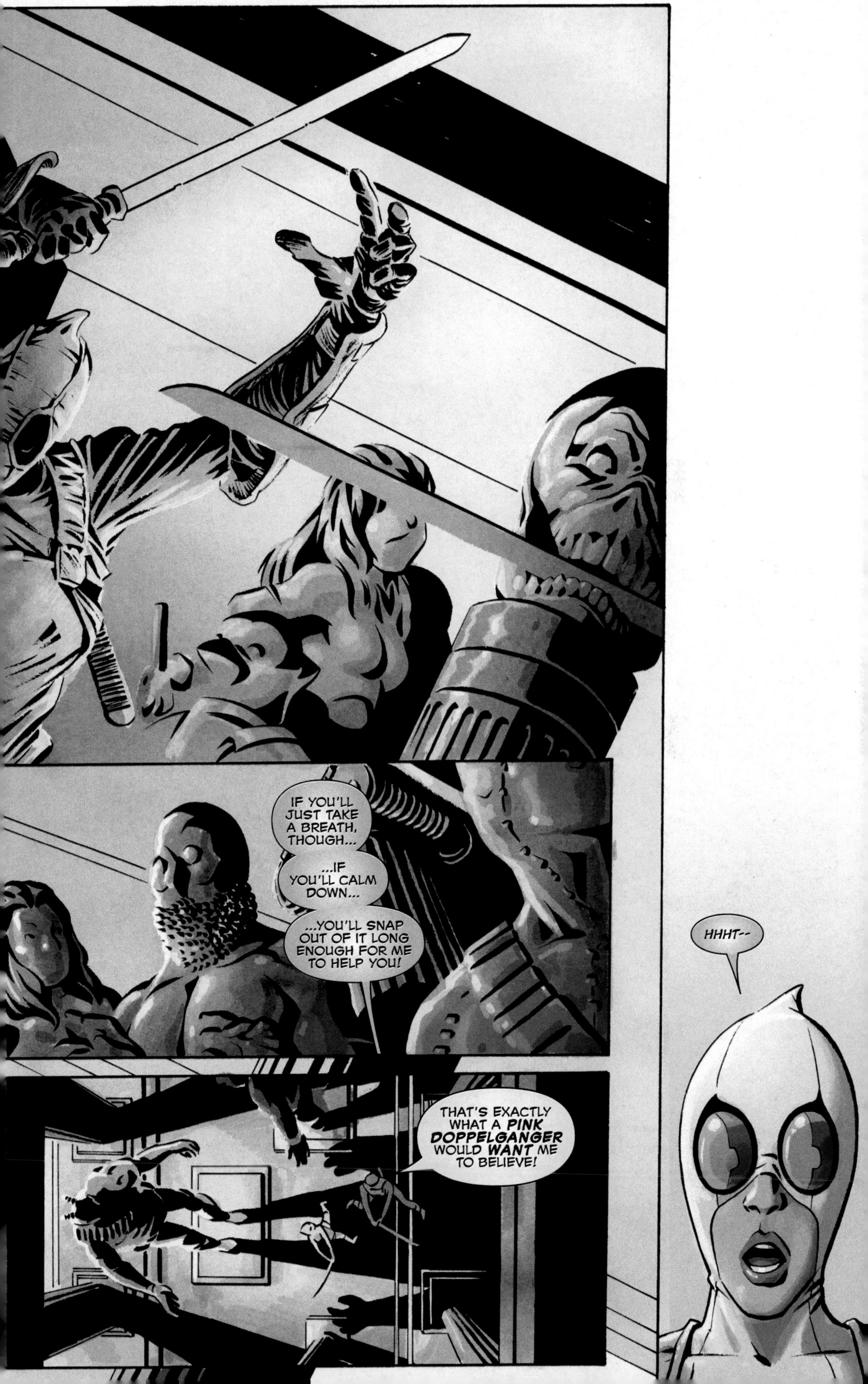
IF YOU'LL JUST TAKE A BREATH, THOUGH...
...IF YOU'LL CALM DOWN...
...YOU'LL SNAP OUT OF IT LONG ENOUGH FOR ME TO HELP YOU!
THAT'S EXACTLY WHAT A PINK DOPPELGANGER WOULD WANT ME TO BELIEVE!
HHHT--

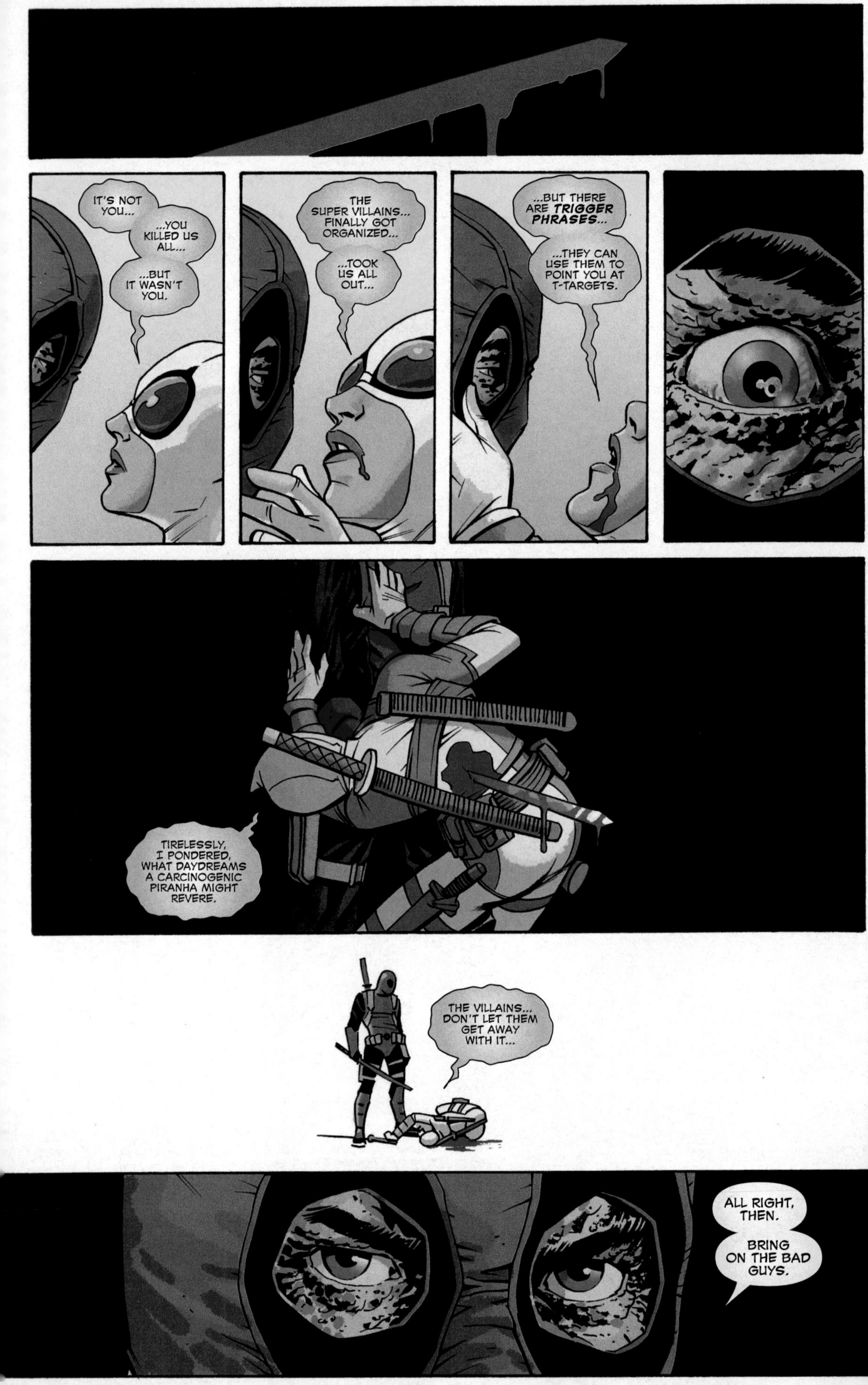
IT'S NOT YOU...
...YOU KILLED US ALL...
...BUT IT WASN'T YOU.
THE SUPER VILLAINS... FINALLY GOT ORGANIZED...
...TOOK US ALL OUT...
...BUT THERE ARE TRIGGER PHRASES...
...THEY CAN USE THEM TO POINT YOU AT T-TARGETS.
TIRELESSLY, I PONDERED, WHAT DAYDREAMS A CARCINOGENIC PIRANHA MIGHT REVERE.
THE VILLAINS... DON'T LET THEM GET AWAY WITH IT...
ALL RIGHT, THEN.
BRING ON THE BAD GUYS.

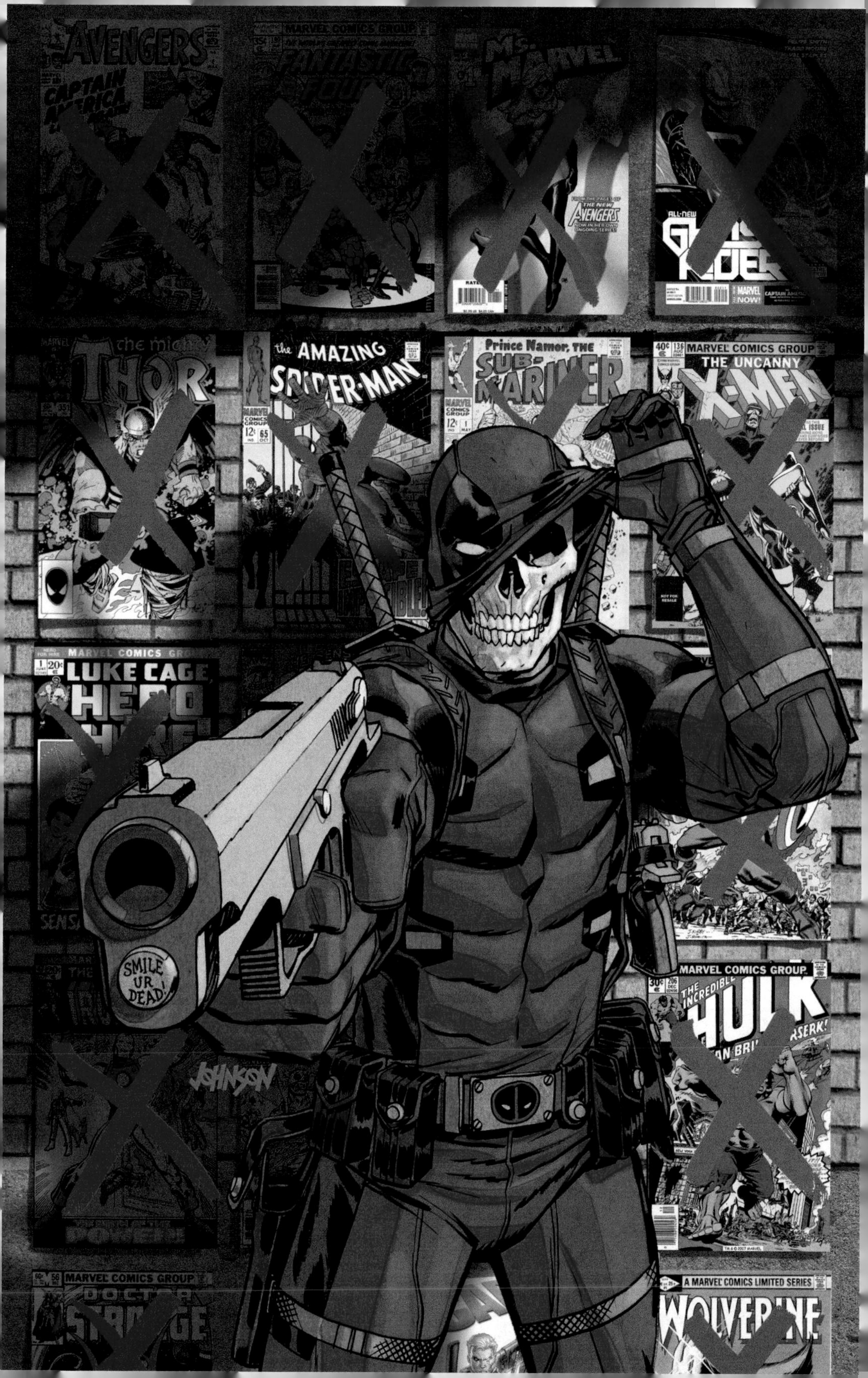
AVENGERS
MARVEL COMICS GROUP
FROM THE PAGES OF THE NEW AVENGERS NOW IN HER OWN ONGOING SERIES!
ALL-NEW
the mighty THOR
the AMAZING SPIDER-MAN
Prince Namor, THE
MARVEL COMICS GROUP
THE UNCANNY
MARVEL COMICS GROUP
LUKE CAGE
SMILE UR DEAD!
JOHNSON
MARVEL COMICS GROUP.
THE INCREDIBLE HULK
MARVEL COMICS GROUP
A MARVEL COMICS LIMITED SERIES

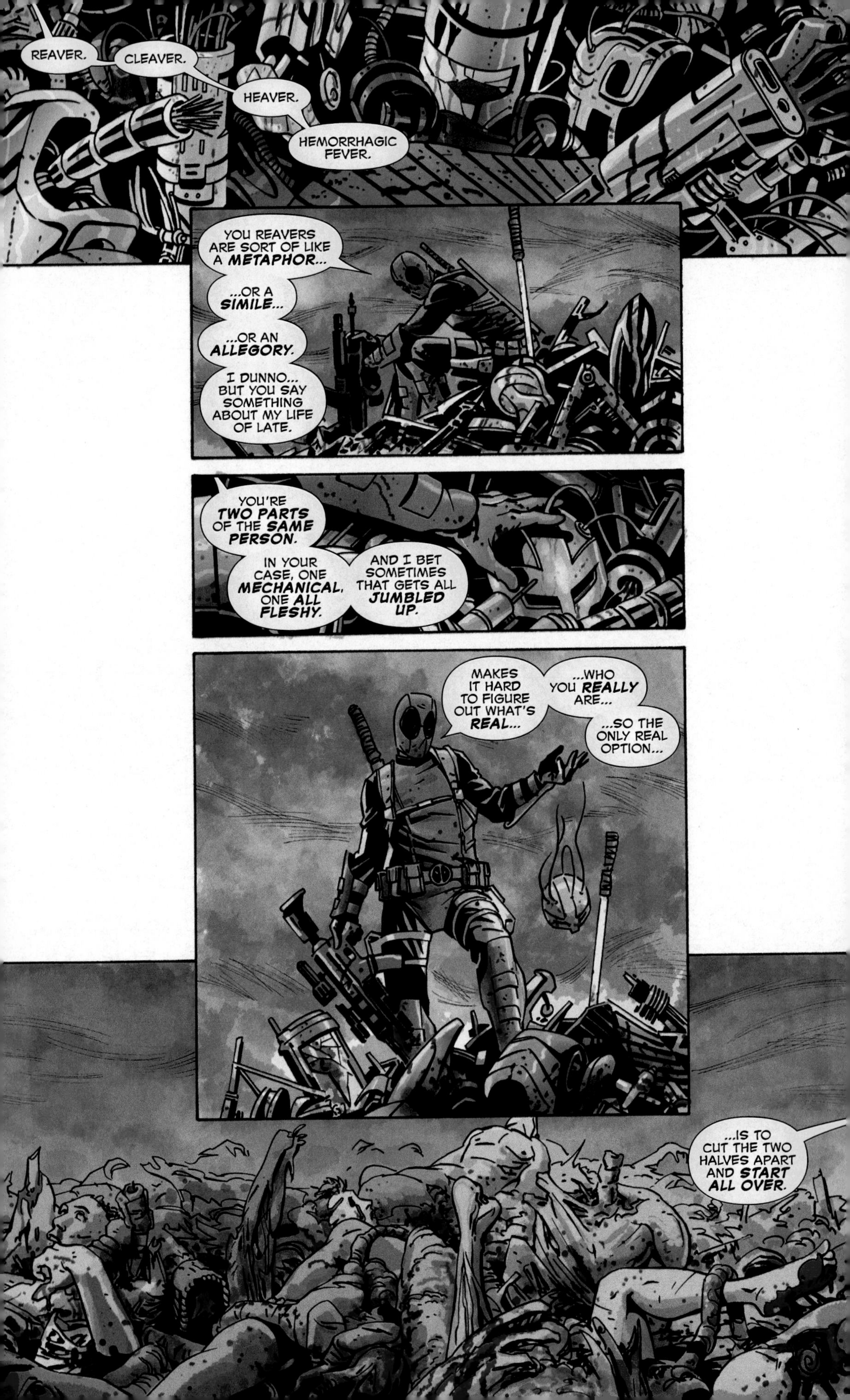
REAVER.
CLEAVER.
HEAVER.
HEMORRHAGIC FEVER.
YOU REAVERS ARE SORT OF LIKE A METAPHOR...
...OR A SIMILE...
...OR AN ALLEGORY.
I DUNNO... BUT YOU SAY SOMETHING ABOUT MY LIFE OF LATE.
YOU'RE TWO PARTS OF THE SAME PERSON.
IN YOUR CASE, ONE MECHANICAL, ONE ALL FLESHY.
AND I BET SOMETIMES THAT GETS ALL JUMBLED UP.
MAKES IT HARD TO FIGURE OUT WHAT'S REAL...
...WHO YOU REALLY ARE...
...SO THE ONLY REAL OPTION...
...IS TO CUT THE TWO HALVES APART AND START ALL OVER.

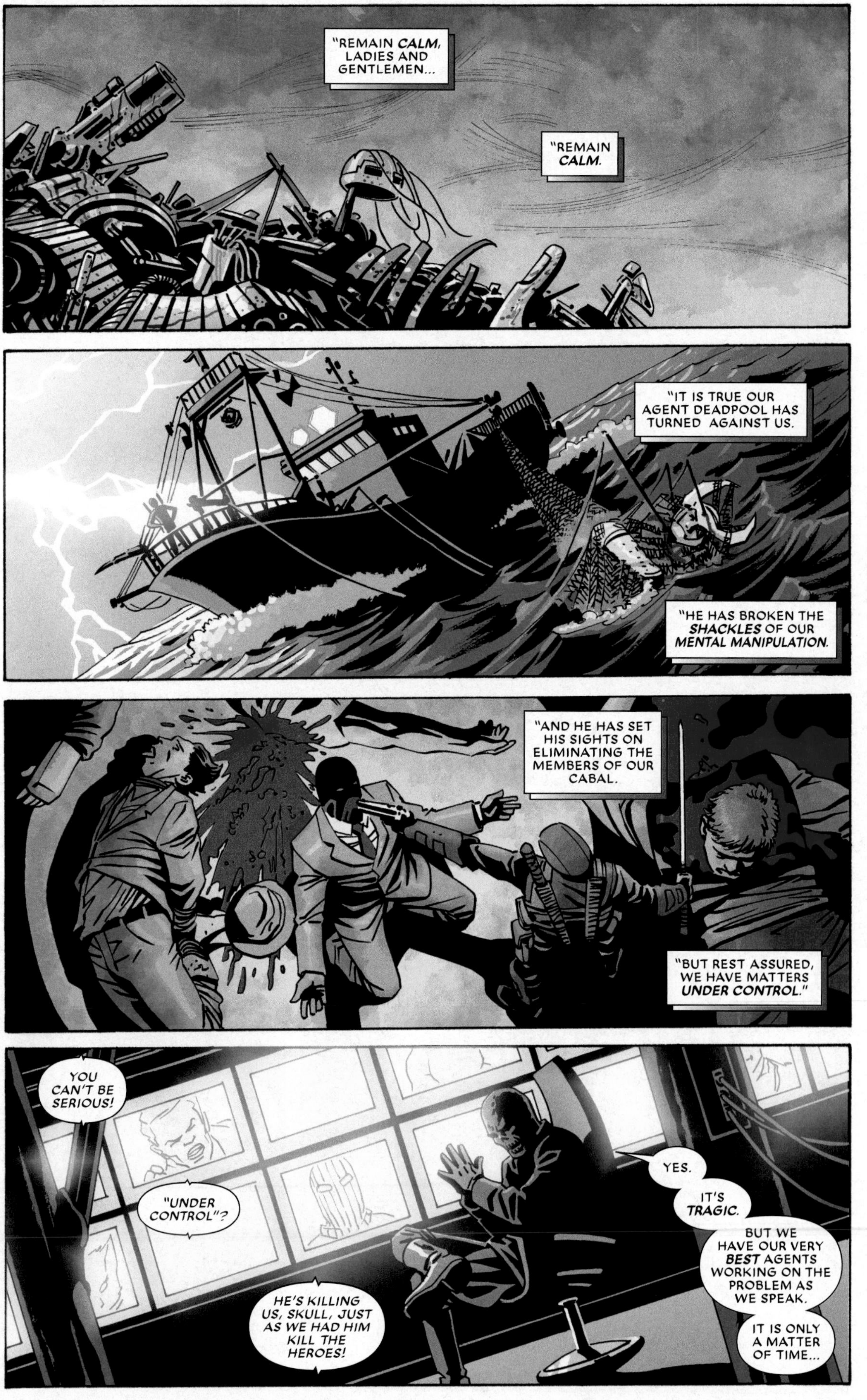
"REMAIN CALM, LADIES AND GENTLEMEN...
"REMAIN CALM.
"IT IS TRUE OUR AGENT DEADPOOL HAS TURNED AGAINST US.
"HE HAS BROKEN THE SHACKLES OF OUR MENTAL MANIPULATION.
"AND HE HAS SET HIS SIGHTS ON ELIMINATING THE MEMBERS OF OUR CABAL.
"BUT REST ASSURED, WE HAVE MATTERS UNDER CONTROL."
YOU CAN'T BE SERIOUS!
"UNDER CONTROL"?
HE'S KILLING US, SKULL, JUST AS WE HAD HIM KILL THE HEROES!
YES.
IT'S TRAGIC.
BUT WE HAVE OUR VERY BEST AGENTS WORKING ON THE PROBLEM AS WE SPEAK.
IT IS ONLY A MATTER OF TIME...

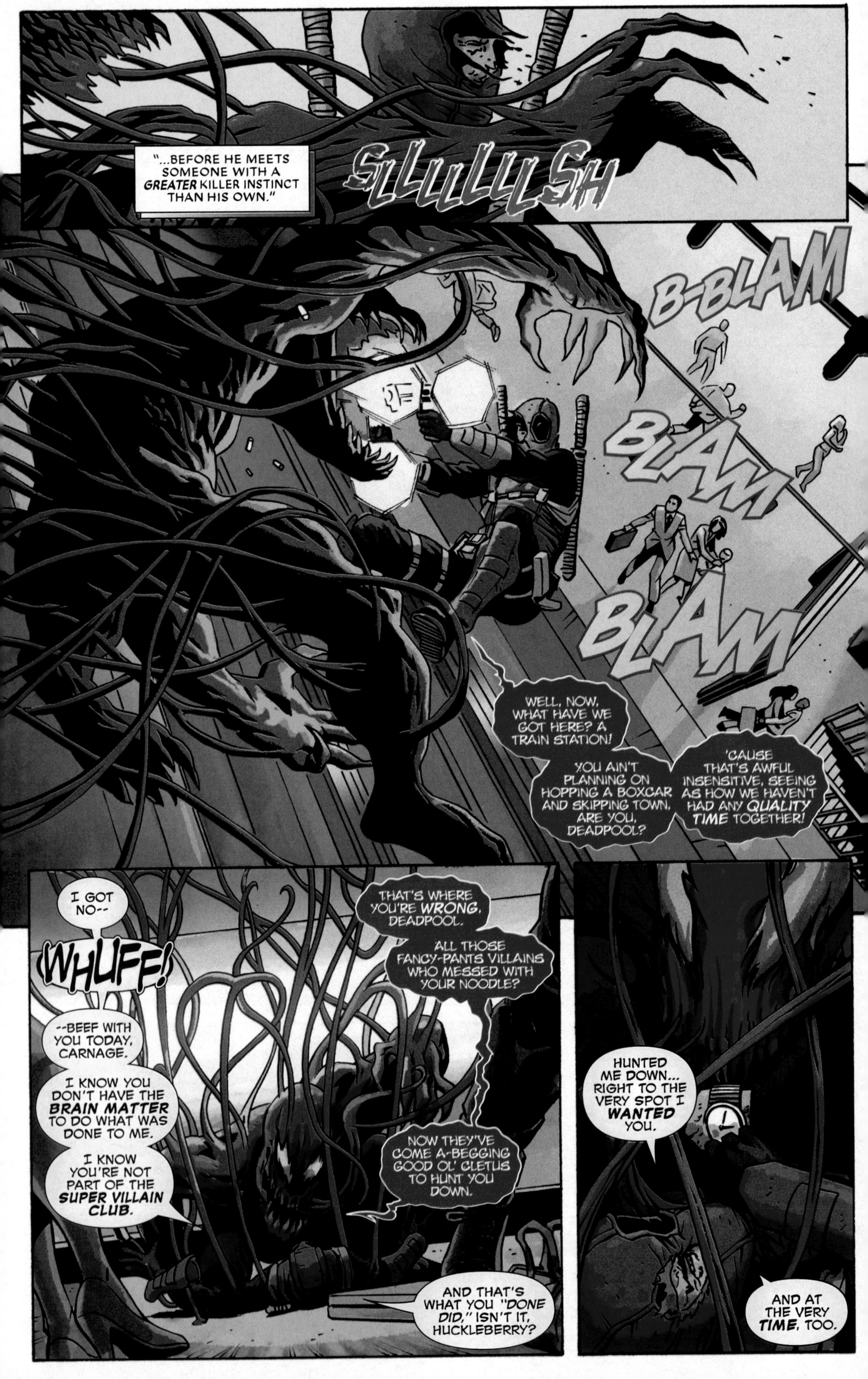
"...BEFORE HE MEETS SOMEONE WITH A GREATER KILLER INSTINCT THAN HIS OWN."
SLLLLLLLSH
B-BLAM
BLAM
BLAM
WELL, NOW, WHAT HAVE WE GOT HERE? A TRAIN STATION!
YOU AIN'T PLANNING ON HOPPING A BOXCAR AND SKIPPING TOWN, ARE YOU, DEADPOOL?
'CAUSE THAT'S AWFUL INSENSITIVE, SEEING AS HOW WE HAVEN'T HAD ANY QUALITY TIME TOGETHER!
I GOT NO--
WHUFF!
--BEEF WITH YOU TODAY, CARNAGE.
I KNOW YOU DON'T HAVE THE BRAIN MATTER TO DO WHAT WAS DONE TO ME.
I KNOW YOU'RE NOT PART OF THE SUPER VILLAIN CLUB.
THAT'S WHERE YOU'RE WRONG, DEADPOOL.
ALL THOSE FANCY-PANTS VILLAINS WHO MESSED WITH YOUR NOODLE?
NOW THEY'VE COME A-BEGGING GOOD OL' CLETUS TO HUNT YOU DOWN.
AND THAT'S WHAT YOU "DONE DID," ISN'T IT, HUCKLEBERRY?
HUNTED ME DOWN... RIGHT TO THE VERY SPOT I WANTED YOU.
AND AT THE VERY TIME, TOO.

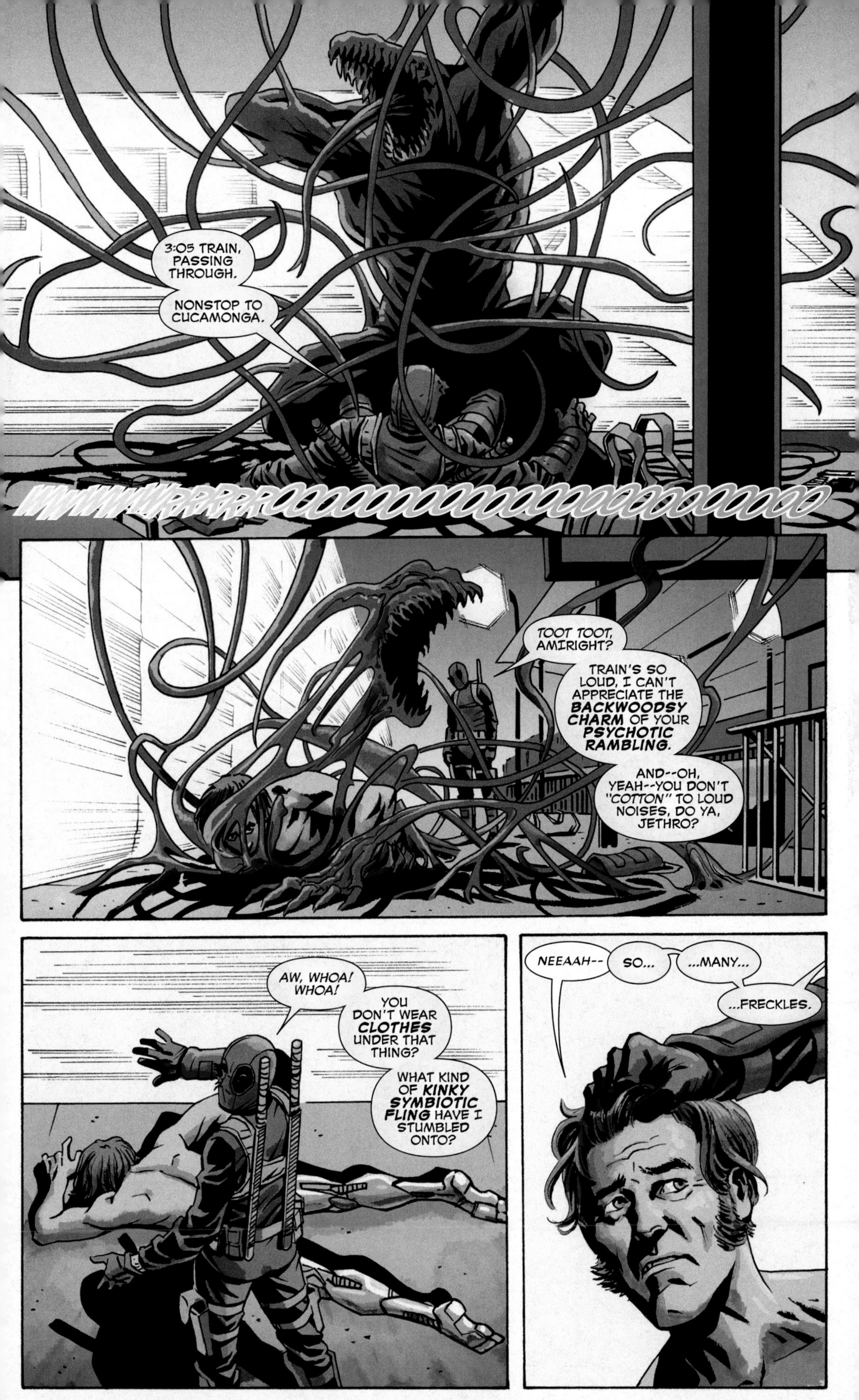
3:05 TRAIN, PASSING THROUGH.
NONSTOP TO CUCAMONGA.
WWWWWWRRRRROOOOOOOOOOOOOOOOOOOOOOOOOOOO
TOOT TOOT, AMIRIGHT?
TRAIN'S SO LOUD, I CAN'T APPRECIATE THE BACKWOODSY CHARM OF YOUR PSYCHOTIC RAMBLING.
AND--OH, YEAH--YOU DON'T "COTTON" TO LOUD NOISES, DO YA, JETHRO?
AW, WHOA! WHOA!
YOU DON'T WEAR CLOTHES UNDER THAT THING?
WHAT KIND OF KINKY SYMBIOTIC FLING HAVE I STUMBLED ONTO?
NEEAAH--
SO...
...MANY...
...FRECKLES.

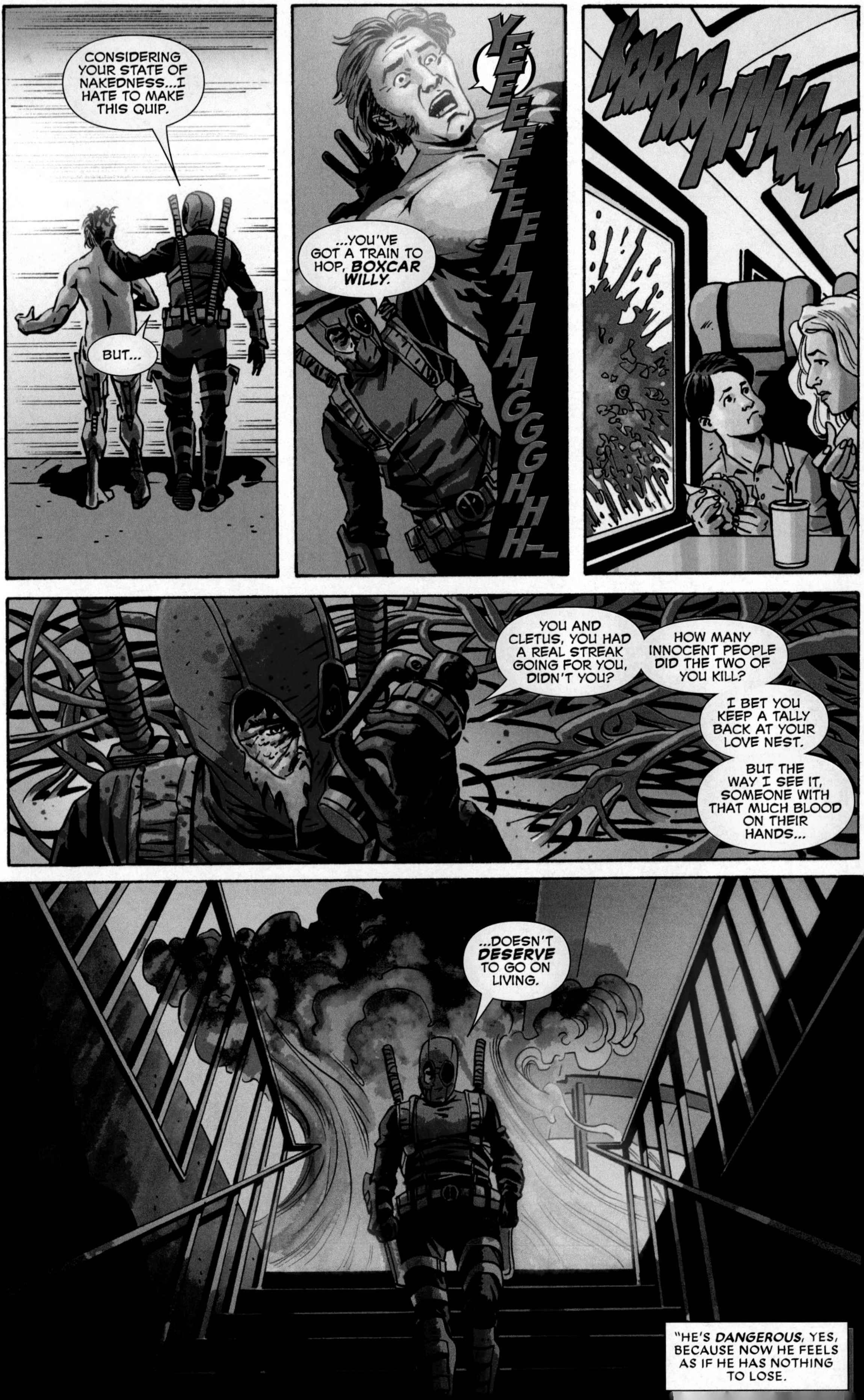

CONSIDERING YOUR STATE OF NAKEDNESS...I HATE TO MAKE THIS QUIP.
BUT...
YEEEEEEEEAAAAAAAGGHHHH--
...YOU'VE GOT A TRAIN TO HOP, BOXCAR WILLY.
KRRRRUNNNCGK
YOU AND CLETUS, YOU HAD A REAL STREAK GOING FOR YOU, DIDN'T YOU?
HOW MANY INNOCENT PEOPLE DID THE TWO OF YOU KILL?
I BET YOU KEEP A TALLY BACK AT YOUR LOVE NEST.
BUT THE WAY I SEE IT, SOMEONE WITH THAT MUCH BLOOD ON THEIR HANDS...
...DOESN'T DESERVE TO GO ON LIVING.
"HE'S DANGEROUS, YES, BECAUSE NOW HE FEELS AS IF HE HAS NOTHING TO LOSE.

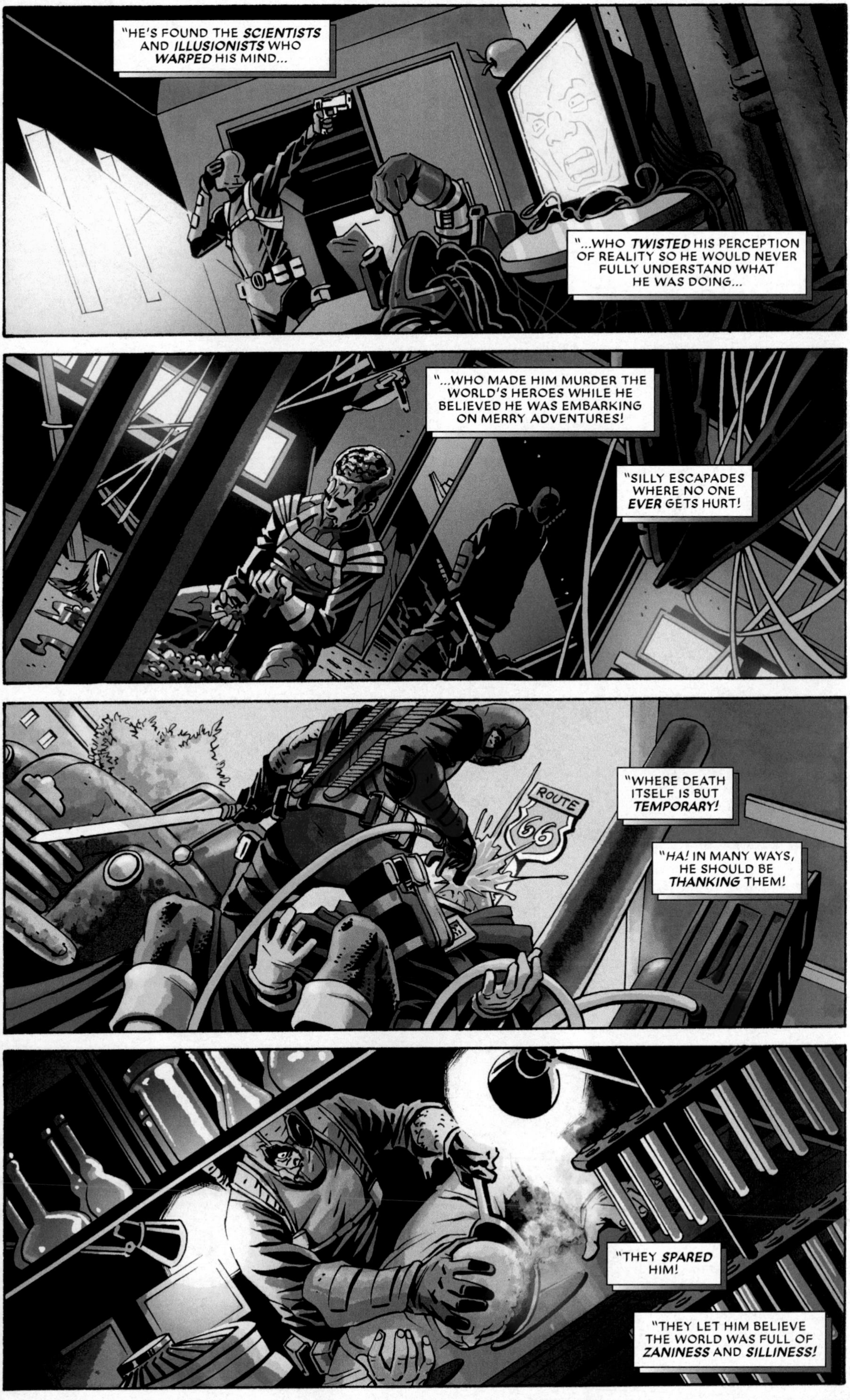
"HE'S FOUND THE SCIENTISTS AND ILLUSIONISTS WHO WARPED HIS MIND...
"...WHO TWISTED HIS PERCEPTION OF REALITY SO HE WOULD NEVER FULLY UNDERSTAND WHAT HE WAS DOING...
"...WHO MADE HIM MURDER THE WORLD'S HEROES WHILE HE BELIEVED HE WAS EMBARKING ON MERRY ADVENTURES!
"SILLY ESCAPADES WHERE NO ONE EVER GETS HURT!
"WHERE DEATH ITSELF IS BUT TEMPORARY!
ROUTE 66
"HA! IN MANY WAYS, HE SHOULD BE THANKING THEM!
"THEY SPARED HIM!
"THEY LET HIM BELIEVE THE WORLD WAS FULL OF ZANINESS AND SILLINESS!

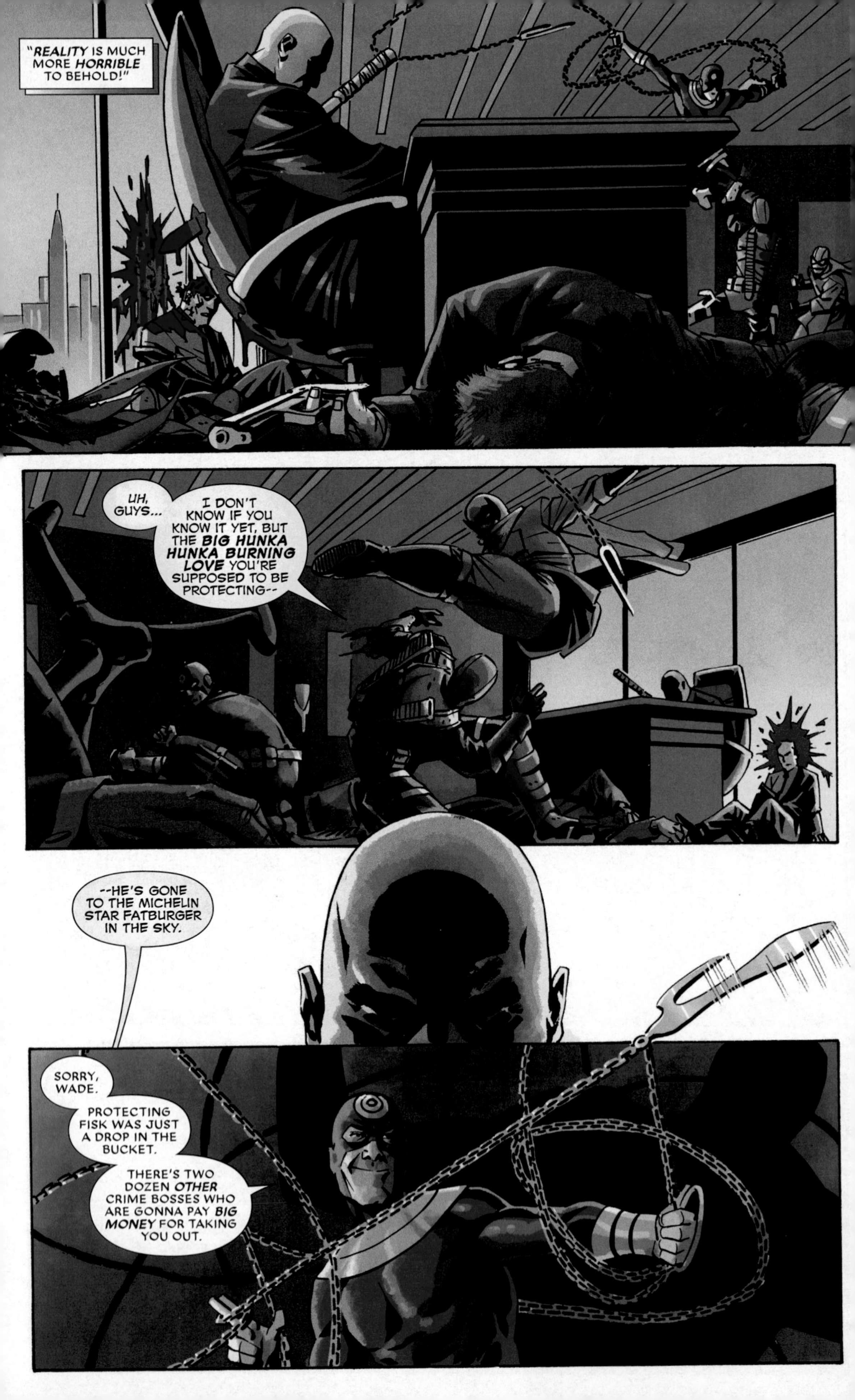
"REALITY IS MUCH MORE HORRIBLE TO BEHOLD!"
UH, GUYS...
I DON'T KNOW IF YOU KNOW IT YET, BUT THE BIG HUNKA HUNKA BURNING LOVE YOU'RE SUPPOSED TO BE PROTECTING--
--HE'S GONE TO THE MICHELIN STAR FATBURGER IN THE SKY.
SORRY, WADE.
PROTECTING FISK WAS JUST A DROP IN THE BUCKET.
THERE'S TWO DOZEN OTHER CRIME BOSSES WHO ARE GONNA PAY BIG MONEY FOR TAKING YOU OUT.

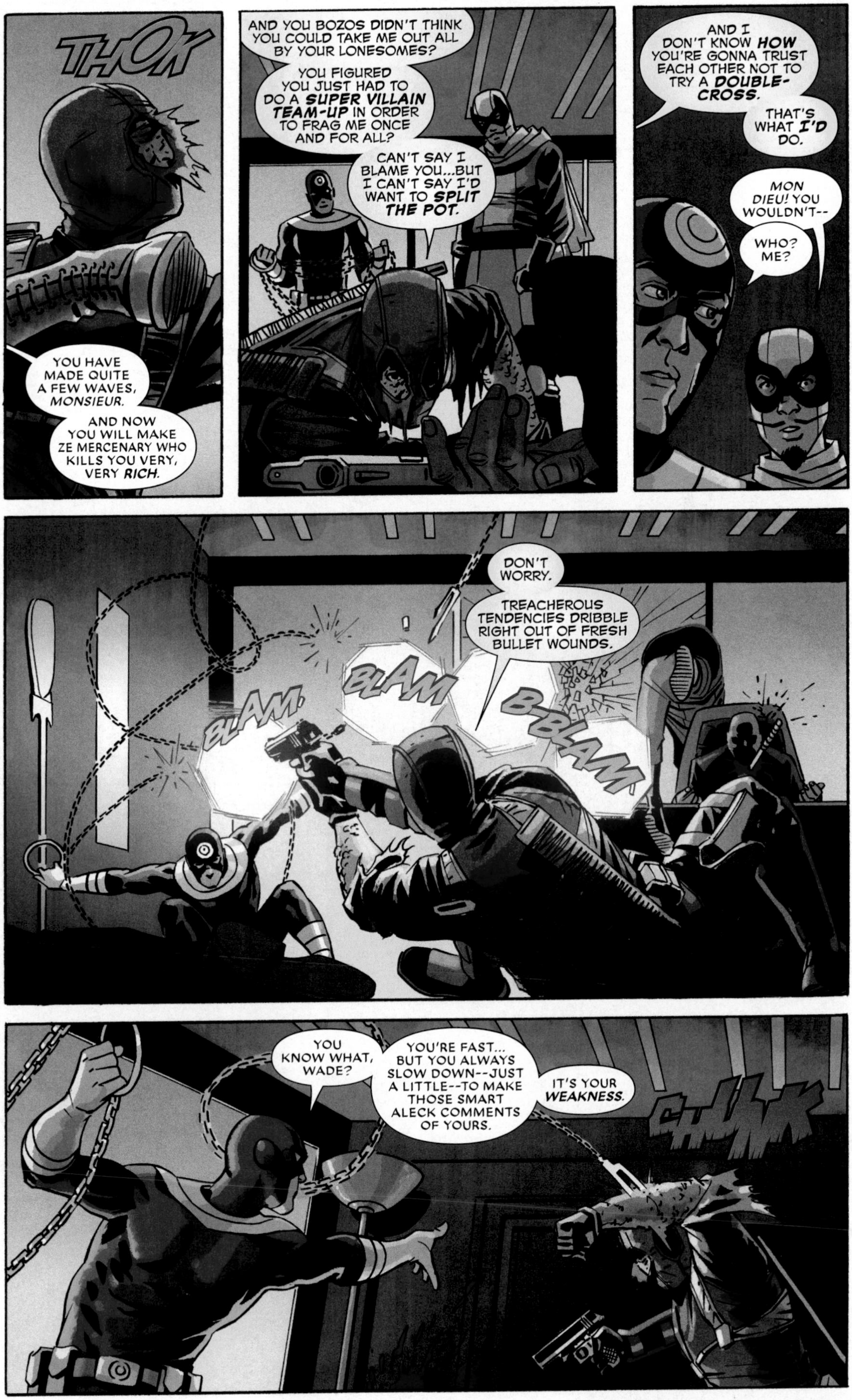
THOK
YOU HAVE MADE QUITE A FEW WAVES, *MONSIEUR.*
AND NOW YOU WILL MAKE ZE MERCENARY WHO KILLS YOU VERY, VERY *RICH*.
AND YOU BOZOS DIDN'T THINK YOU COULD TAKE ME OUT ALL BY YOUR LONESOMES?
YOU FIGURED YOU JUST HAD TO DO A **SUPER VILLAIN TEAM-UP** IN ORDER TO FRAG ME ONCE AND FOR ALL?
CAN'T SAY I BLAME YOU...BUT I CAN'T SAY I'D WANT TO **SPLIT THE POT**.
AND I DON'T KNOW **HOW** YOU'RE GONNA TRUST EACH OTHER NOT TO TRY A **DOUBLE-CROSS**.
THAT'S WHAT **I'D** DO.
MON DIEU! YOU WOULDN'T--
WHO? ME?
DON'T WORRY.
TREACHEROUS TENDENCIES DRIBBLE RIGHT OUT OF FRESH BULLET WOUNDS.
BLAM
BLAM
B-BLAM
YOU KNOW WHAT, WADE?
YOU'RE FAST... BUT YOU ALWAYS SLOW DOWN--JUST A LITTLE--TO MAKE THOSE SMART ALECK COMMENTS OF YOURS.
IT'S YOUR **WEAKNESS**.
CHUNK

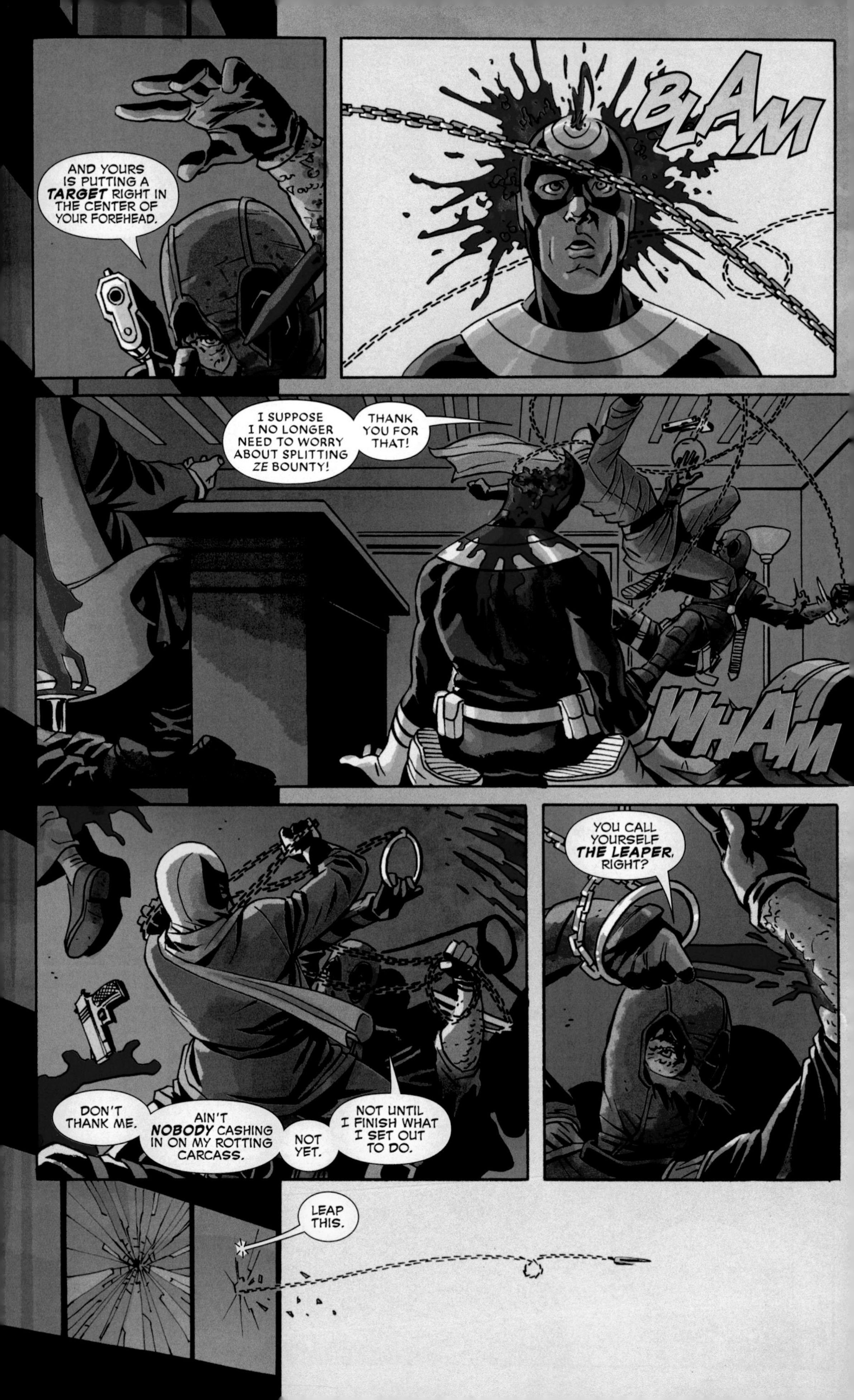
AND YOURS IS PUTTING A **TARGET** RIGHT IN THE CENTER OF YOUR FOREHEAD.
BLAM
I SUPPOSE I NO LONGER NEED TO WORRY ABOUT SPLITTING *ZE* BOUNTY!
THANK YOU FOR THAT!
WHAM
DON'T THANK ME.
AIN'T **NOBODY** CASHING IN ON MY ROTTING CARCASS.
NOT YET.
NOT UNTIL I FINISH WHAT I SET OUT TO DO.
YOU CALL YOURSELF **THE LEAPER**, RIGHT?
LEAP THIS.

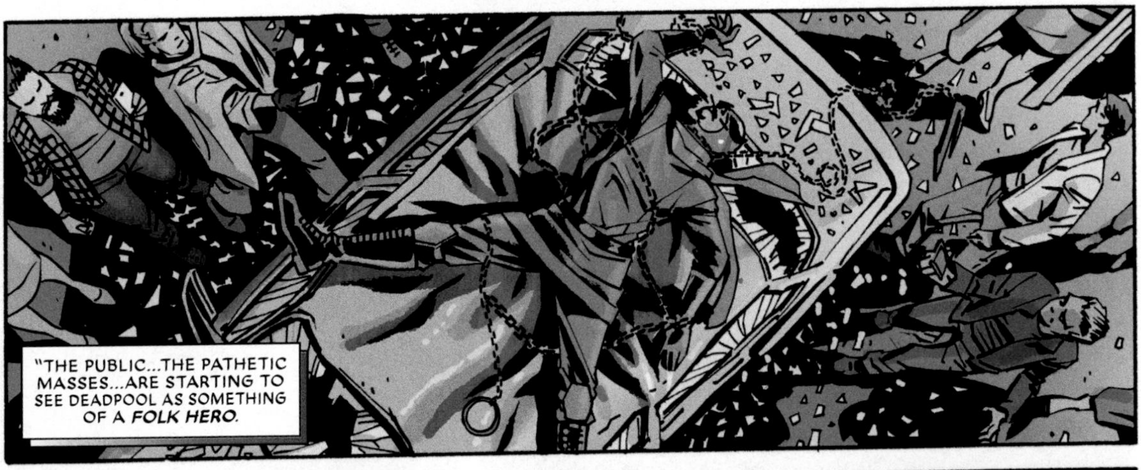
"THE PUBLIC...THE PATHETIC MASSES...ARE STARTING TO SEE DEADPOOL AS SOMETHING OF A *FOLK HERO*.

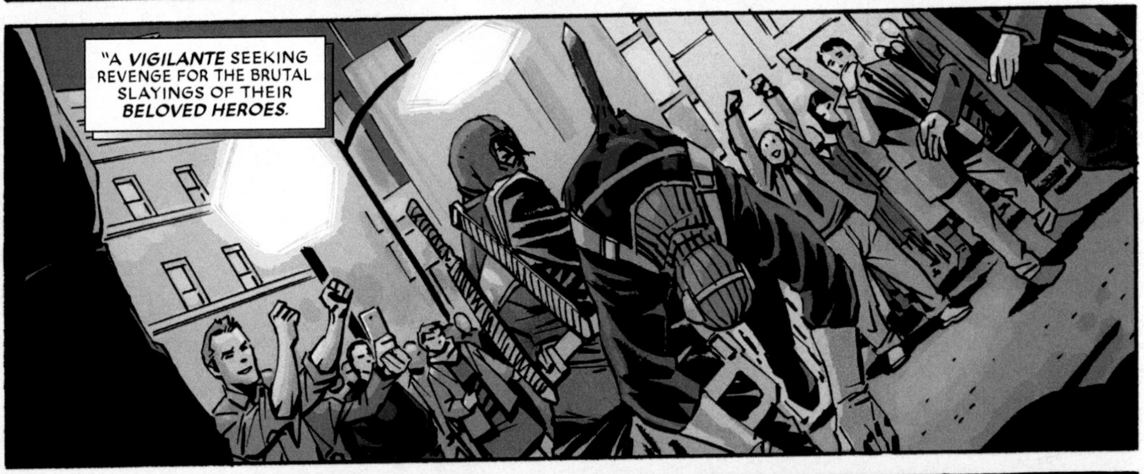
"A *VIGILANTE* SEEKING REVENGE FOR THE BRUTAL SLAYINGS OF THEIR *BELOVED HEROES*.

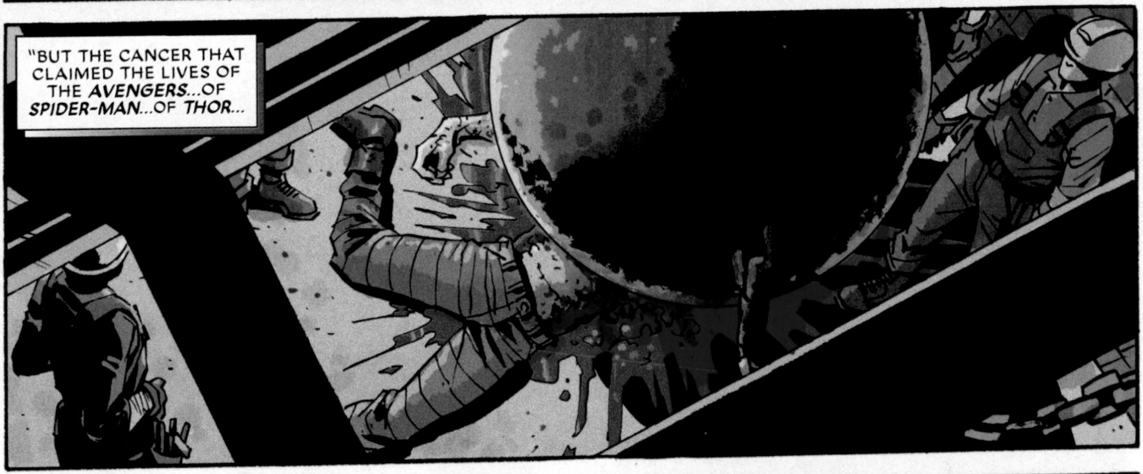
"BUT THE CANCER THAT CLAIMED THE LIVES OF THE *AVENGERS*...OF *SPIDER-MAN*...OF *THOR*...

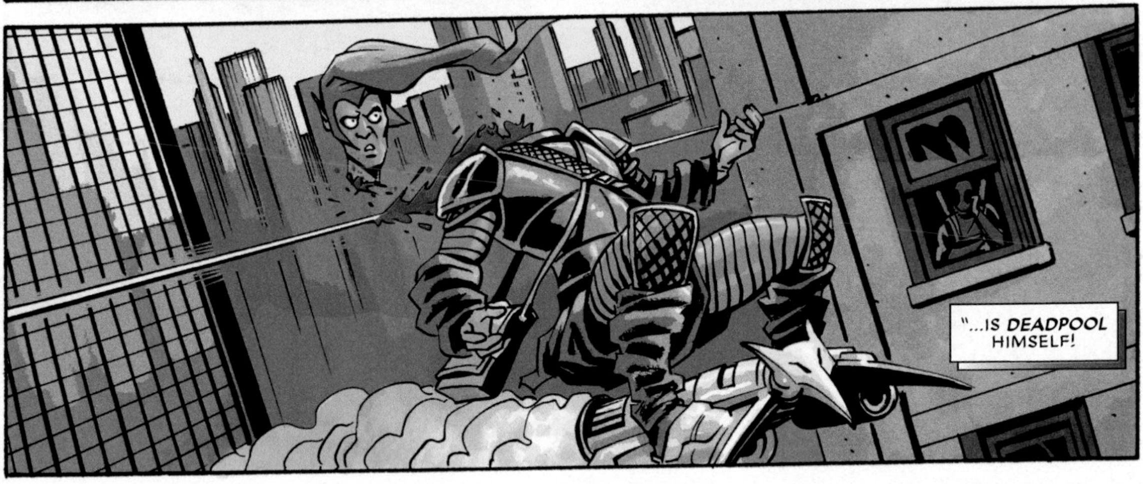
"...IS *DEADPOOL* HIMSELF!

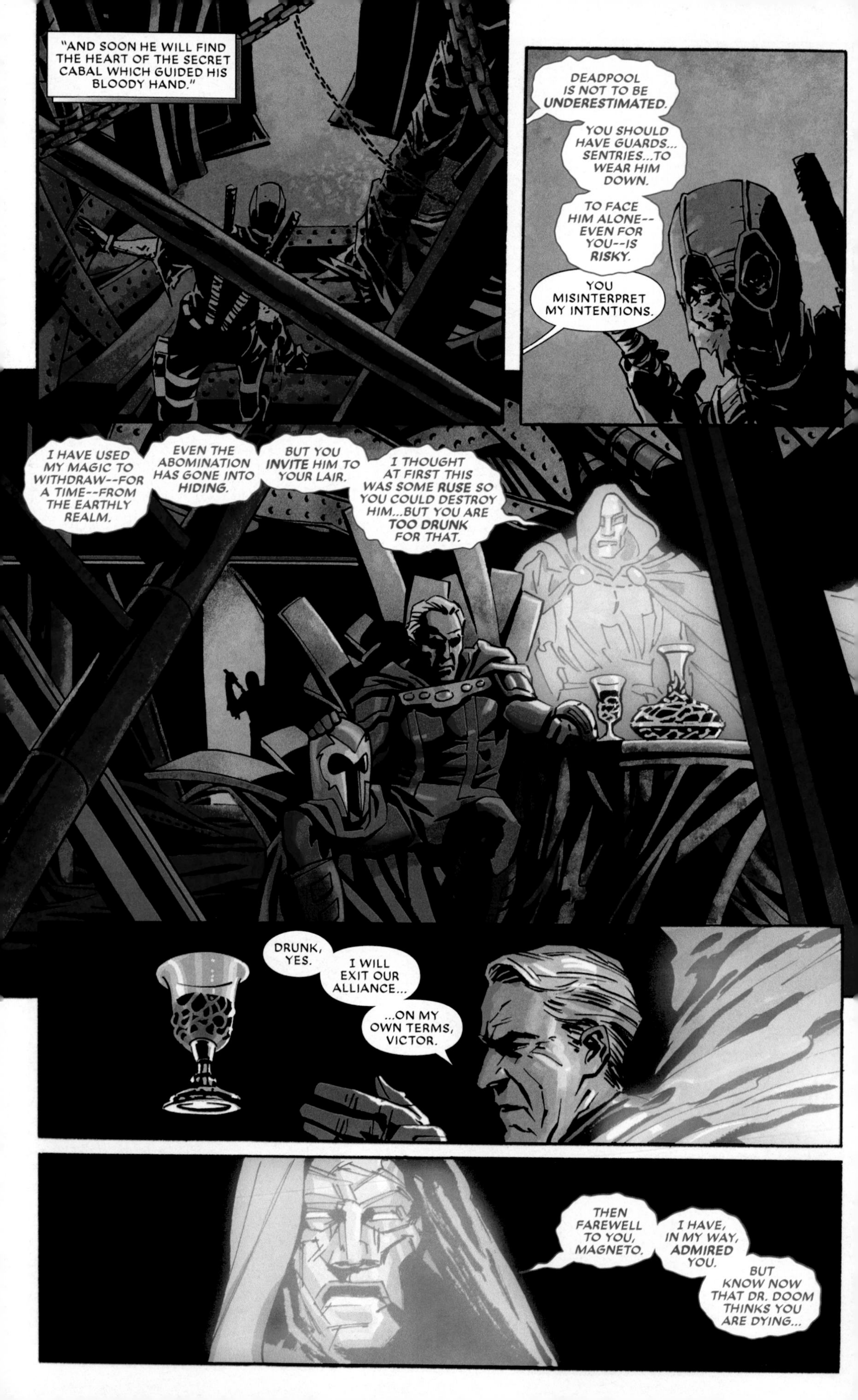
"AND SOON HE WILL FIND THE HEART OF THE SECRET CABAL WHICH GUIDED HIS BLOODY HAND."
DEADPOOL IS NOT TO BE UNDERESTIMATED.
YOU SHOULD HAVE GUARDS... SENTRIES...TO WEAR HIM DOWN.
TO FACE HIM ALONE-- EVEN FOR YOU--IS RISKY.
YOU MISINTERPRET MY INTENTIONS.
I HAVE USED MY MAGIC TO WITHDRAW--FOR A TIME--FROM THE EARTHLY REALM.
EVEN THE ABOMINATION HAS GONE INTO HIDING.
BUT YOU INVITE HIM TO YOUR LAIR.
I THOUGHT AT FIRST THIS WAS SOME RUSE SO YOU COULD DESTROY HIM...BUT YOU ARE TOO DRUNK FOR THAT.
DRUNK, YES.
I WILL EXIT OUR ALLIANCE...
...ON MY OWN TERMS, VICTOR.
THEN FAREWELL TO YOU, MAGNETO.
I HAVE, IN MY WAY, ADMIRED YOU.
BUT KNOW NOW THAT DR. DOOM THINKS YOU ARE DYING...

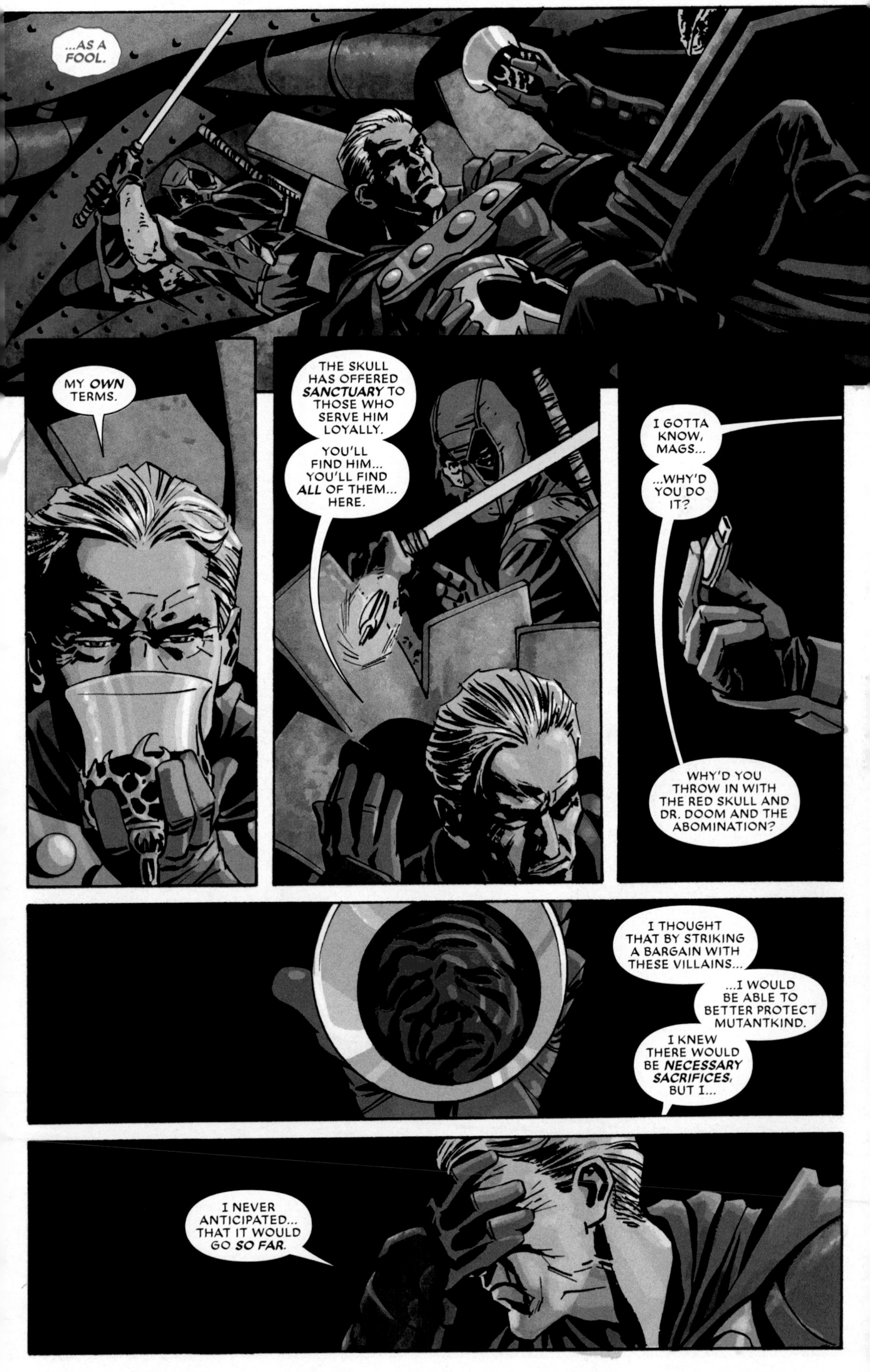
...AS A FOOL.
MY OWN TERMS.
THE SKULL HAS OFFERED SANCTUARY TO THOSE WHO SERVE HIM LOYALLY.
YOU'LL FIND HIM... YOU'LL FIND ALL OF THEM... HERE.
I GOTTA KNOW, MAGS...
...WHY'D YOU DO IT?
WHY'D YOU THROW IN WITH THE RED SKULL AND DR. DOOM AND THE ABOMINATION?
I THOUGHT THAT BY STRIKING A BARGAIN WITH THESE VILLAINS...
...I WOULD BE ABLE TO BETTER PROTECT MUTANTKIND.
I KNEW THERE WOULD BE NECESSARY SACRIFICES, BUT I...
I NEVER ANTICIPATED... THAT IT WOULD GO SO FAR.

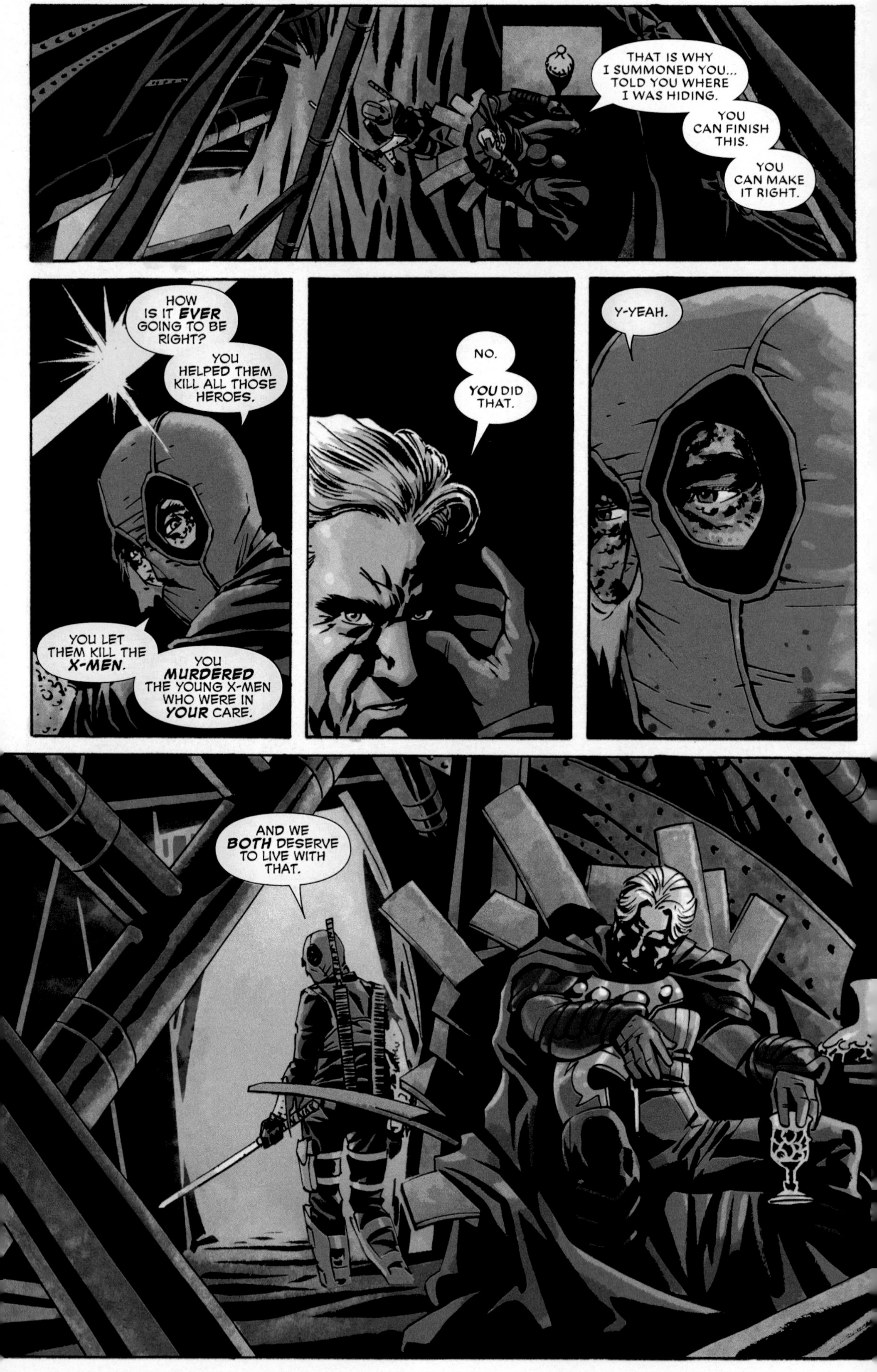
THAT IS WHY I SUMMONED YOU... TOLD YOU WHERE I WAS HIDING.
YOU CAN FINISH THIS.
YOU CAN MAKE IT RIGHT.
HOW IS IT EVER GOING TO BE RIGHT?
YOU HELPED THEM KILL ALL THOSE HEROES.
YOU LET THEM KILL THE X-MEN.
YOU MURDERED THE YOUNG X-MEN WHO WERE IN YOUR CARE.
NO.
YOU DID THAT.
Y-YEAH.
AND WE BOTH DESERVE TO LIVE WITH THAT.

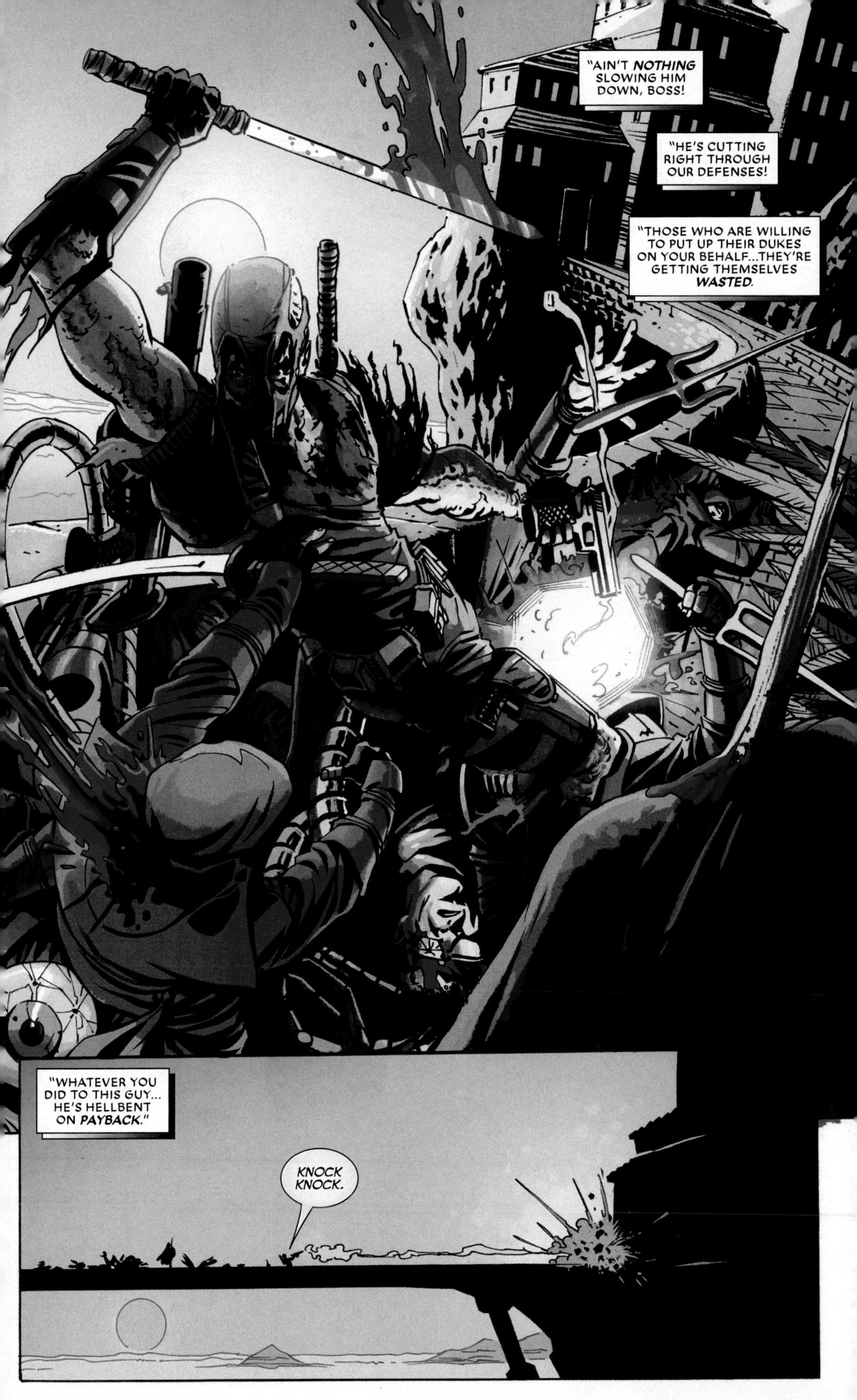
"AIN'T NOTHING SLOWING HIM DOWN, BOSS!
"HE'S CUTTING RIGHT THROUGH OUR DEFENSES!
"THOSE WHO ARE WILLING TO PUT UP THEIR DUKES ON YOUR BEHALF...THEY'RE GETTING THEMSELVES WASTED.
"WHATEVER YOU DID TO THIS GUY... HE'S HELLBENT ON PAYBACK."
KNOCK KNOCK.

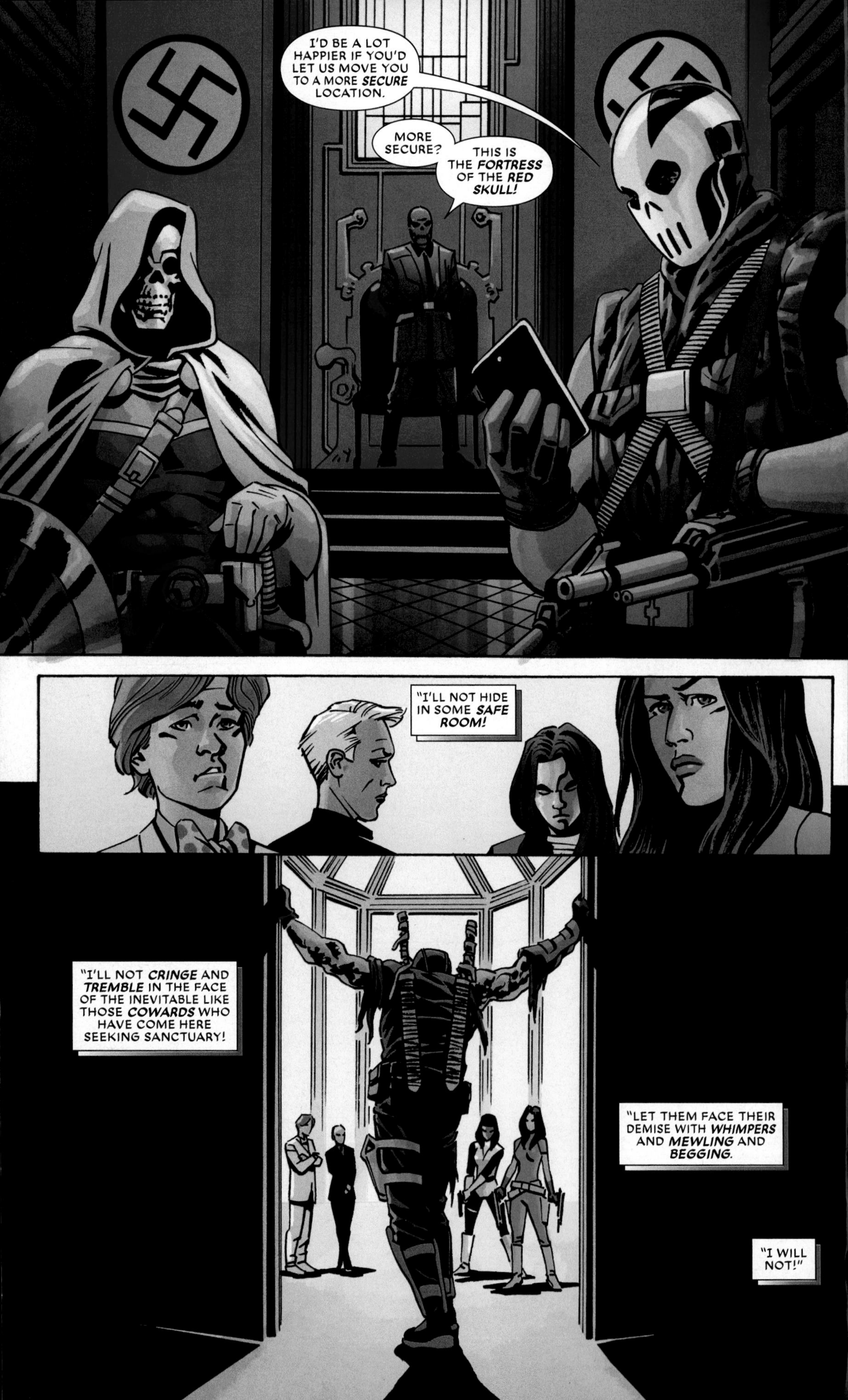
I'D BE A LOT HAPPIER IF YOU'D LET US MOVE YOU TO A MORE *SECURE* LOCATION.
MORE SECURE?
THIS IS THE *FORTRESS* OF THE *RED SKULL!*
"I'LL NOT HIDE IN SOME *SAFE ROOM!*
"I'LL NOT *CRINGE* AND *TREMBLE* IN THE FACE OF THE INEVITABLE LIKE THOSE *COWARDS* WHO HAVE COME HERE SEEKING SANCTUARY!
"LET THEM FACE THEIR DEMISE WITH *WHIMPERS* AND *MEWLING* AND *BEGGING*.
"I WILL NOT!"

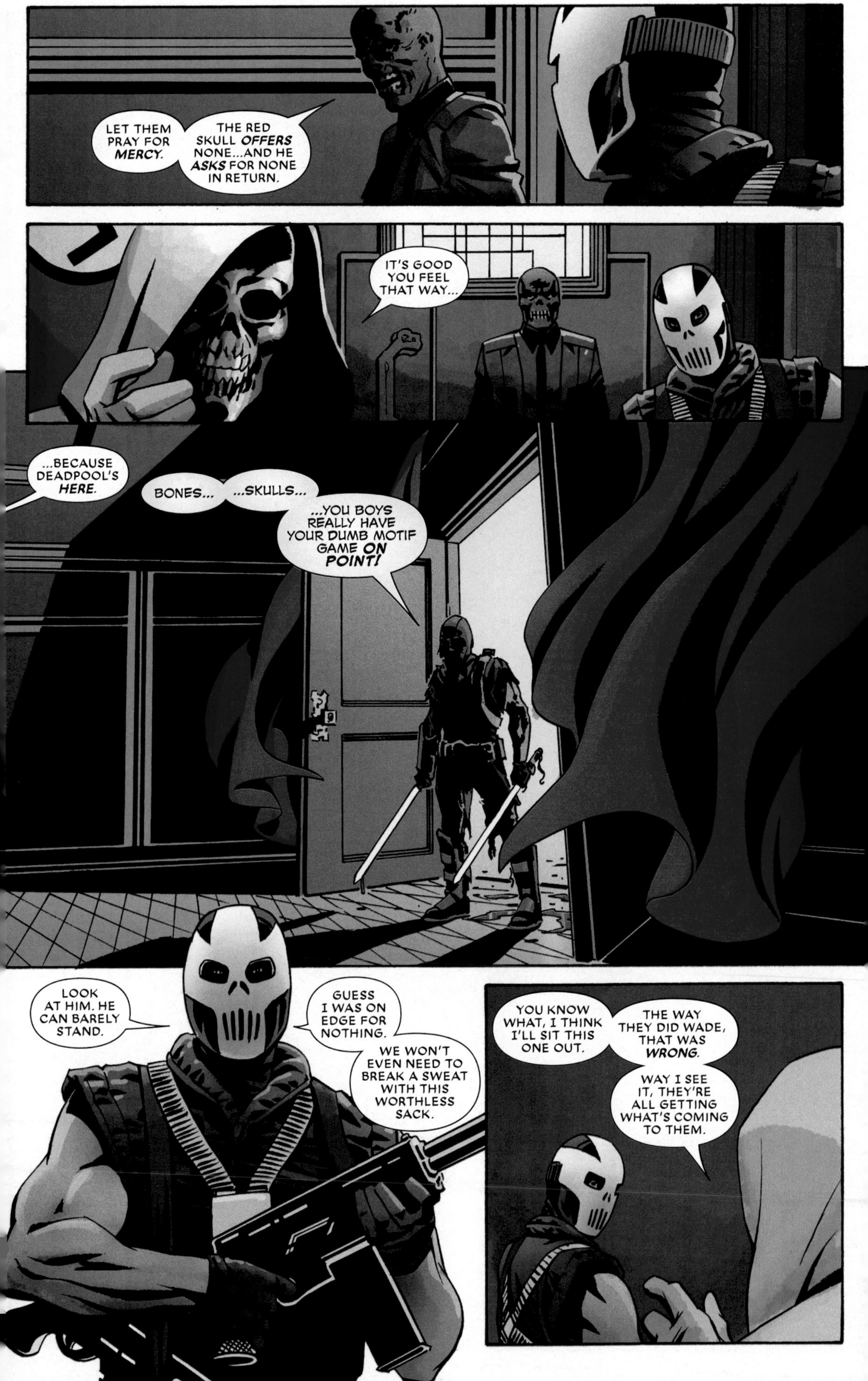
LET THEM PRAY FOR MERCY.
THE RED SKULL OFFERS NONE...AND HE ASKS FOR NONE IN RETURN.
IT'S GOOD YOU FEEL THAT WAY...
...BECAUSE DEADPOOL'S HERE.
BONES...
...SKULLS...
...YOU BOYS REALLY HAVE YOUR DUMB MOTIF GAME ON POINT!
LOOK AT HIM. HE CAN BARELY STAND.
GUESS I WAS ON EDGE FOR NOTHING.
WE WON'T EVEN NEED TO BREAK A SWEAT WITH THIS WORTHLESS SACK.
YOU KNOW WHAT, I THINK I'LL SIT THIS ONE OUT.
THE WAY THEY DID WADE, THAT WAS WRONG.
WAY I SEE IT, THEY'RE ALL GETTING WHAT'S COMING TO THEM.

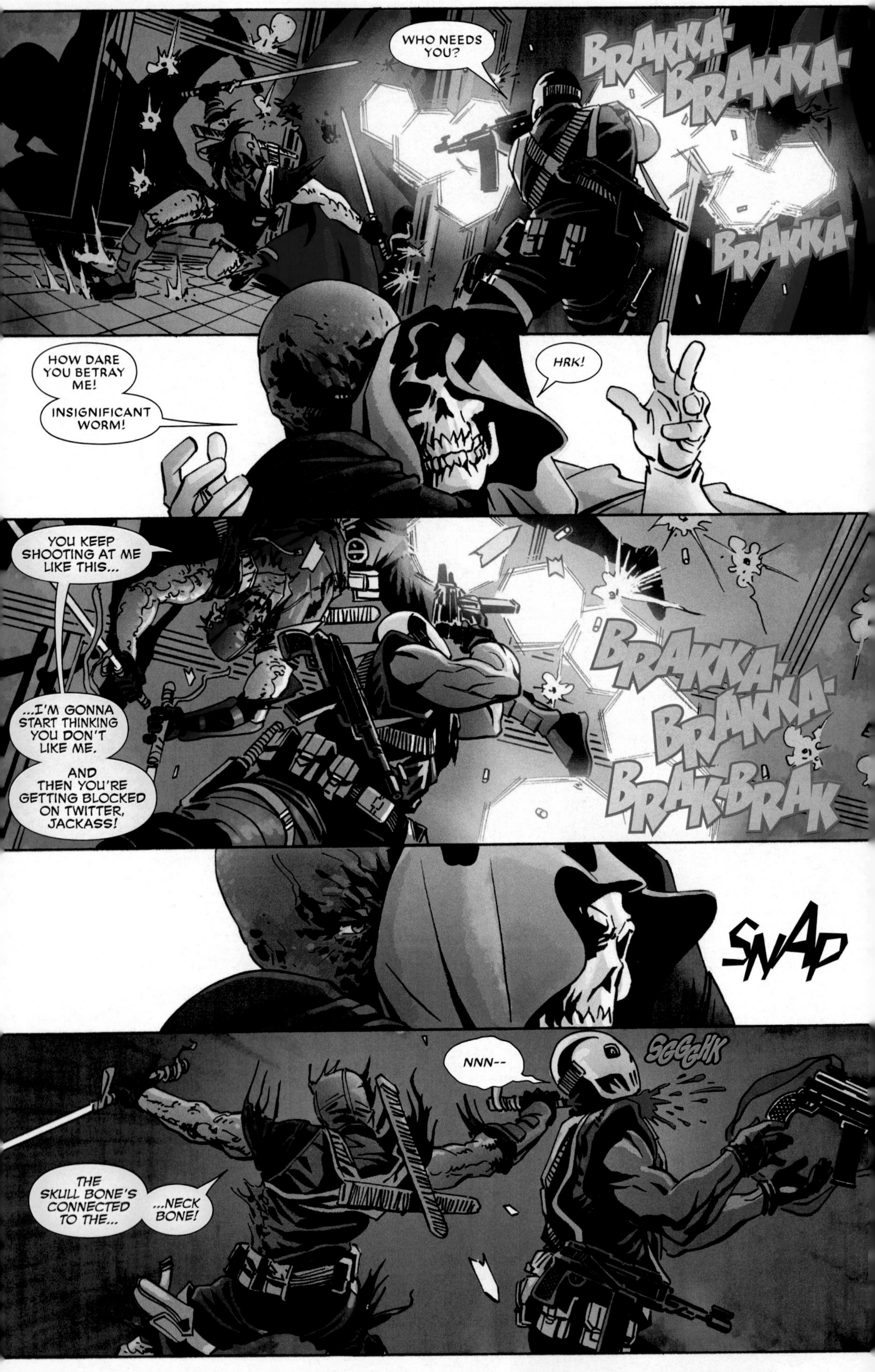
WHO NEEDS YOU?
BRAKKA-BRAKKA-BRAKKA-
HOW DARE YOU BETRAY ME!
INSIGNIFICANT WORM!
HRK!
YOU KEEP SHOOTING AT ME LIKE THIS...
...I'M GONNA START THINKING YOU DON'T LIKE ME.
AND THEN YOU'RE GETTING BLOCKED ON TWITTER, JACKASS!
BRAKKA-BRAKKA-BRAK-BRAK
SNAP
NNN--
SGGGHK
THE SKULL BONE'S CONNECTED TO THE...
...NECK BONE!

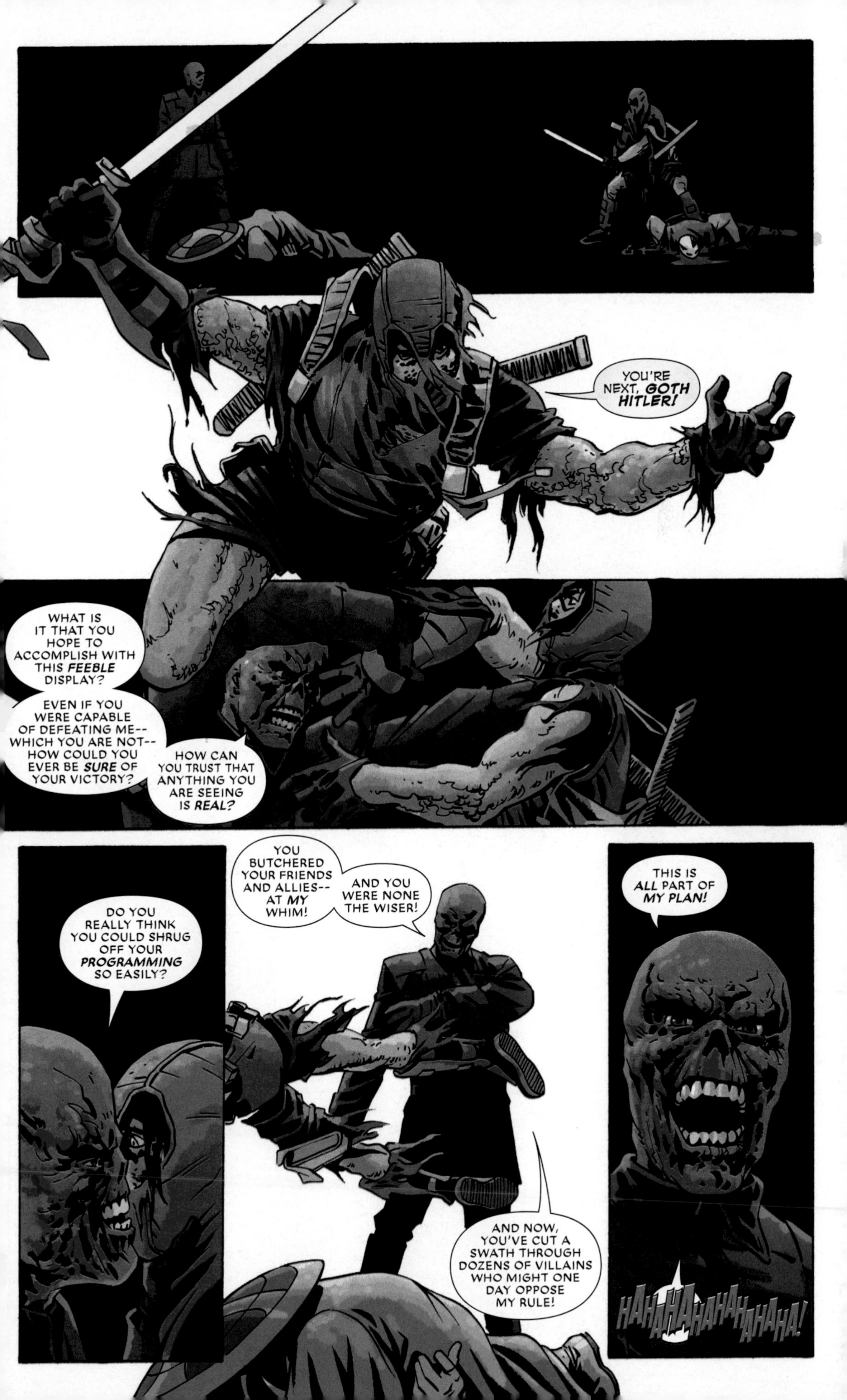
YOU'RE NEXT, GOTH HITLER!
WHAT IS IT THAT YOU HOPE TO ACCOMPLISH WITH THIS FEEBLE DISPLAY?
EVEN IF YOU WERE CAPABLE OF DEFEATING ME-- WHICH YOU ARE NOT-- HOW COULD YOU EVER BE SURE OF YOUR VICTORY?
HOW CAN YOU TRUST THAT ANYTHING YOU ARE SEEING IS REAL?
DO YOU REALLY THINK YOU COULD SHRUG OFF YOUR PROGRAMMING SO EASILY?
YOU BUTCHERED YOUR FRIENDS AND ALLIES-- AT MY WHIM!
AND YOU WERE NONE THE WISER!
AND NOW, YOU'VE CUT A SWATH THROUGH DOZENS OF VILLAINS WHO MIGHT ONE DAY OPPOSE MY RULE!
THIS IS ALL PART OF MY PLAN!
HAHAHAHAHAHAHAHAHA!

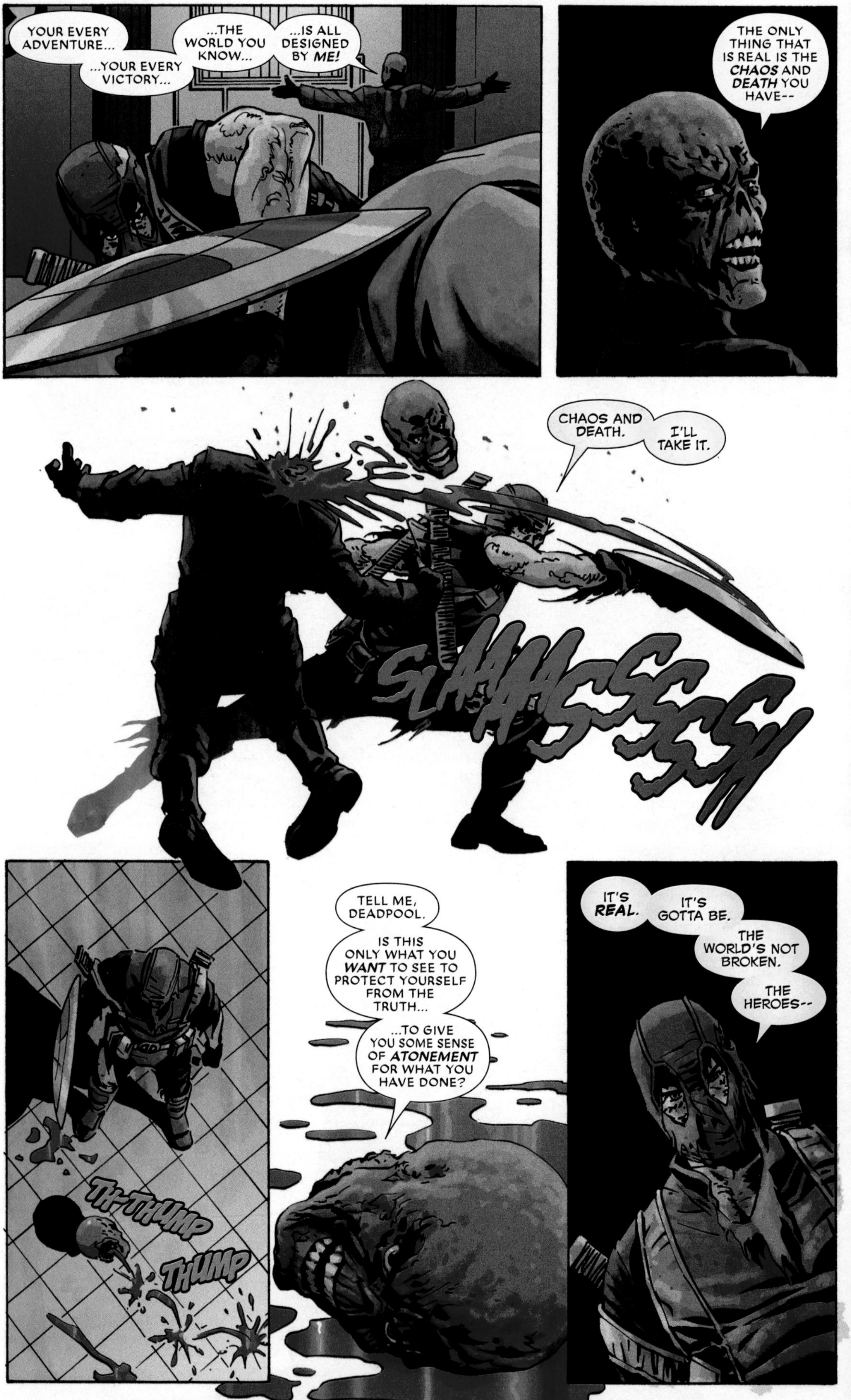
YOUR EVERY ADVENTURE...
...YOUR EVERY VICTORY...
...THE WORLD YOU KNOW...
...IS ALL DESIGNED BY *ME!*
THE ONLY THING THAT IS REAL IS THE *CHAOS* AND *DEATH* YOU HAVE--
CHAOS AND DEATH.
I'LL TAKE IT.
SLAAAHSSSSSH
TH-THUMP
THUMP
TELL ME, DEADPOOL.
IS THIS ONLY WHAT YOU *WANT* TO SEE TO PROTECT YOURSELF FROM THE TRUTH...
...TO GIVE YOU SOME SENSE OF *ATONEMENT* FOR WHAT YOU HAVE DONE?
IT'S *REAL.*
IT'S GOTTA BE.
THE WORLD'S NOT BROKEN.
THE HEROES--

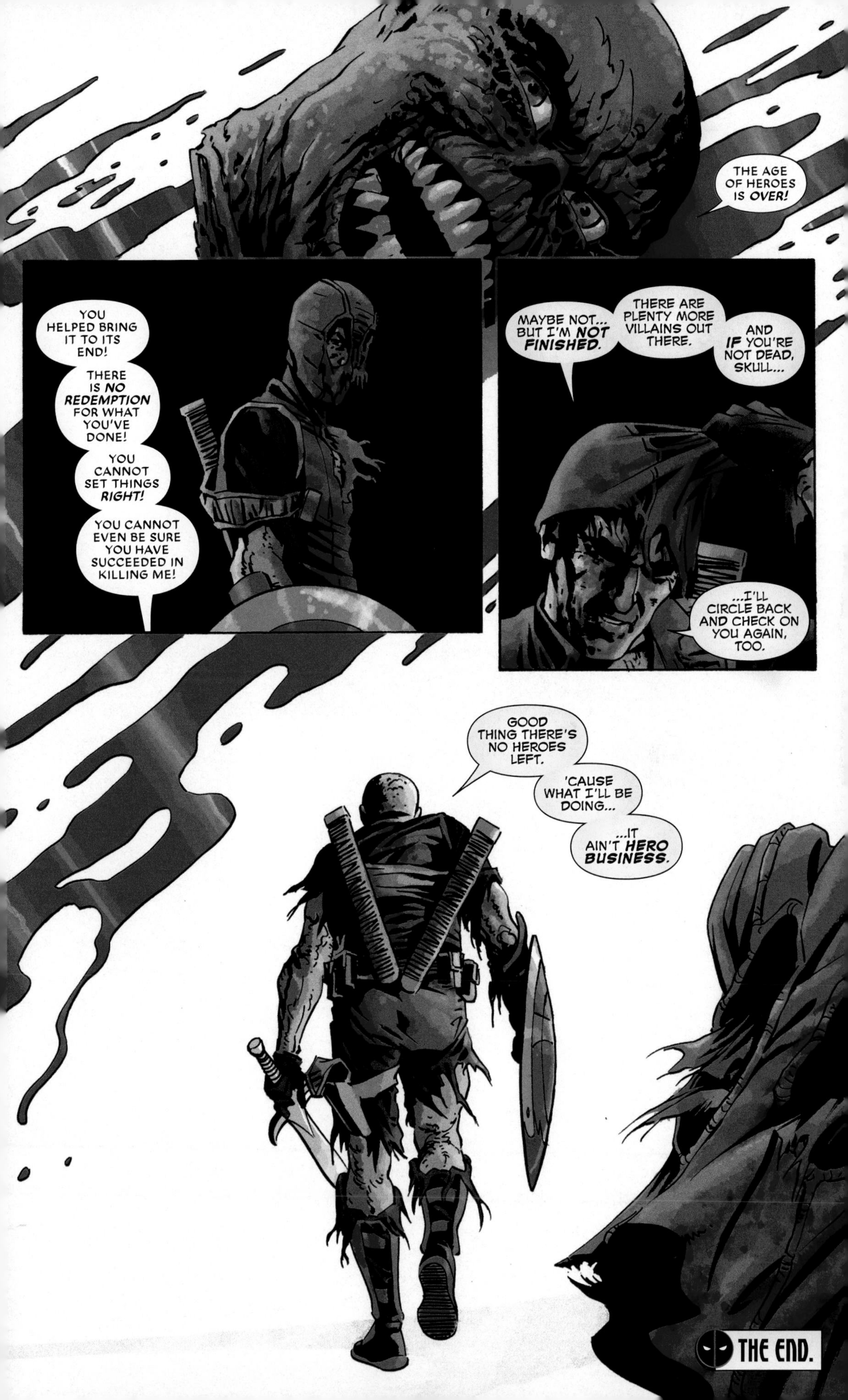
THE AGE OF HEROES IS OVER!
YOU HELPED BRING IT TO ITS END!
THERE IS NO REDEMPTION FOR WHAT YOU'VE DONE!
YOU CANNOT SET THINGS RIGHT!
YOU CANNOT EVEN BE SURE YOU HAVE SUCCEEDED IN KILLING ME!
MAYBE NOT... BUT I'M NOT FINISHED.
THERE ARE PLENTY MORE VILLAINS OUT THERE.
AND IF YOU'RE NOT DEAD, SKULL...
...I'LL CIRCLE BACK AND CHECK ON YOU AGAIN, TOO.
GOOD THING THERE'S NO HEROES LEFT.
'CAUSE WHAT I'LL BE DOING...
...IT AIN'T HERO BUSINESS.
THE END.

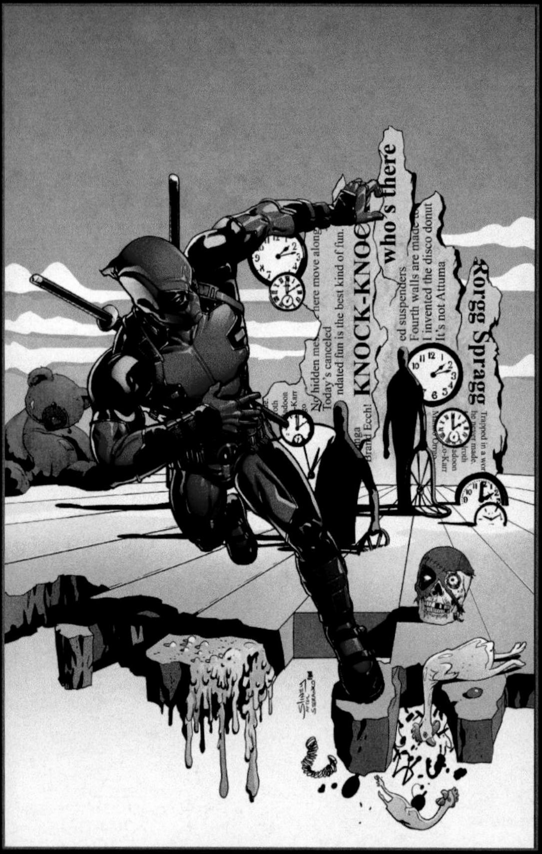
KNOCK-KNOC
who's there
Korgg Spragg
ed suspenders
Fourth walls are made
I invented the disco donut
It's not Attuma
Today's canceled
Brand Ecch!

NO. 1 VARIANT BY
WILL SLINEY & FRANK D'ARMATA

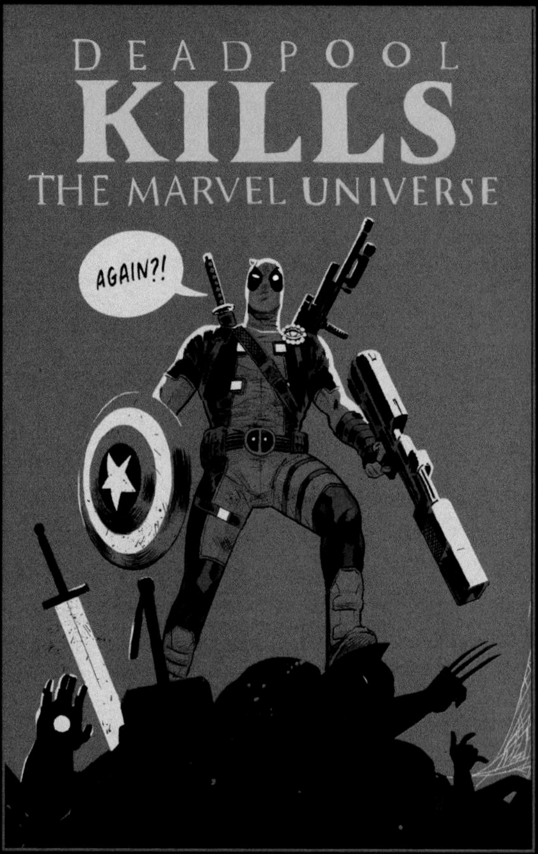
DEADPOOL
KILLS
THE MARVEL UNIVERSE
AGAIN?!

NO. 1 VARIANT BY
MICHAEL WALSH

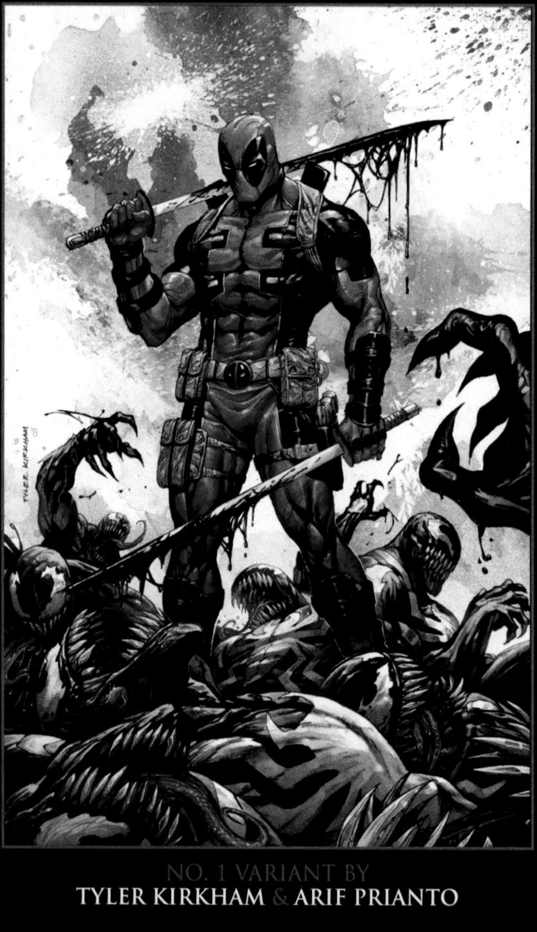

NO. 1 VARIANT BY
TYLER KIRKHAM & ARIF PRIANTO

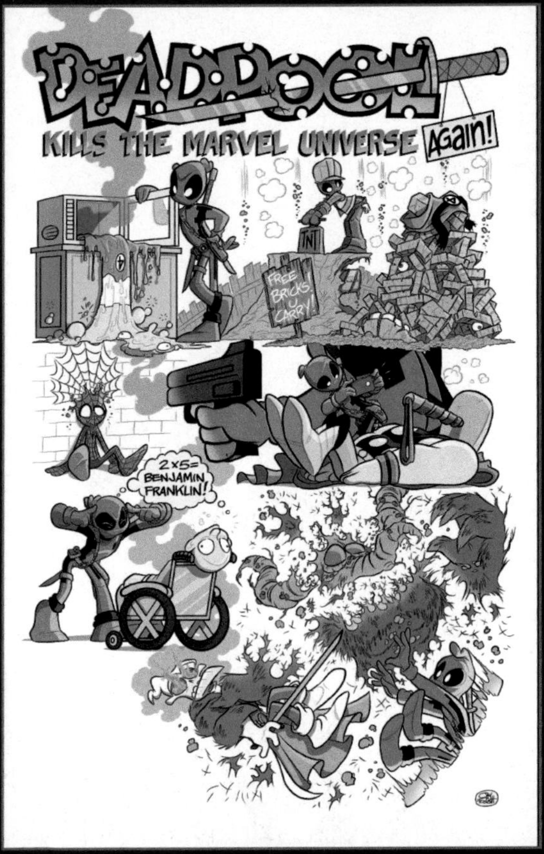
DEADPOOL
KILLS THE MARVEL UNIVERSE AGAIN!
FREE BRICKS U CARRY!
2x5= BENJAMIN FRANKLIN!

NO. 1 VARIANT BY
JAY FOSGITT

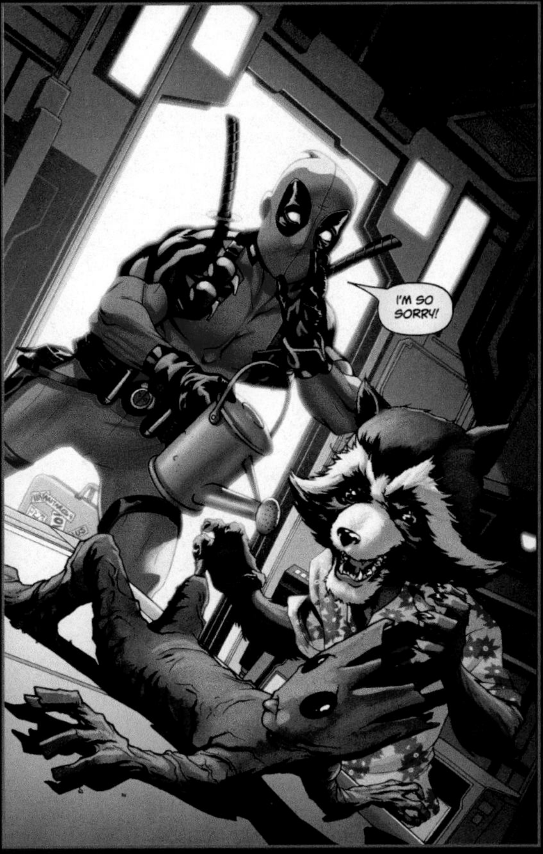
I'M SO SORRY!

NO. 1 VARIANT BY
MIKE McKONE & RACHELLE ROSENBERG

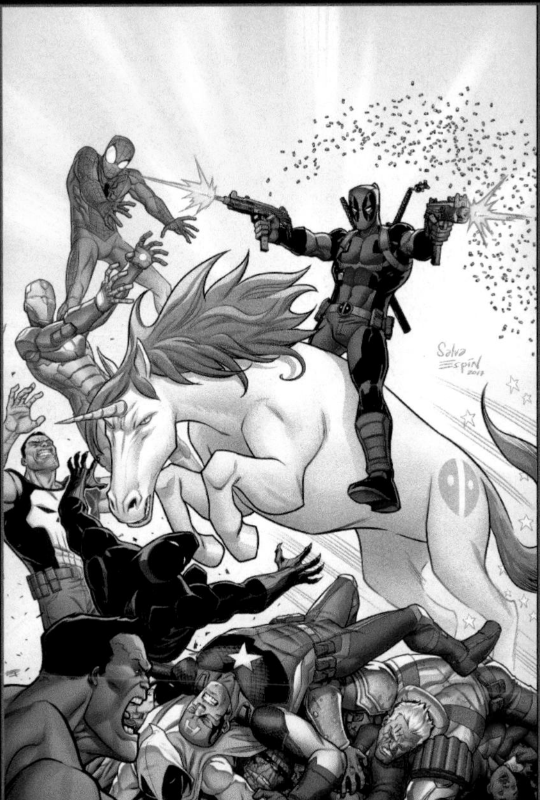

NO. 2 VARIANT BY
SALVA ESPIN & GURU-eFX

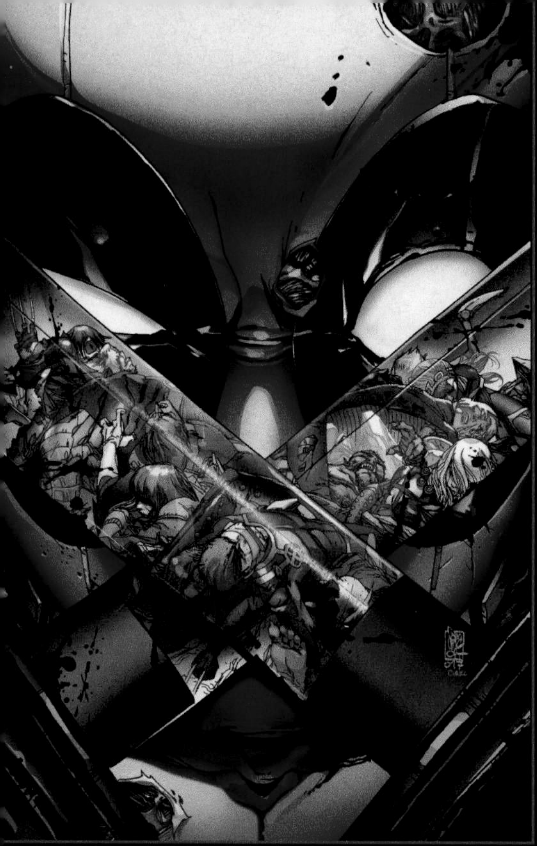

NO. 3 VARIANT BY
GIUSEPPE CAMUNCOLI & DAVID CURIEL

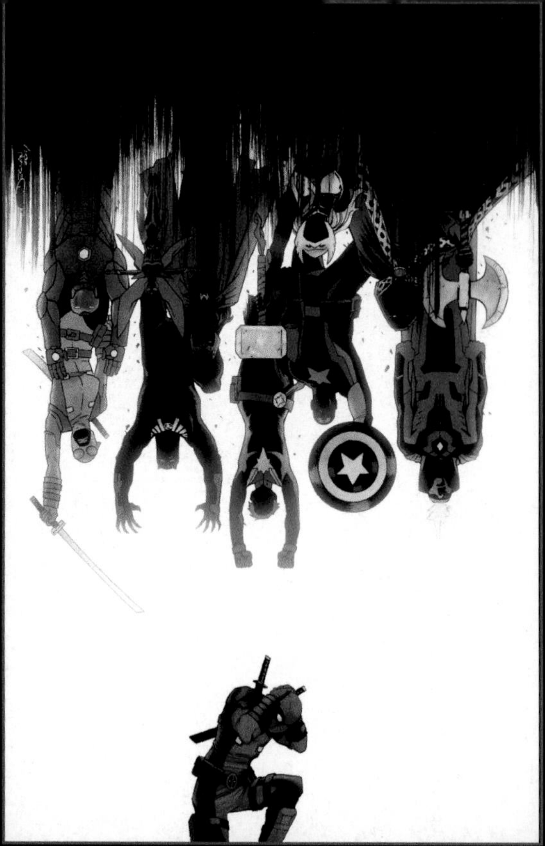

NO. 4 VARIANT BY
DECLAN SHALVEY & JORDIE BELLAIRE

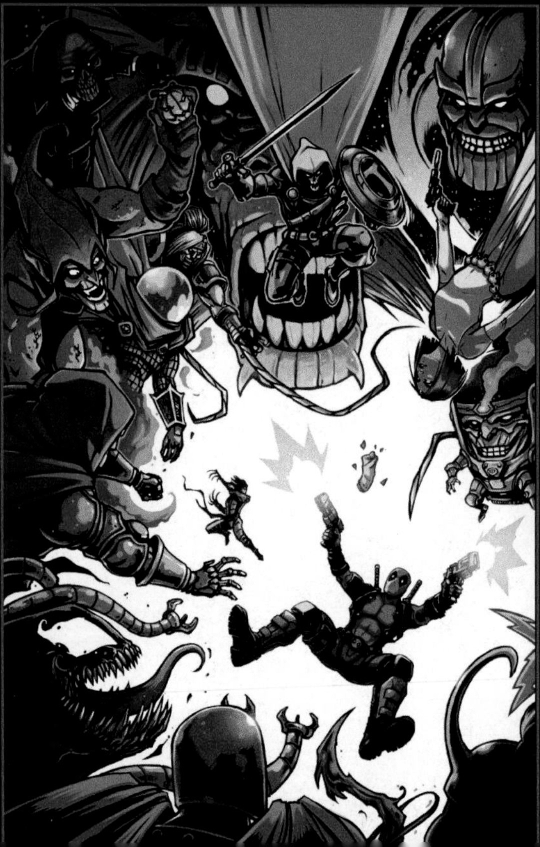